Cyberpatterns

Clive Blackwell · Hong Zhu

Editors

Cyberpatterns

Unifying Design Patterns with Security and Attack Patterns

Springer

Editors
Clive Blackwell
Department of Computing and
   Communication Technologies
Oxford Brookes University
Oxford
UK

Hong Zhu
Department of Computing and
   Communication Technologies
Oxford Brookes University
Oxford
UK

ISBN 978-3-319-35218-3   ISBN 978-3-319-04447-7   (eBook)
DOI 10.1007/978-3-319-04447-7
Springer Cham Heidelberg New York Dordrecht London

Printed on acid-free paper

Springer is part of Springer Science+Business Media (www.springer.com)

Contents

Part VI Pattern Recognition

Part VII The Future

Contributors

Muhammad Asim School of Computing and Mathematical Sciences, Liverpool John Moores University, Liverpool, UK

Julian Bangert Dartmouth College, Hanover, NH, USA

Ian Bayley Department of Computing and Communication Technologies, Oxford Brookes University, Wheatley Campus, Wheatley, Oxford, UK

Daniel Bilar Siege Technologies, Manchester, NH, USA

Clive Blackwell Department of Computing and Communication Technologies, Oxford Brookes University, Wheatley Campus, Wheatley, Oxford, UK

Sergey Bratus Dartmouth College, Hanover, New Hampshire, USA

Natalie Coull School of Science, Engineering, and Technology, University of Abertay Dundee, Dundee, UK

Renato Cordeiro de Amorim Department of Computing, Glyndŵr University, Wrexham, UK

Paul Ekblom Design Against Crime Research Centre, Central Saint Martins College of Art and Design, London, UK

Shamal Faily Bournemouth University, Poole, UK

Ian Ferguson School of Science, Engineering, and Technology, University of Abertay Dundee, Dundee, UK

Alexandar Gabrovsky Dartmouth College, Hanover, NH, USA

Nathan Griffiths Department of Computer Science, University of Warwick, Coventry, UK

David Hutchison School of Computing and Communications, Lancaster University, Lancaster, UK

Paul J. Kearney BT Technology, Service and Operations, Ipswich, UK

Peter Komisarczuk School of Computing Technology, University of West London, London, UK

Harjinder Singh Lallie Warwick Manufacturing Group (WMG), University of Warwick, Coventry, UK

David Lamb School of Computing and Mathematical Sciences, Liverpool John Moores University, Liverpool, UK

K. Lano Department of Informatics, King's College London, London, UK

David Llewellyn-Jones School of Computing and Mathematical Sciences, Liverpool John Moores University, Liverpool, UK

Michael E. Locasto University of Calgary, Alberta, Canada

John Lyle University of Oxford, Oxford, UK

Andreas Mauthe School of Computing and Communications, Lancaster University, Lancaster, UK

Madjid Merabti School of Computing and Mathematical Sciences, Liverpool John Moores University, Liverpool, UK

Allan Milne School of Science, Engineering, and Technology, University of Abertay Dundee, Dundee, UK

Faye Rona Mitchell Department of Computing and Communication Technologies, Oxford Brookes University, Wheatley Campus, Wheatley, Oxford, UK

Simon Parkin University College London, London, UK

Martin Ruskov Information Security Resarch Group, University College London, London, UK

M. Angela Sasse Information Security Resarch Group, University College London, London, UK

Alberto Schaeffer-Filho Institute of Informatics, Federal University of Rio Grande do Sul, Porto Alegre, Brazil

Qi Shi School of Computing and Mathematical Sciences, Liverpool John Moores University, Liverpool, UK

Noor-ul-hassan Shirazi School of Computing and Communications, Lancaster University, Lancaster, UK

Anna Shubina Dartmouth College, Hanover, NH, USA

David A. Sinclair School of Computing, Irish Software Engineering Research Centre, Dublin City University, Dublin 9, Ireland

Paul Smith Safety and Security Department, AIT Austrian Institute of Technology, Seibersdorf, Austria

Sebastian Wagner Institute of Architecture of Application Systems, University of Stuttgart, Stuttgart, Germany

Nick Walker School of Science, Engineering, and Technology, University of Abertay Dundee, Dundee, UK

Bo Zhou School of Computing and Mathematical Sciences, Liverpool John Moores University, Liverpool, UK

Hong Zhu Department of Computing and Communication Technologies, Oxford Brookes University, Wheatley Campus, Wheatley, Oxford, UK

Part I
Introduction

Chapter 1
Cyberpatterns: Towards a Pattern Oriented Study of Cyberspace

Hong Zhu

Abstract A pattern represents a discernible regularity in the world or in manmade designs. In the prescriptive point of view, a pattern is a template from which instances can be created; while in the descriptive point of view, the elements of a pattern that repeat in a predictable manner can be observed and recognised. Similar to theories in sciences, patterns explain and predict regularities in a subject domain. In a complicated subject domain like cyberspace, there are usually a large number of patterns that each describes and predicts a subset of recurring phenomena, yet these patterns can interact with each other and be interrelated and composed with each other. The pattern-oriented research method studies a subject domain by identifying the patterns, classifying and categorising them, organising them into pattern languages, investigating the interactions between them, devising mechanisms and operations for detecting and predicting their occurrences, and facilitating their instantiations. This chapter illustrates this research methodology through a review of the research on software design patterns as an example of successful application of the methodology. It then discusses its possible applications to the research on cyberpatterns, i.e. patterns in cyberspace. It defines the scope of research, reviews the current state of art and identifies the key research questions.

1 Motivation

Since the first occurrence of the word cyberspace in 1980s in science fictions, cyberspace has expanded significantly and is expanding ever faster than before nowadays. During this period, the uses of the Internet, computer networks, and digital communication have been growing dramatically and the term "cyberspace" has been

H. Zhu (✉)
Department of Computing and Communication Technologies, Oxford Brookes University,
Wheatley Campus, Wheatley, Oxford OX33 1HX, UK
e-mail: hzhu@brookes.ac.uk

C. Blackwell and H. Zhu (eds.), *Cyberpatterns*, DOI: 10.1007/978-3-319-04447-7_1,
© Springer International Publishing Switzerland 2014

used to represent the new ideas and phenomena that have emerged. In this virtual space, individuals can interact, exchange ideas, share information, provide social support, conduct business, direct actions, create artistic media, play games, engage in political discussion, and so on, as a social experience. With the emerging of sensor networks, the Internet of things, mobile computing and cloud computing, cyberspace is now no longer isolated from the real world. The term cyberspace has become a conventional means to describe anything associated with the Internet and the diverse Internet culture.

More importantly, the computational medium in cyberspace is an augmentation of the communication channel between real people. One of the core characteristics of cyberspace is that it offers an environment that consists of many participants with the ability to affect and influence each other. It is not simply a consensual hallucination experienced daily by billions of legitimate operators in every nation. In this space, children are being taught mathematics, natural and social sciences, and concepts and knowledge of all disciplines through, for example, Mass Open Online Courses. Social events that are big and small ranging from a family birthday party to a revolutionary protest are organised, for example, through social networks like YouTube and Facebook. Millions of business transactions are completed, employing e-commerce platforms like eBay and Amazon, etc. Yet, hacking for unauthorised access of computer systems, the spread of computer viruses and various forms of computer crimes also happen at every minute. Cyberspace is unthinkably complex and of great importance. The United States as well as many other countries have recognised the interconnected information technology operating across this space as part of the national critical infrastructure.

However, the enormous scale, the notorious complexity, the intangibility of the virtual world and its complicated relations to the real world have imposed grave challenges to the researchers to operate, manage, protect and further develop this space. The notion of cyberpatterns (i.e. patterns in cyberspace) was thus proposed to meet such challenges as a new concept as well as a new research methodology for the study of cyberspace.

This chapter gives an introduction to the book by explaining the notion of cyberpatterns, defining its scope and domain, outlining the so-called pattern-oriented research method based on the notion of pattern, and discussing the key research questions to be answered in the study of cyberpatterns.

The chapter is organised as follows. Section 2 defines the notion of pattern, and Sect. 3 explains the pattern oriented research methodology, which is illustrated by a brief review of the research on software design patterns as an example of a successful application of the methodology. Section 4 explores the potential applications of pattern-oriented research methods to the study of cyberspace and related subject areas.

2 The Notion of Pattern

Pattern is a word widely uses in many subject domains of computer science and technology as well as many other scientific and technological disciplines. For example, in artificial intelligence, pattern recognition is an active and fruitful research topic in image processing and machine learning. In software engineering, research on design patterns has been an active research topic since the 1990s. It aims at systematically representing codified and reusable design knowledge. It has been extended into research on requirement analysis patterns, process patterns, testing patterns, and so forth. The notion of software design patterns are in fact borrowed from a theory of architectural designs proposed by Alexander [2] in the 1970s.

Generally speaking, a pattern means a template from which instances can be created. Such a view of pattern is called the *prescriptive view*, because it provides a means for generating the instances of the pattern. Natural patterns such as spirals, meanders, waves, foams, tilings, cracks, etc., can be created by operations such as symmetries of rotation and reflection.

Another core characteristic of the notion of pattern is that a pattern represents a discernible regularity in the world or in a manmade design. As such, the elements of a pattern repeat in a predictable manner. Not only can such repetition be generated using operators as in the prescriptive view, but also be observed and recognised. For patterns in nature and art, the regularity can often be directly observed by any of the five senses. But patterns in cyberspace are more like the abstract patterns in science, mathematics, or language, which may be observable only by analysis. This leads to the *descriptive view* of patterns, which is an alternative to the prescriptive view. In this view, a pattern describes the instances of the pattern, thus providing a means to recognise whether an element in the domain is an instance of the pattern.

Nature patterns are often chaotic, never exactly repeating, and often involve fractals. This means that the predictions can be less accurate as one may expect. However, all such patterns have an underlying mathematical structure through which regularities manifest themselves as mathematical theories and functions. Therefore, scientific experiments can be carried out to demonstrate the regularity that a pattern predicts to validate the correctness of the documentation and specification of the pattern. This is similar to the sciences, where theories explain and predict regularities in the world. However, as one of the main differences from science theories, a subject domain may have a large number of patterns that each describes and predicts one subset of phenomena, yet these patterns can interact with each other and be interrelated and composed with each other. Such a set of validated patterns formulates a scientific foundation for the study of a space of phenomena. Thus, patterns are classified, categorised, and organised into pattern languages through assigning a vocabulary to the patterns in a subject domain.

3 Pattern-Oriented Research Methodology

These general features of patterns suggest that the notion of pattern is useful to investigate on the following types of research questions:

- finding the regularities of the complicated phenomena in a subject domain like cyberspace,
- understanding such repeating phenomena through discovery of the underlying mathematical structures,
- facilitating the observations of the phenomena in order to detecting the occurrences of a repeating phenomena,
- defining the operations to detect, predict and prevent and/or reproduce such phenomena,
- determining the relationships between various repeating phenomena,
- devising the mechanisms for classifying and categorising such phenomena,
- standardising the vocabulary of such phenomena to form pattern languages, etc.

Systematically studying all aspects of patterns in a subject domain is a research methodology that we believe is suitable for the research of cyberspace's related subjects. This methodology is called *pattern-oriented* in the sequel.

To illustrate how this research methodology works, this section briefly reviews the research on software design patterns. It is perhaps the most advanced subject domain in which pattern-oriented research methodology is applied.

3.1 Software Design Patterns: An Example of Applying the Pattern-Oriented Research Method

Software, as the most complex manmade artefact, is difficult to design and implement. There are a great number of software systems that have been developed for a vast range of different application domains. Some are very successful; while some others completely fail. A key research question is therefore:

- *Can design knowledge contained in the successful software systems be extracted and reused in the design of other systems?*

The pattern-oriented research methodology answers this question by regarding such successful design knowledge as patterns. In particular, design patterns are regarded as codified reusable solutions to recurring design problems [3, 18]. In the past two decades, much research on software design patterns has been reported in the literature. The following briefly reviews the existing work on software design patterns to illustrate how the pattern-oriented research method works.

3.1.1 Identification and Documentation of Design Patterns

Design patterns are mostly identified by experienced software designers manually by recognising the recurring design problems and the successful examples of design solutions. These samples of successful solutions are abstracted into a template so that it can be applied to a wide range of applications but of the same design problem. Typically, such a template of design solutions consists of a number of software components, called *participants* of the solution, and they are connected to each other in certain specific configurations. The instantiation of the template is also illustrated by some typical examples. The applicability of the pattern, alternative designs and relations to other patterns are also made explicit as a part of the pattern.

Usually, such a pattern is documented in the so-called *Alexandrian format*. In this format, design principles are first explained in informal English, and then clarified with illustrative diagrams and specific code examples [18]. The diagrams serve as the template and show how the participants interact with each other and the configuration of the connections. The specific code examples show the typical instances of the pattern. This format is informative for humans to understand the design principle underlying the pattern and to learn how to apply patterns to solve their own design problems.

3.1.2 Catalogues of Patterns and Pattern Languages

Design patterns are not only identified and documented in isolation, but also systematically categorised and their relationships charted. Among many types of design patterns that have been studied are object-oriented program designs [17, 18, 20, 21], enterprise system designs [3, 22, 24, 37, 42], real-time and distributed systems [10, 16, 42], fault tolerance architectures [23], pattern-oriented software architectures [8, 9], and program code for implementing security feature [36, 37], etc.

The most important relationships between design patterns include:

- *Sub-pattern*: Pattern *A* is a sub-pattern of pattern *B* means that every instances of pattern *A* is also an instance of pattern *B*.
- *Uses*: Pattern *A* uses pattern *B* means that certain participants (i.e. the components) in pattern *A* is designed and implemented by using pattern *B*.
- *Composition*: Pattern *A* is a composition of pattern *B*, *C* and so on, if pattern *A* is formed by put pattern *B* and *C* etc. together.
- *Alternative Choice*: Pattern *A* and pattern *B* are alternative choices, if they serve certain common design goals and solve some common design problems, but they also have some different properties thus used in difference situations.

The systematic categorising of design patterns has led to a set of vocabulary of design terminology, which forms the so-called pattern languages.

3.1.3 Formal Specification of Design Patterns

The documentation of design patterns in Alexandrian format is informal and hence brings such ambiguity that it is often a matter of dispute whether an implementation conforms to a pattern or not. Empirical studies show that poor documentation of patterns can lead to poor system quality, and can actually impede software maintenance and evolution [26]. Mathematical notations are thus employed to help eliminate this ambiguity by clarifying the underlying notions. Several formalisms for formally specifying OO design patterns have been advanced [1, 6, 19, 32, 39].

In spite of differences in these formalisms, the underlying ideas are quite similar. That is, patterns are specified by constraints on what are its valid instances via defining their structural features and sometimes their behavioural features too. The structural constraints are typically assertions that certain types of components exist and have a certain configuration of the structure. The behavioural constraints, on the other hand, detail the temporal order of messages exchanged between the components.

Formally, a design pattern P can be defined abstractly as a tuple $\langle V, Pr_S, Pr_D \rangle$, where $V = \{v_1:T_1, \ldots, v_n:T_n\}$ declares the components in the pattern, while Pr_S and Pr_D are predicates that specify the structural and behavioural features of the pattern, respectively. Here, v_i in V is a variable that ranges over the type T_i of software elements, such as class, method, and attribute. The predicates are constructed from primitive predicates either manually defined, or systematically induced from the meta-model of software design models. The semantics of a specification is the ground formula $\exists V \cdot (Pr_S \wedge Pr_D)$. Such a formalism for the specification of design patterns enables the conformation of a design or an implementation of a software system to a pattern be formally verified and automatically detected. This is in fact a descriptive view of design patterns.

An alternative approach to the formal specification of design patterns is the so-called transformational approach. In this approach, a design pattern is defines as a transformation rule that when applied to a flawed design (or implementation) results in a new design (or implementation) that conforms to the pattern [30]. Such a specification of pattern is prescriptive.

3.1.4 Development of Software Tools

With the documentation of design patterns, a large number of software tools have been developed to support various uses of design patterns in software engineering, which include

- Detection of design patterns in program code for reverse engineering [7, 15, 25, 31, 33, 34] and in designs represented as UML models [27–29, 44, 45]. Such tools are useful to reverse engineering.
- Instantiation of patterns for software design. Such tools are employed as parts of modelling tools and included as plug-ins in integrated software development environments, such as Eclipse, NetBeans, etc.

- Visual and graphical representation of patterns. For example, Dong et al. implemented a tool [14] for computer-aided visualisation of the application of design patterns in UML class diagrams. Their tool, deployed as a web service, identifies pattern applications, and does so by displaying stereotypes, tagged values, and constraints. Their experiments show that the tool reduces the information overload faced by designers.

3.1.5 Composition of Design Patterns

Although each pattern is documented and specified separately, they are usually to be found composed with each other with overlaps except in trivial cases [35]. Thus, pattern composition plays a crucial role in the effective use of design knowledge.

Composition of design patterns has been studied informally by many authors, for example, in [8, 35]. Visual notations, such as the *Pattern:Role* annotation and a forebear based on Venn diagrams, have been proposed by Vlissides [41] and widely used in practice. They indicate where, in a design, patterns have been applied so that their compositions are comprehensible.

Pattern compositions have also been studied formally through formalisation and extension of the *Pattern:Role* graphic notation by considering pattern compositions as overlaps between pattern applications [4, 11–13, 38, 40]. A set of six operators on design patterns were defined with which the composition and instantiation of design patterns can be accurately and precisely expressed [5]. The algebraic laws of these pattern operators were also studied so that the equivalence of two pattern composition and instantiation expressions can be proved via equational reasoning [43].

Pattern decomposition, i.e. to work out how a design or a pattern is composed from a set of known patterns, is of particular importance in software engineering, especially in software reverse engineering. This is achieved through recognising the instances of patterns in the program code or in the design model represented in UML.

In summary, software design is a highly complicated domain. The research on design patterns started with the definition of the notion of design patterns as repeating phenomena in this domain, i.e. the solutions of recurring design problems. This notion of pattern is consolidated by the identification of certain design patterns and demonstration of their uses in software design. The research further developed with such a notion of pattern as the central concept to answer various research questions like how to document and specify design patterns, how patterns relate to each other and interact with each other, how to detect patterns when given a design or implementation, how find applicable design patterns and to instantiate a design pattern when given a design problem, etc.

3.2 Advantages and Benefits

The fruitful research on software design patterns and its wide applications in software development shows the following advantages and benefits of pattern-oriented research method.

1. Patterns represent domain knowledge in fine granularity, in which the complicated knowledge of the subject domain (such as software design) is divided into self-contained composable pieces.
2. Patterns, being self-contained, can be described and documented with high readability and learnability.
3. Each pattern as a piece of domain knowledge can also be easily validated and formally specified relatively independent of the other patterns.
4. Patterns codify domain knowledge in such a way that each pattern's applicability can be easily recognised and they can be flexibly combined through pattern composition.
5. The relationships between the patterns and the way patterns are composed and combined are also important parts of the domain knowledge, which can also be formally defined, specified, and applied.
6. Automated tools can be developed and employed for various uses of the knowledge.
7. A complete knowledge of the subject domain can be developed incrementally by gradually identifying more and more patterns and the whole picture of the domain knowledge emerges in the form of catalogues of the patterns when a sufficient number of patterns are identified. Meanwhile, the incompleteness of a set of patterns does not affect the usefulness of the known knowledge.

In the next section, we discuss how the pattern-oriented research methodology exemplified above can be applied to the research on cyberspace.

4 Patterns in Cyberspace

The notion of cyberpattern advocates the application of the pattern-oriented research methodology to the study of cyberspace. Here, we discuss the scope of the research, the core research questions to be addressed as a road map for the future research.

4.1 What are Patterns in Cyberspace?

The first key research questions to be addressed in pattern-oriented research is:

- *What are the patterns in cyberspace?*

As discussed previously, cyberspace is a complicated subject domain. There is a vast range of phenomena that can be observed, recorded and detected as patterns.

The following are just some examples of the patterns that have already been studied by researchers in various research communities.

- *User behaviour patterns*: Users of particular resources and applications on the internet tend to demonstrate certain regularities. Such regularities can be described as patterns, detected if abnormal behaviour occurs, for example, for intruder detection.
- *Workload patterns*: The workload on a particular server or a particular application on the internet varies, but often demonstrates certain pattern of variation, for example, due to the common behaviour of the users. Such patterns can be used to improve system performance and efficiency through load balancing and power management of the cluster.
- *Network traffic patterns*: The communication traffic on a particular network also exhibit clear patterns of variation according to the time and date as the users of the network have common behaviour patterns. Such patterns are useful for network optimisation.
- *Social network patterns*: People connecting with each other through social networks demonstrate certain patterns, for example, to form a network that observes the so-called Small World and Power Law of scale-free networks. The information propagates through such a social network in certain patterns, too.
- *Attack patterns*: The hackers attack the resource on the internet use certain information techniques. Thus, their behaviours also have certain dynamic characteristics that repeat inevitably.
- *Security design patterns*: To combat malicious attacks over the internet to attack computer facilities and resources, online systems employ security facilities to prevent, detect and mitigate security attacks. The vast range of such security facilities and mechanisms has certain common structures and implementations that can be represented as patterns like software design patterns.
- *Patterns of vulnerabilities*: The security facilities and mechanisms employed to protect internet resources often have weakness and vulnerabilities. Efforts have been made in the research on cybersecurity to identify, classify and categorise such vulnerabilities. Each type of vulnerability is in fact a pattern although they are not called so in the literature.
- *Digital forensic patterns*: In the investigation of cybercrime and more generally digital computer crimes, common investigation processes and guidelines have been developed for various types of crimes. They can be regarded as patterns, too.

Further research should be directed to answer questions like:

- *How can various types of cyberpatterns be identified?*
- *How should various types of cyberpatterns be described, documented and specified?*
- *How can cyberpatterns of various types be classified and catalogued systematically?*

Fig. 1 Potential relationships between different types of cyberpatterns

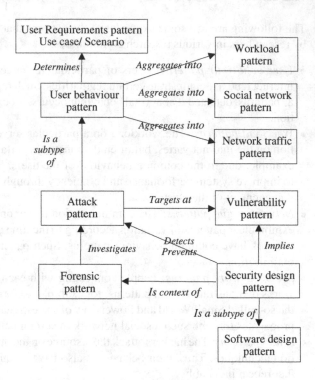

The standards for the documentation and specification of various types of cyber-patterns are of particular importance to answer the following research question:

- *How can various types of cyberpatterns be stored, retrieved and applied with the support of computer software tools and used automatically?*

4.2 How do Cyberpatterns Interrelate and Interact with Each Other?

The pattern-oriented research methodology not only studies patterns individually, but also the relationship between them and the interaction they may have. A key research question to be addressed is therefore:

- *What are the relationships between various types of cyberpatterns?*
- *How cyberpatterns of the same type and across different types interact and inter-relate with each other?*

For each type of patterns, one pattern may be related to another as its sub-pattern, and one is composed of some others, etc., as in the design patterns. In addition to such relationships, patterns in cyberspace of different types may also be related to each other in more complicated forms. Figure 1 shows some ideas about the relationships between the types of patterns.

Fig. 2 Potential relationships between different types of cyberpatterns

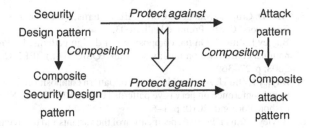

Understanding these relationships will significantly improve our understanding of cyberspace and the effectiveness of using and protecting the infrastructure and resources on the Internet.

For example, consider the relationships between security design patterns and attack patterns. Security designs are often made by composing a number of design patterns that each pattern protects against one or more type of attack patterns. As illustrated in Fig. 2, a problem that worth studying is to prove that *the composition of security design patterns can protect against the composition of attack patterns*.

5 Conclusion

A pattern represents a discernible regularity in a subject domain. It is a template from which instances can be created. It represents knowledge of recurring phenomena that can be observed and recognised. Similar to theories in sciences, patterns explain and predict regularities in certain phenomena. In a complicated subject domain like cyberspace, there are usually a large number of patterns that each describes and predicts a subset of recurring phenomena, yet these patterns can interact with each other and be interrelated and composed with each other.

The pattern oriented research method studies a subject domain by identifying the patterns, classifying and categorising them, organising them into pattern languages, investigating the interactions between them, devising mechanisms and operations for detecting and predicting their occurrences, and facilitating their instantiations. It is applicable to complicated subject domain like cyberspace.

References

1. Alencar PSC, Cowan DD, de Lucena CJP. A formal approach to architectural design patterns. In: Gaudel MC, Woodcock J, editors. In: Proceedings of the third international symposium of formal methods Europe on industrial benefit and advances in formal methods (FME'96), Lecture Notes In Computer Science, Springer-Verlag; 1996. p. 576–594.
2. Alexander C. A pattern language: towns, buildings, construction. New York: Oxford University Press; 1977.

3. Alur D, Crupi J, Malks D. Core J2EE Patterns: Best Practices and Design Strategies, 2nd ed. Englewood Cliffs: Prentice Hall; 2003.
4. Bayley I, Zhu H. On the composition of design patterns. In: Proceedings of the eighth international conference on quality software (QSIC 2008). IEEE Computer Society, Oxford, UK; 2008: p. 27–36.
5. Bayley I, Zhu H. A formal language of pattern composition. In: Proceedings of the 2nd international conference on pervasive patterns (PATTERNS 2010), XPS (Xpert Publishing Services), Lisbon, Portugal; 2010: p. 1–6.
6. Bayley I, Zhu H. Formal specification of the variants and behavioural features of design patterns. J Syst Software. 2010;83(2):209–21.
7. Blewitt A, Bundy A, Stark I. Automatic verification of design patterns in Java. In: Proceedings of the 20th IEEE/ACM international conference on automated software engineering (ASE 2005), ACM Press, Long Beach, California, USA; 2005: p. 224–232. http://www.inf.ed.ac.uk/stark/autvdp.html.
8. Buschmann F, Henney K, Schmidt DC. Pattern-oriented software architecture: on Patterns and pattern languages, vol. 5. Chichester: Wiley; 2007.
9. Buschmann F, Henney K, Schmidt DC. Pattern-oriented software architecture: a pattern language for distributed computing, vol. 4. West Sussex: Wiley; 2007.
10. DiPippo L, Gill CD. Design patterns for distributed real-time systems. New York: Springer; 2005.
11. Dong J, Alencar PS, Cowan DD. Ensuring structure and behavior correctness in design composition. In: Proceedings of the IEEE 7th annual international conference and workshop on engineering computer based systems (ECBS 2000), IEEE CS Press, Edinburgh, Scotland; 2000: p. 279–287.
12. Dong J, Alencar PS, Cowan DD. A behavioral analysis and verification approach to pattern-based design composition. Softw Syst Model. 2004;3:262–2.
13. Dong J, Alencar PSC, Cowan DD. Correct composition of design components. In: Proceedings of the 4th international workshop on component-oriented programming in conjunction with ECOOP99; 1999.
14. Dong J, Yang S, Zhang K. Visualizing design patterns in their applications and compositions. IEEE Trans Softw Eng. 2007;33(7):433–3.
15. Dong J, Zhao Y, Peng T. Architecture and design pattern discovery techniques—a review. In: Arabnia HR, Reza H, editors. In: Proceedings of the 2007 international conference on software engineering research and practice (SERP 2007), vol. II. Las Vegas Nevada, USA: CSREA Press; 2007. p. 621–27.
16. Douglass BP. Real time design patterns: robust scalable architecture for real-time systems. Boston: Addison Wesley; 2002.
17. Fowler M. Patterns of enterprise application architecture. Boston: Addison Wesley; 2003.
18. Gamma E, Helm R, Johnson R, Vlissides J. Design patterns—elements of reusable object-oriented software. Reading: Addison-Wesley; 1995.
19. Gasparis E, Eden AH, Nicholson J, Kazman R. The design navigator: charting Java programs. In: Proceedings of ICSE'08, Companion Volume; 2008. p. 945–46
20. Grand M. Patterns in Java, vol. 2. New York: Wiley; 1999.
21. Grand M. Java enterprise design patterns. New York: Wiley; 2002.
22. Grand M. Patterns in Java: a catalog of reusable design patterns illustrated with UML, vol. 1. New York: Wiley; 2002.
23. Hanmer RS. Patterns for fault tolerant software. West Sussex: Wiley; 2007.
24. Hohpe G, Woolf B. Enterprise integration patterns: designing, building, and deploying messaging solutions. Boston: Addison Wesley; 2004.
25. Hou D, Hoover HJ. Using SCL to specify and check design intent in source code. IEEE Trans Softw Eng. 2006;32(6):404–23.
26. Khomh F, Gueheneuc YG. Do design patterns impact software quality positively? In: Proceedings of the 12th European Conference on Software Maintenance and Reengineering (CSMR 2008), IEEE, Athens, Greece; 2008. p. 274–78.

27. Kim DK, Lu L. Inference of design pattern instances in UML models via logic programming. In: Proceedings of the 11th international conference on engineering of complex computer systems (ICECCS 2006), IEEE Computer Society, Stanford, California, USA; 2006. p. 47–56.

28. Kim DK, Shen W. An approach to evaluating structural pattern conformance of UML models. In: Proceedings of the 2007 ACM symposium on applied computing (SAC'07), ACM Press, Seoul, Korea; 2007. p. 1404–08.

29. Kim DK, Shen W. Evaluating pattern conformance of UML models: a divide-and-conquer approach and case studies. Software Qual J. 2008;16(3):329–9.

30. Lano K, Bicarregui JC, Goldsack S. Formalising design patterns. In: BCS-FACS Northern formal methods workshop, Ilkley, UK; 1996.

31. Mapelsden D, Hosking J, Grundy J. Design pattern modelling and instantiation using DPML. In: CRPIT '02: Proceedings of the fortieth international conference on tools pacific, Australian Computer Society, Inc.; 2002. p. 3–11.

32. Mikkonen T. Formalizing design patterns. In: Proceedings of ICSE'98, Kyoto, Japan, IEEE CS; 1998. p. 115–24.

33. Niere J, Schafer W, Wadsack JP, Wendehals L, Welsh J. Towards pattern-based design recovery. In: Proceedings of the 22nd international conference on software engineering (ICSE 2002), IEEE CS, Orlando, Florida, USA; 2002. p. 338–48.

34. Nija Shi N, Olsson R. Reverse engineering of design patterns from java source code. In: Proceedings of ASE'06, Tokyo, Japan, IEEE Computer Society; 2006. p. 123–34.

35. Riehle D. Composite design patterns. In: Proceedings of the 1997 ACM SIGPLAN conference on object-oriented programming systems., Languages and Applications (OOPSLA'97) Atlanta, Georgia: ACM Press; 1997. p. 218–28.

36. Schumacher M, Fernandez E, Hybertson D, Buschmann F. Security patterns: integrating security and systems engineering. West Sussex: Wiley; 2005.

37. Steel C. Applied J2EE security patterns: architectural patterns and best practices. Upper Saddle River: Prentice Hall PTR; 2005.

38. Taibi T. Formalising design patterns composition. IEE Proc Software. 2006;153(3):126–53.

39. Taibi T, Check D, Ngo L. Formal specification of design patterns—a balanced approach. J Object Technol. 2003;2(4):127–40.

40. Taibi T, Ngo DCL. Formal specification of design pattern combination using BPSL. Inf Softw Technol. 2003;45(3):157–70.

41. Vlissides, J. Notation, notation, notation. C++ Report; 1998.

42. Voelter M, Kircher M, Zdun U. Remoting patterns. West Sussex: Wiley; 2004.

43. Zhu H, Bayley I. An algebra of design patterns. ACM Trans Softw Eng Methodol. 2013;22(3):Article 23.

44. Zhu H, Bayley I, Shan L, Amphlett R. Tool support for design pattern recognition at model level. In: Proceedings of COMPSAC'09, IEEE Computer Society, Seattle, Washington, USA; 2009. p. 228–33.

45. Zhu H, Shan L, Bayley I, Amphlett R. A formal descriptive semantics of UML and its applications. In: Lano K, editor. UML 2 semantics and applications. Chichester: Wiley; 2009. ISBN-13: 978–0470409084.

Chapter 2
Towards a Conceptual Framework for Security Patterns

Clive Blackwell

Abstract We introduce security patterns as the most mature domain within cyberpatterns, and outline a conceptual framework to help understand and develop good security patterns. Security patterns help us move from an improvised craft to engineering discipline because they transfer knowledge about proven solutions in an understandable and reusable format to experienced users and novices alike. Although security patterns are widely known, many questions remain unanswered regarding their conceptual foundation and practical use. We characterise the current pattern schemes using the Zachman Framework for enterprise architecture modelling, which allows us to structure and pose questions about both the problem domain and corresponding solutions provided by security patterns. We propose a parallel security plane overlaying the entire Zachman grid allowing the separate consideration of security within the security plane using the interrogative questions (who, what, where, when, why and how) to evaluate the six aspects. The integration between security and functional concerns is similarly aided by using the correspondence between aspects in the security and functional planes to decompose and examine the relationship between security patterns and problem context. We also briefly discuss security patterns as transformations, and related concepts such as tactics that may usefully be applied to security. We conclude with a set of unsolved challenges for security patterns. This discussion is relevant to other types of cyberpattern such as attack patterns, and may aid the eventual development of a comprehensive framework for cyberpatterns.

C. Blackwell (✉)
Department of Computing and Communication Technologies, Oxford Brookes University,
Wheatley Campus, Wheatley, Oxford OX33 1HX, UK
e-mail: CBlackwell@brookes.ac.uk

C. Blackwell and H. Zhu (eds.), *Cyberpatterns*, DOI: 10.1007/978-3-319-04447-7_2,
© Springer International Publishing Switzerland 2014

1 Introduction and Rationale

Designing a secure system is a hard endeavour requiring unique skills that we cannot expect from typical development teams. It would be helpful if there were a set of easily usable building blocks that provide a foundation for secure systems, without users needing to grasp the finer points of security engineering. Security patterns aim to provide these blocks by providing realisable solutions to help solve known recurrent security problems.

A pattern can be characterised as a solution to a problem that arises within a specific context. Each pattern expresses a relation between a problem context, a set of unwanted forces that occurs repeatedly in that context, and a system configuration that allows these forces to be resolved [1]. Similarly, a security pattern encapsulates security expertise in the form of vetted solutions to recurring problems [2], as in the 'Gang of Four' (GoF) Design Patterns book [3]. A security pattern describes a solution to the problem of controlling specific threats through the application of some security mechanisms in a given context [4].

Security patterns organise and preserve this knowledge in an understandable and reusable format, so that less proficient developers may benefit. This may help us move from a craft to engineering discipline, because patterns transfer knowledge and understanding about proven solutions to the community and thereby help to establish security on a sounder footing.

2 Pattern Classification

2.1 Zachman Framework

We propose the use of the Zachman Framework [5] to model security patterns and their various classification schemes. The Zachman Framework [6] is a widely used and influential framework for enterprise system architecture, and is displayed as a matrix or table providing different system scopes and levels of abstraction in the horizontal rows and different system aspects in the vertical columns, as shown in Table 1.

The framework comprehensively models all horizontal scopes and levels of abstraction from global in the top row down to the operational or data scope. When used to develop enterprise systems, the development lifecycle starts with high-level analysis of the system goals and context in the top row progressing down through the rows until very detailed concerns are addressed in the operational system. The columns allow comprehensive analysis of different system aspects using particular methods or tools to answer the question relevant to the particular concern. Each cell analyses the syl suitable for the concerns of the column aspect with an appropriate level of detail for the row.

Table 1 Zachman framework for security patterns (some row names altered)

Scope	Aspect Question	Data What?	Function How?	Network Where?	People Who?	Time When?	Motivation Why?
Global							
Enterprise							
Architecture							
Design							
Implementation							
Operation or data							

2.2 Modelling Security Patterns

We use the Zachman Framework somewhat differently for modelling security patterns and so the names of some of the rows have been changed to match their new use. A key point is that the implementation of an enterprise system employs all the framework rows with clear relationships between them, where analysis in a lower row breaks down the model for the next higher row into more detail.

A security pattern lives at one or possibly two rows only, but does relate to a system problem also represented in the same row of the Zachman Framework. The framework has been used to model attack patterns [7] by mapping various attack pattern sections to the six Zachman aspects. The same idea for security patterns helps integration of security patterns into the systems they protect by matching the six aspects between the pattern solution and system problem. The connection between patterns of different horizontal scopes is not examined further, but we suggest that one relationship is pattern aggregation where a broader pattern such as an architectural pattern encapsulates narrower patterns such as design patterns.

The crucial link is between security and system concerns in the third dimension. We are inspired by the SABSA (Sherwood Applied Business Security Architecture) model [8] of an entire plane devoted to security replicating all the elements of the Zachman Framework from a security perspective. The separate security plane is displayed in the third dimension parallel to the original functional Zachman matrix. The different aspects help to answer the questions who, what, why, where, when and how about both the system problem and security pattern solution. The Zachman aspects of the security pattern in the security plane must constrain the undesirable problem behaviour by resolving the security forces, and match the aspects of the problem context in the functional plane for compatibility.

The security plane promotes both separation and integration of security and the other system concerns. The parallel plane allows the separate consideration of security by decomposing security analysis into the six column aspects, as in the SABSA model [8]. This allows comprehensive investigation of security aspects within the plane, and thereby helps security pattern specialisation and composition to address pure security concerns.

Table 2 Zachman framework for security patterns (development lifecycle perspective)

Level	Aspect Question	Data What?	Function How?	Network Where?	People Who?	Time When?	Motivation Why?
Analysis							
Requirements							
Architecture							
Design							
Implementation							
Deployment							

The matching between the functional and security planes on the other hand allows the integration of security with the system concerns. The relationships between the planes enable integration, because the security aspect in a cell in the security plane must be compatible with the functional aspect in the corresponding cell in the functional domain. In particular, the security patterns and the system context must be at the same level of abstraction and have compatible horizontal scope.

We can model security patterns at all six different scopes from the wider global scope right down to the very narrow operation or data scope, extending beyond their existing use spanning the enterprise down to implementation rows. Then, the six scopes of security pattern (with example security issues in brackets) are in descending order: Global (social engineering), Enterprise (insider threat), Architecture (man-in-the-middle), Design (SQL injection), Implementation (buffer overflow), and Operation or Data (malware operation detected by signature).

The Zachman grid does not distinguish the horizontal scope of analysis in each row from the stage in the system development lifecycle, as they usually match when building enterprise IT systems. The broader abstract system concerns are considered first before moving down to more and more detailed and narrow functionality eventually finishing with the deployed system in the bottom row.

However, the horizontal scope and lifecycle stages need to be considered separately when the framework is used for patterns, as the lifecycle stage does not necessarily bear a close connection to the pattern scope. For example, an early-lifecycle analysis pattern could apply narrowly to a small component, whereas a late-lifecycle deployment pattern could suggest a broad system solution involving architectural restructuring. Therefore, we can also consider the levels of abstraction in pattern development using a staged lifecycle process and map its various phases to the Zachman hierarchy as shown in Table 2. The relationship between horizontal scope and level of abstraction therefore needs more thought for security patterns.

Fernandez et al. proposed a methodology that incorporates security patterns in all the lifecycle stages [9], which we relate to the Zachman Framework levels. A development methodology for security patterns is required, as many security pattern catalogues do not provide clear information about when or where to apply them. This methodology proposes guidelines for incorporating security patterns within the requirements, analysis, design, implementation, testing and deployment phases of development. Our methodology contains the analysis, requirements, architecture, design, implementation and deployment phases, as shown in the rows of Table 2.

This suggests more research in needed for security patterns outside the design and architectural stages where most work has occurred so far. For example, the answers to the aspect questions depend crucially on the lifecycle stage and level of abstraction. In addition, the processes involved in each stage are also important, and common techniques may be abstracted and modelled as behavioural patterns.

3 History and Classification of Security Patterns

3.1 Basic Pattern Catalogues

This is not intended to be a comprehensive survey of security patterns, so the cited sources should be consulted as several have extensive bibliographies. We describe the simpler pattern arrangements that are not full classification schemes in this section summarised in Table 3, before discussing multifaceted schemes in the next section. Yoder and Barcalow [10] wrote the first paper on security patterns in 1997, introducing seven patterns using the GoF (Gang of Four) template and structuring them as a pattern language.

The pattern community developed a large number of security patterns over a number of years for workshops at the Pattern Languages of Programs (PLoP) conferences. Subsequently, a working group was established under Markus Schumacher with the results published as a book [4] in 2005 that was the first to categorise most known security patterns. Their systematic collection of 46 security patterns covered multiple scopes and levels of abstraction, including several enterprise patterns for risk assessment and mitigation, as well as the usual architectural and design patterns. Graham [11] studied more general business patterns creating a pattern language containing 42 patterns with several that could be specialised as procedural security patterns.

Finally, Munawar Hafiz worked with Ward Cunningham and the Microsoft Patterns and Practices group on a comprehensive catalogue of all known security patterns following the path started at the PLOP workshops and continued by Schumacher's book. The current catalogue currently contains nearly 100 security patterns by culling duplicate, poor quality and out-of-scope patterns, which were then classified and organised into a pattern language [12].

There are several other security pattern repositories, collections and surveys. The Security Patterns Repository Version 1.0 (the only version) [2] is a book-length technical report published in 2002 consisting of a comprehensive description of 29 patterns. They considered the patterns under two broad classes of structural and procedural patterns, with 16 structural patterns for implementing secure applications and 13 procedural patterns for the development process.

The procedural patterns are not the same as the behavioural patterns in the GoF book, as they have a broader scope involving people performing activities such as

Table 3 Simple security pattern schemes

Authors	Purpose	Classification criteria	Scope
Kienzle et al. [2]	General pattern repository attempting to document known patterns and improve pattern quality	Two classes of structural and procedural (manual security processes)	Enterprise (procedural patterns), architectural and design (mainly structural patterns)
Open Group [14]	Aiding security and availability (against unintentional causes not just deliberate denial of service)	Two categories of security and availability (availability is distinguished from the other security objectives)	Architectural and design. Availability patterns have the wider goal of aiding dependability
Steel et al. [17]	To aid implementation of Web services on Java platforms	By architectural tier (web, business, web service and identity tiers) in the system domain	Architectural, design and implementation, but restricted to Web services only
Microsoft's Patterns and Practices group [18]	To aid implementation of Web services using Microsoft technologies	By security purposes (eg. authentication) and indirectly by protection target (eg. resource in resource access)	Architectural, design and implementation, but restricted to Web services only
Yoshioka et al. [15]	A survey paper establishing the current state of the art and performing gap analysis to identify future research directions	By system development phases	Spanning all scopes from enterprise to implementation as befits a survey
Dougherty et al. [16]	To protect existing design patterns by decoration with security aspects	Secure design patterns are specialised from existing architectural, design and implementation patterns	Architectural, design and implementation

documentation, testing and patching, similar to Graham's business patterns. Hafiz [13] discovered very few procedural patterns in his comprehensive classification, so this might be an area for future pattern discovery, both in security and possibly in the emerging domain of digital forensics.

The Open Group Guide to Security Patterns book [14] in 2004 contains architectural and design patterns following the GoF template [3]. The catalogue classifies 13 patterns into two broad groups based on the protection objective with eight patterns for security and five for availability. The security patterns aim to protect valuable assets against unauthorised use, disclosure, or modification, whereas the five availability patterns aim to provide predictable and uninterrupted access to services and resources against both deliberate and unintentional causes, rather than just for the narrow security objective of defeating intentional denial of service attacks.

Yoshioka et al. [15] produced a comprehensive survey that investigated the various approaches to security patterns and proposed future research directions. They characterised security patterns according to the software development phases and analysed the adequacy of patterns by their conformance to established security concepts. They identified the need to ground analysis in actual risks by keeping attacks in mind when developing security patterns. However, it is difficult to find specific security threats before implementation, and therefore, we need to establish a way of discussing attacks abstractly at the design stage to help us develop corresponding security patterns.

The Software Engineering Institute guide to Secure Design Patterns [16] in 2009 describes various secure design patterns addressing security issues in the architectural, design and implementation phases of the development lifecycle. Secure design patterns are distinguished from security patterns, as they do not describe specific security mechanisms (eg. access control, authentication, and authorisation), but simply adapt and extend existing functional patterns.

Finally, two books take a more practical technological viewpoint. Steel et al. [17] developed an extensive collection of security patterns in 2005, specifically for developing Web services on Java platforms at quite a detailed level of granularity ready for implementation. They classified 23 security patterns according to logical architectural tiers; namely, web, business, web service and identity tiers. These are logical functions in the system decomposed into separate components within the Web services domain.

Microsoft's Patterns and Practices group published a security patterns book [18] for Web services in 2006 with 18 patterns focussing on implementation with Microsoft technologies. The patterns are classified mainly by security purpose with classes for Authentication, Message protection, Transport and message layer security, Resource access, Service boundary protection and Service deployment. These categories mention both security objectives and protection targets, unlike the Steel book that classifies patterns according to system functionality alone (Table 4).

3.2 Multi-Dimensional Classification Schemes

Pattern classification schemes are needed for organisation, classification, comparison and selection of patterns. We proceed to discuss the more complex classification schemes using multiple criteria and indicate their place within the Zachman framework.

MITRE [19] introduced the use of the Zachman Framework in 2002 to help characterise and classify security patterns. They invented a seventh column for the framework to represent the Information Assurance perspective (which we consider synonymous with security here). The Information Assurance column enables the separate self-contained consideration of security concerns in every row of the framework.

Table 4 Security pattern classification schemes using the Zachman framework

Authors	Purpose	Classification criteria	Scope
MITRE [19]	Captures security best practices as reusable knowledge at all scopes of the enterprise from broad concerns down to implementation	Firstly by row in the Zachman table and secondly by security objective	Spanning all scopes from enterprise to implementation
Microsoft [20]	Aiding the development of products using Microsoft technologies	Classification by rows and then by subdivision into roles within each row, and finally by their Zachman aspects in the vertical dimension	General functional patterns at the bottom five rows of the Zachman framework
Schumacher [4]	Catalogued and documented known good quality patterns to support a firmer theoretical foundation for security patterns and aid their use by developers	Mainly by security objective, but other aspects such as resource being protected intrude into the classification. They place these groups of patterns within a diagram of horizontal sections resembling the Zachman rows, and different vertical columns that partition each row according to specific criteria appropriate for that level or scope	Enterprise, architectural and design, but not implementation
Hafiz et al. [13]	To consolidate and organise security patterns using a variety of classification criteria	By application context referring to where the pattern is applied relative to the system (core, perimeter, exterior), by Zachman aspect, by STRIDE category of security threat, and by fundamental security objective (confidentiality, integrity and availability)	Architectural, design and implementation
Hafiz [12]	Catalogued and documented all known good quality patterns and formed them into a pattern language	Final classification is by application context (core, perimeter, exterior) and then by STRIDE threat category	Architectural, design and implementation
Fernandez[a] [24]	Developed a methodology for building secure systems using patterns, and catalogued and documented good quality patterns including several new ones	Main criteria for patterns are firstly by security concern (security objective or application domain) and secondly by computer layer where the pattern is deployed. Several other classification criteria were also discussed	Architectural and design

[a]Does not explicitly mention the Zachman Framework

Secondly, the elements of the Information Assurance perspective are considered to form a plane overlaying the entire Zachman framework. This allows the integration of security and functional concerns as well, as the security concerns can be linked to the functional concerns in each of the other six columns. Our framework extends this with an explicit security plane overlaying the entire Zachman table cell-for-cell to model each of the six security aspects within their own cells, thus comprehensively decomposing and clarifying the relationships between the functional and security concerns.

They further subdivided the Information Assurance concerns into the classes of Identification and Authentication (Authentication), Access Control, Integrity, Denial of Service (Availability) and IA Accounting (Accountability) to aid detailed analysis. Confidentiality is a crucial omission, and Denial of Service is a threat not a security service (with the corresponding Availability service and the more common names for the other services given in brackets).

The Microsoft Patterns and Practices team [20] in 2004 adapted and extended the Zachman Framework to describe 110 patterns classified as Enterprise (64 patterns), Data (16 patterns) or Integration Patterns (30 patterns) for use in some of their products. The patterns are for modelling functional rather than security concerns, but the classification is similar to several of the security pattern schemes presented in this section.

They also have five levels that are roughly comparable to the bottom five rows of the Zachman Framework, which are (from the top): Business, Integration, Application, Operational and Development Architectures (the last two levels are ordered the opposite way in the Zachman Framework). The top row of the Zachman Framework is purely conceptual covering organisational objectives and the external environment and so has no architecture.

Their classification system goes a step further by dividing the rows according to specific roles giving particular use cases for each role, as originally described in the IEEE Standard 1471 for software architecture [21]. For example, the four roles given at the Business Level are CEO, General Manager, Process Owner and Process Worker who all clearly need different use cases to model the specific activities required to achieve their differing objectives, which can be analysed in detail by answering the questions associated with the various aspects.

It also includes a seventh column for testing called Scorecard that indicates test methods and success criteria appropriate to the purpose of the use cases and their level of abstraction. This is similar to MITRE [19], but Microsoft's conception has a narrower focus as the patterns are developed for implementation rather than conceptual analysis. They explicitly trace the tests to the purpose column for validation against desired objectives, rather than having relationships between the seventh column and all the other cells in the same row. Furthermore, they used the seven columns along with the roles in each row to classify each security pattern within a particular cell. However, this does not appear to be very useful, as most of the patterns were classified by function (how) with some by data (what) and a few by network (where) with no patterns classified within the remaining four columns.

Schumacher et al. [4] in 2005 structured their security pattern classification by overlaying collections of related patterns onto Zachman's levels of information models from the enterprise to design levels. They faithfully reproduced MITRE's idea of a seventh column, but changed its name to Security and gave it the question 'what security' or 'what protection'. Their security model has four explicit levels mapping to the upper five rows in the Zachman hierarchy (shown in brackets): Security strategy and policy (rows 1 and 2), Services (row 3), Mechanisms and Implementations (row 4), and an unnamed row for products and tools not containing any patterns (row 5).

They categorised the patterns mostly by security objective, although some other aspects such as the resource being protected (eg. a firewall) are sometimes incorporated as well. The classes are Enterprise security and risk management, Identification and authentication, Access control, Accounting, Firewall architecture, and secure Internet applications. The enterprise security and risk management patterns are at the enterprise scope, whereas most of the others are at both of the Services level (mapping to Zachman's architectural row) and Mechanisms and Implementations level (mapping to Zachman's design row).

They also partitioned each level by different criteria according to the theme for the level, and then placed the pattern classes (mentioned above) within these divisions. For example, the Mechanisms and Implementation level (design row) was partitioned according to the mechanisms supported, with the patterns classified into management support, automated, physical and procedural mechanisms. However, they discovered that all their patterns at this level were automated mechanisms, so there is ample scope for pattern discovery within the other categories.

Hafiz et al. [13] proposed several ways to classify and organise security patterns by:

- The application context referring to where the pattern is applied relative to the system
- Zachman aspect like Microsoft's general pattern scheme [21]
- The STRIDE threat model [22] devised by Microsoft
- Security objectives of confidentiality, integrity and availability.

The application context classifies the security patterns by their location within the system core, on the system perimeter or exterior in the system environment. It is the horizontal location where the pattern is applied, and is not to be confused with the vertical application level at layer 7 in the OSI network model. One issue is that most patterns fall into the system core category and the scheme does not provide a way to separate them into smaller unified groups.

The Zachman aspects were proposed for classifying security patterns based on the ideas put forward by Microsoft discussed earlier [20]. Nearly all security patterns are classified by the functional and data aspects with a few by the network aspect, which is not very useful for classification as we already mentioned. In addition, the Zachman table could not uniquely classify many patterns whose classification occupied multiple cells vertically or horizontally. Others employing the Zachman Framework used the column aspects to characterise different facets of patterns rather than for classification.

They included a seventh column for testing correctness or verification, not validation as proposed by Microsoft [20] or the wider sense of considering the different security concerns for all of the aspects as proposed by MITRE [19]. The testing column also houses separate testing patterns consistent with their classification scheme by aspect, whereas most others only used the seventh column for posing questions about the adequacy of patterns described in the other columns.

Furthermore, they classified patterns based on the problems they try to overcome in the security domain using Microsoft's threat modelling scheme. STRIDE [22] is an acronym that categorises the different types of threats to systems: Spoofing, Tampering, Repudiation, Information disclosure, Denial of service and Elevation of privilege. Once again, many patterns fall into several classes.

The final classification method is by the fundamental security objectives of confidentiality, integrity and availability. This is not a good classification scheme either, as there are many other security requirements such as authentication, authorisation and accountability, and several patterns have overlapping objectives even within even this restricted set, so it does not classify security patterns either completely or uniquely.

They finally settled on a hierarchical classification criteria using the two concepts of location first and then STRIDE security issue, discarding the Zachman aspects and security objective classifiers from their earlier work because they were not discriminating enough. The two dimensional schema overcomes to an extent the inadequate and incomplete classification provided by the single classifiers.

They then used the classification criteria to build a large security pattern language cataloguing all known patterns [23], and succeeded in classifying around 80 % of the around 100 unique patterns. The rest were generic patterns that they called higher-level patterns that could not be classified uniquely according to the two criteria. They weeded out poor quality and duplicate patterns, grouped the patterns using the criteria to help classification and selection, and identified and documented the relationships between the patterns in a pattern language displayed visually in pattern diagrams.

Fernandez [24] extends the ideas developed in the previous book with Schumacher et al. [4] adding many new patterns, and developing a methodology for utilising security patterns in building secure systems. Fernandez's schema does not mention the Zachman Framework, but is still able to be classified within its organisational structure*.

He discussed patterns at different levels (not scopes), thinking of a computer system as a hierarchy of layers (as in the 7-layer OSI network model), including the metalayer (people), application layer, system layer (operating system and database), distribution layer and hardware configuration [25]. These are the levels where patterns are deployed in the system domain, not the levels of abstraction in problem detail described in the rows of the Zachman Framework.

They then refined the basic classification using a multi-dimensional matrix of categories [26]. One dimension corresponds to lifecycle stages, including domain analysis, requirements, problem analysis, design, implementation, integration, deployment, operation, maintenance and disposal. They gave a mapping of patterns to the different computer levels along with the different lifecycle phases as the two main classification criteria. This separates out the Zachman horizontal row into two separate concepts divorcing level from lifecycle stage, as the levels considered by Fernandez are in the system domain where patterns are deployed, not levels of abstraction in problem detail as in the Zachman Framework that is correlated with the lifecycle stage.

Fernandez also indicates a dimension of security concern [24] that typically refers to security objective (eg. access control) in the security domain or application area in the system domain (eg. cloud computing). The security concerns are Identity Management, Authentication, Access control, Process Management, Execution and File Management, Operating System Architecture and Administration, Networks, Web Services, Cryptography, Middleware, and Cloud Computing that are the topics of several of the chapters of his book. Fernandez finally settles on a mapping of patterns that are firstly grouped by security concern, and within that, different computer levels as the two main classification criteria.

4 More Pattern Types and Related Concepts

4.1 Security Tactics and Specialisation

The less familiar idea of tactics [27] playing the role of design primitives may complement the broader pattern construct. A tactic is a design decision that influences the achievement of a quality attribute (aka non-functional requirement). The focus is on the attribute with little consideration of the wider concerns seen in patterns, such as problem context or trade-off analysis. Tactics are simpler and therefore, it is argued, easier to devise and apply.

The tactics idea has been applied to security, which we consider a quality for the purposes of this paper. There are four classes of security tactics: Detect, Resist, React and Recover [28, Chap. 9]. For example, within the Detect Attack class, we have Detect Intrusion, Detect Service Denial, Verify Message Integrity and Detect Message Delay. Security tactics are quite restricted and therefore ought to be more easily characterised and analysed than security patterns. We suggest that security tactics can adapt or compose with existing functional or security patterns to address particular security concerns.

Secure design patterns [16] were created by adding security services to several of the design patterns in the Gang of Four (GoF) book [3]. Secure design patterns are distinguished from security patterns, as they do not describe separate security mechanisms, but simply adapt and extend existing patterns (possibly using security tactics). This is a specialisation of an existing pattern to create a secure design pattern decorated with security concerns, whereas a standalone security pattern has to be composed with a design pattern to provide protection.

4.2 Transformational Patterns

Refactoring is the process of altering the internal structure of existing code to improve its quality without changing its externally observable behaviour [28]. Refactoring is generally simpler than a pattern as it makes more tactical rather than systemic improvements to code. For example, each refactoring in Fowler's catalogue [28] has a name, motivation, mechanics and examples rather than a dozen or more sections typical in a pattern template.

Lano [29] proposed a novel representation of design patterns as transformation rules that refactor a system to improve its quality. A refactoring is a transformation pattern if it describes a recurrent problem and its solution along with consequences [29], so it is more generic and has wider concerns than basic refactoring. When applied, the pattern transforms a given situation in which a particular problem is present into another situation where it is resolved or attenuated. To clarify, the transformation is the pattern and the source and target of the transformation may not be patterns.

The concept of transformational patterns seems to apply equally well to security as other quality or non-functional concerns. For example, Fowler's catalogue [28] contains several refactorings that can remove the security flaws from existing object-oriented programs. Hafiz considered his catalogue of patterns as security-oriented program transformations [30]. These transformations may ease the task of retro-fitting security to existing systems, which is a crucial benefit because many deployed systems cannot be easily replaced.

5 Pattern Organisation

5.1 Pattern Templates

Patterns are usually described using a template with predefined sections to document the different aspects. The template design is important, because it defines the type and characteristics of the information collected about the pattern and the problems it attempts to resolve. The level of detail in patterns templates differs considerably; although some templates provide very detailed explanations, others are quite concise. There is a strong correlation between poorly documented and inferior quality patterns. Short informal textual patterns may be useful for experienced designers to remind them of the different issues and possibilities, but they are not detailed or precise enough to aid implementation or acquire understanding by inexperienced users.

The GoF pattern template [3] is the de facto standard template for describing design patterns, and the POSA (Pattern-Oriented Software Architecture) format [31] is common for architectural patterns. However, there is no agreed standard format for describing security patterns and little consistency in the level of detail prescribed within the various templates. Patterns using ad hoc templates make the job of selecting and applying patterns much harder.

Some security patterns are structured using the GoF [3] or POSA [32] formats without significant adaptation or extension to incorporate security aspects. This is a sensible starting point because many security patterns aim to solve particular design and architectural problems. However, these general formats may not be specific enough to capture particular security concerns making it difficult to design, select and implement suitable security patterns that resolve the particular security issues satisfactorily. We may need to adapt or extend the sections in a standard template for each level of abstraction to address the distinctive security concerns in each stage of the development lifecycle.

5.2 Pattern Spaces and Diagrams

Patterns resolve problems by shaping their environments by configuring elements that exhibit suitable behaviour to resolve the forces displayed by the problem. However, implementing a pattern in a specific way creates a concrete situation whose context narrows the potential solution space for resolving problems remaining within the system context or brought about by the design solution.

Security patterns are usually secondary to objective concerns, which is awkward as the system environment or problem context may make it difficult to apply adequate security because of prior system commitments. Therefore, a structured way of thinking about the functional and security problems together using patterns is helpful to connect the security requirements to the system objectives they serve.

The patterns community structures and organises pattern spaces with pattern catalogues [3], pattern systems [31] and pattern languages [32]. One objective is to elaborate how security patterns can be combined into meaningful structures with other types of pattern.

We need to extend pattern combination to multiple spaces with security patterns composing with or specialising functional patterns. This requires understanding how the languages in the two domains can interoperate, with the functional pattern describing purposeful activities and the security pattern constraining potential undesirable behaviour allowed by the system context or functional pattern.

We can describe the relationships between patterns using a pattern diagram in which rounded rectangles represent patterns and arrows indicate the contribution of a pattern to another [31]. The basic pattern diagram can be extended with the generalisation notation from UML class diagrams [24] to indicate patterns that are subpatterns or specialisations of other patterns. As already mentioned, a Carnegie Mellon group invented secure design patterns [16] by simply specialising existing design patterns into secure design patterns by adapting and extending the basic pattern with security features. We can extend pattern diagrams in the UML notation to show the specialisation of design patterns into secure design patterns across pattern spaces.

The typical view of a security pattern is as a separate concept from design patterns, so patterns from both classes may need to be composed together to resolve problems. The security forces present in the problem domain are resolved by the security pattern in the security domain. We invent some new relationships between patterns with 'protects' between security and design patterns, and 'defeats' for the oppositional relationship between security and attack patterns. Hafiz [12] used pattern diagrams to express the associations between all known security patterns in his classification system, which we can extend to display these new relationships across pattern spaces as indicated by Zhu [33].

6 Conclusions and Further Work

The Zachman Framework is a metamodel for developing enterprise architectures as it incorporates the concepts needed for representing system models at all levels of investigation. We have demonstrated that it can similarly be seen as a metamodel for understanding and developing security patterns as it contains the concepts needed to classify all existing schemes and indicate their limitations. Our framework extends the basic Zachman framework with a parallel security plane overlaying the entire Zachman grid cell-for-cell to model each security aspect within its own column, allowing analysis of its compatibility with the problem context in the corresponding columns in the functional plane.

We highlight some of the key benefits of the Zachman Framework for modelling security patterns before elucidating some of the challenges. The advantages include:

- Separation of security from functional concerns using the separate security plane allowing for their independent analysis, as in the SABSA model [8]
- Integration of security and functional concerns by analysing the relationships between the corresponding aspects in the security and functional planes
- Extension to different horizontal scopes using the top row to model global patterns on the Internet, and the bottom row for modelling data patterns
- A meta-classification structure using the three dimensions of the framework (rows, aspects, planes) supporting examination of existing multidimensional schemes
- Aiding pattern selection as the solution pattern aspects in the security plane must be compatible with the corresponding functional aspects of the problem context.

The challenges regarding both the conceptual foundation and practical use of security patterns include:

- Clarifying their description to help both experienced and novice developers
- Determining the underlying concepts for their proper expression in a suitable ontology, possibly aided by the existing ontology for the Zachman Framework [34]
- Characterising their interrelationships in an adequate and complete pattern language

- Producing agreed classification criteria, unlike current pattern catalogues that use a variety of different attributes without giving a persuasive rationale
- Better coverage of the problem space identified from categorising existing patterns within the various rows, aspects and planes of the framework
- Providing a precise formalism for verifying the protection offered by security patterns against various attacks
- Developing tool support to enable pattern selection and formal reasoning
- Exploring the inconsistency between the horizontal scope of the problem compared with the lifecycle stage when the pattern is developed and its level of abstraction
- Establishing a systematic methodology with guidelines for incorporating security patterns within the various development stages to aid their differing objectives
- Developing patterns within fresh domains and applications such as data patterns
- Abstracting and modelling the processes and techniques involved in each lifecycle stage to extract common procedures into behavioural patterns
- Needing to distinguish pattern development from use in operational systems
- Needing to understand the relationships to descriptive patterns like attack patterns that are observed and inferred from their operational activities
- Analysing the relationships to other pattern types such as attack patterns by comparing their corresponding aspects using additional planes for each type
- Determining the utility of security patterns as transformations of insecure system configurations or observed attack activities into safe situations
- Possible development of related techniques such as security tactics for situations where patterns are unsatisfactory.

Relationships between patterns in different conceptual spaces can be advantageously considered [33] in addition to the existing relationships between security patterns such as generalisation, aggregation and conflict employed in security pattern languages [12]. The current use of specialisation in decorating design patterns with security concerns [16] and composition of patterns with tactics [27] can both be extended with a 'protects' relationship between complete security and design patterns.

The patterns in the various spaces must be compatible for the relationships between them to have practical utility. The integration and separation of security and functional concerns by using separate planes can be extended to other types of cyberpattern. We can again use aspects for analysis of the 'protects' relationship to match the characteristics of the design pattern in the functional plane and security pattern in the security plane, analogous to their use to overcome system problems with compatible security pattern solutions discussed earlier.

In addition, attack and security patterns can be modelled in oppositional planes connected by the 'defeats' relationship. The Zachman Framework has already been used for the decomposition of attack patterns [7] by their various aspects, and it is possible to use aspects to establish the likely success of attack instances in the prevailing system context. The idea now is to make the attack pattern incompatible with the system context using a security pattern that 'defeats' the attack pattern by preventing or overcoming the attack behaviour (how question) or another crucial aspect such as its motivation (why). This allows consideration of a broader set of protection mechanisms such as deterrence rather than focussing exclusively on malicious actions.

In addition, the patterns in the various spaces must also be compatible as pattern constructs for the relationships between them to have meaning. For example, pattern types match when they have the same operations, which may occur for base class operations inherited from a cyberpattern superclass. There has been some formal work to show compatibility between design and security patterns [35] and an indication that the main classes of cyberpattern including attack patterns may be compatible with each other [36]. A uniform framework for cyberpatterns is a significant and credible objective integrating formalisation with a strong conceptual basis along the lines discussed here.

References

1. Gabriel RP. Patterns of software: tales from the software community. New York: Oxford University Press; 1996. http://www.dreamsongs.com/Files/PatternsOfSoftware.pdf. Accessed 10 Nov 2013.
2. Kienzle DM, Elder MC, Tyree D, Edwards-Hewitt J. Security patterns repository version 1.0. Washington DC: DARPA; 2002. www.scrypt.net/~celer/securitypatterns/repository.pdf. Accessed 7 Nov 2013.
3. Gamma E, Helm R, Johnson R, Vlissides J. Design patterns: elements of reusable object-oriented software. Reading: Addison-Wesley; 1995.
4. Schumacher M, Fernandez-Buglioni E, Hybertson D, Buschmann F, Sommerlad P. Security patterns: integrating security and systems engineering. Chichester: John Wiley; 2005.
5. Zachman JA. A framework for information systems architecture. IBM Syst J. 1987;26(3): 276–92.
6. Zachman JA. John Zachman's concise definition of The Zachman framework^{TM}. Zachman International, Inc. 2008. http://www.zachman.com/about-the-zachman-framework. Accessed 28 Oct 2013.
7. Blackwell C. A strategy for formalising attack patterns. 1st cyberpatterns workshop. 2012. In cyberpatterns: unifying design patterns with security and attack patterns. Springer; 2014.
8. Sherwood J, Clark A, Lynas D. Enterprise security architecture, a business driven approach. San Francisco: CMP Books; 2005.
9. Fernandez EB, Larrondo-Petrie MM, Sorgente T, VanHilst M. A methodology to develop secure systems using patterns. Chapter V: Integrating security and software engineering: advances and future vision. IGI; 2006. p. 107–26.
10. Yoder J, Barcalow J. Architectural patterns for enabling application security. In: Proceedings of the 4th annual conference on pattern languages of programs (PLoP 1997). 1997.
11. Graham I. Business rules management and service oriented architecture: a pattern language. Chichester (WSX): John Wiley; 2007.
12. Hafiz M. Security pattern catalog. www.munawarhafiz.com/securitypatterncatalog. Accessed 30 Oct 2013 (15 March 2013).
13. Hafiz M, Adamczyk P, Johnson RE. Organising security patterns. IEEE Softw. 2007;24(4): 52–60.
14. Blakely B, Heath C. Security design patterns. Berkshire, UK: The Open Group; 2004.
15. Yoshioka N, Washizaki H, Maruyama K. A survey on security patterns. Prog Inf. 2008;5(5): 35–47.

16. Dougherty CR, Sayre K, Seacord R, Svoboda D, Togashi K. Secure design patterns. Software engineering institute. Paper 47. 2009. http://repository.cmu.edu/sei/47. Accessed 8 Nov 2013.
17. Steel C, Nagappan R, Lai R. Core security patterns: best practices and strategies for J2EE, web services, and identity management. Englewood Cliffs: Prentice Hall; 2005.
18. Hogg J, Smith D, Chong F, Taylor D, Wall L, Slater P. Web service security: scenarios, patterns, and implementation guidance for web services enhancements (WSE) 3.0. Redmond (WA): Microsoft Press; 2006.
19. Heaney J, Hybertson D, Reedy A, Chapin S, Bollinger T, Williams D, Kirwan Jr. M. Information assurance for enterprise engineering. In: Proceedings of the 8th annual conference on pattern languages of programs (PLoP'02). 2002.
20. Trowbridge D, Cunningham W, Evans M, Brader L, Slater P. Describing the enterprise architectural space. MSDN. June 2004. msdn.microsoft.com/en-us/library/ff648192.aspx. Accessed 8 Nov 2013.
21. Maier MW, Emery D, Hilliard R. Software architecture: introducing IEEE standard 1471. IEEE Comput. 2001;34(4):107–9.
22. Swiderski F, Snyder W. Threat modelling. Redmond (WA): Microsoft Press; 2004.
23. Hafiz M, Adamczyk P, Johnson RE. Growing a pattern language (for security). In: Proceedings of the 27th object-oriented programming, systems, languages and applications (OOPSLA 2012). 2012.
24. Fernandez-Buglioni E. Security patterns in practice: designing secure architectures using software patterns (Wiley software patterns series). New York: John Wiley; 2013.
25. Fernandez EB, Pan R. A pattern language for security models. In: Proceedings of the 8th annual conference on pattern languages of programs (PLoP 2001). 2001.
26. VanHilst M, Fernandez EB, Braz F. A multidimensional classification for users of security patterns. J Res Pract Inf Tech. 2009;41(2):87–97.
27. Bass L, Clements P, Kazman R. Software architecture in practice. Boston: Addison-Wesley; 2012.
28. Fowler M. Refactoring: improving the design of existing code. Boston: Addison-Wesley; 1999.
29. Lano K. Design patterns: applications and open issues. 1st cyberpatterns workshop. 2012. In cyberpatterns: unifying design patterns with security and attack patterns. Springer; 2014.
30. Hafiz M. Security on demand. PhD dissertation. University of Illinois. 2011. http://munawarhafiz.com/research/phdthesis/Munawar-Dissertation.pdf. Accessed 6 Nov 2013.
31. Buschmann F, Meunier R, Rohnert H, Sommerlad P, Stal M. Pattern-oriented software architecture volume 1: a system of patterns. Chichester: John Wiley; 1996.
32. Buschmann F, Henney K, Schmidt DC. Pattern-oriented software architecture volume 4: a pattern language for distributed computing. Chichester: John Wiley; 2007.
33. Zhu H. Cyberpatterns: a pattern oriented research methodology for studying cyberspace. In cyberpatterns: unifying design patterns with security and attack patterns. Springer; 2014.
34. Sowa J, Zachman JA. Extending and formalizing the framework for information systems architecture. IBM Syst J. 1992;31(3):590–616.
35. Zhu H. Design space-based pattern representation. 1st cyberpatterns workshop. 2012. In unifying design patterns with security and attack patterns. Springer; 2014.
36. Bayley I. Challenges for a formal framework for patterns. 1st cyberpatterns workshop. 2012. In unifying design patterns with security and attack patterns. Springer; 2014.

Part II
Pattern Representation

Hong Zhu

As discussed in Chap. 1, patterns are reusable, self-contained and composable knowledge that discern repeated occurrences of phenomena in a subject domain. Therefore, how to represent patterns is a knowledge representation problem, which has profound impact on the expressiveness and usefulness of such knowledge.

Ideally, a good pattern representation formalism should be expressive for encoding the domain knowledge to cover a wide variety of phenomena that are interesting to a wide range of usages with little ambiguity. Second, it must provide strong support to the discovery and use of the knowledge, such as efficient machine support of reasoning as well as the discovery and recognition of such knowledge mechanically. Moreover, a good formalism for the representation of patterns in a subject domain must also be readable, thus enabling patterns to be digested by human beings in knowledge transfer and application, such as in education and training.

Patterns almost always relate to each other and compose with each other in reality. They also interact with patterns of different types in complicated ways. Another challenge in the research on pattern representation is how to represent the relationships and interactions between patterns of the same type and across different subject domains. A particular question is how such pattern representation formalism can support the classification and categorization of patterns, and their composition.

Part II contains three chapters addressing the pattern representation problem. Chapter 3, "Design Patterns: Application and Open Issues" authored by Lano, reviews the recent development in the research on software design patterns and identifies some remaining theoretical and practical issues with the use of design patterns. In particular, Lano analysed the strength and weakness of the Alexandrian representation and its formalization of design patterns as solutions of recurring design problems. He then proposed a novel representation of design patterns as transformation rules that refactor the system to improve design quality. He pointed out that, in this approach, design patterns can be verified for their improvement of quality while preserving the semantics of the design, and be applied mechanically when the design quality problem is recognized through employing quality measurement metrics.

Chapter 4, "Challenges for a Formal Framework for Patterns" authored by Bayley, is concerned with the formalization of design patterns in mathematical notation; in particular, formal predicate logic. Bayley analysed the similarities and differences among software design patterns and security and attack patterns, and discussed the potential benefits and barriers of a general formal framework of pattern representations for all these sub-domains of cyberspace. He concluded that a unified model of design, security and attack patterns should define a pattern as a modification of existing systems. Such a representation of patterns should support pattern composition, instantiation as well as intention satisfaction, and facilitate formal reasoning about patterns with tool support.

Chapter 5, "Towards a General Theory of Patterns" authored by Zhu, proposed a domain-independent formal approach to pattern representation based on the notion of design space. A design space consists of a family of types of design elements and a set of relationships between such elements. A particular design comprises a set of elements, where each design element may have a number of properties, and relate to and interact with other elements through the relationships. Such designs are instances of design patterns. They correspond to the phenomena in a subject domain. A pattern is then represented as a subset of such instances that satisfy certain conditions. In this approach, a design space is defined through a meta-modelling notation called GEBNF, which stands for *Graphically Extended BNF*. A pattern is defined as a predicate on design space that characterizes the set of instances. Zhu demonstrated that both object-oriented software design patterns and security design patterns can be represented in such a language. Zhu also pointed out that the algebra of software design patterns proposed in the previous work with Bayley [1] is also applicable to patterns defined in this generalized approach.

Reference

1. Zhu H, Bayley I. An algebra of design patterns. ACM Trans. Software Eng. Methodol. 2013;22(3). Article 23 (2013) doi: 10.1145/2491509.2491517.

Chapter 3
Design Patterns: Applications and Open Issues

K. Lano

Abstract The field of software design patterns has grown extensively since the first work on patterns in the 1990s. Design patterns have proved useful as encodings of good design practice and expert knowledge in a wide variety of domains, from enterprise information systems to software security. We look at some recent developments in the application of patterns, and identify some remaining theoretical and practical issues with the use of patterns.

1 Introduction

The concept of software design patterns originated in the late 1980s and early 1990s, based on analogy with the architectural design patterns which had been formulated by Christopher Alexander in his series of books [1, 2].

The key text introducing software design patterns to software engineers and developers was "Design Patterns" by Gamma, Helm, Vlissides, Johnson, published in 1994 [7]. This introduced 23 patterns, such as Observer, Visitor, Singleton, Iterator, Template Method, classified into the three general categories of Creational, Structural and Behavioural patterns. Subsequently there has been widespread identification and application of patterns in a wide range of software domains.

Classic design patterns include:

– Template method, Observer, Strategy (Behavioural)
– Facade, Adapter (Structural)
– Singleton, Builder (Creational).

A design pattern expresses a characteristic solution to a common design problem: the pattern describes classes, objects, methods and behaviour which constitute the

K. Lano (✉)
Department of Informatics, King's College London, London, UK
e-mail: kevin.lano@kcl.ac.uk

C. Blackwell and H. Zhu (eds.), *Cyberpatterns*, DOI: 10.1007/978-3-319-04447-7_3, 37
© Springer International Publishing Switzerland 2014

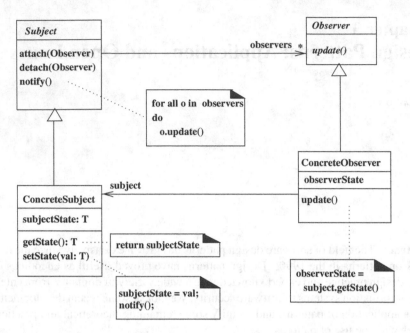

Fig. 1 Observer pattern

solution. The solution is intended to be an improvement on the system without the pattern: more flexible and adaptable, more modular, easier to understand, etc.

For example, the Observer pattern describes a way to organise a system which involves a data source (of arbitrary complexity) and multiple views or representations of that data. The pattern separates out the data and views into independent hierarchies of classes, connected by an association which represents the observation relationship (Fig. 1).

The pattern improves the modularity of the system by separating the system code into two distinct components which have clearly distinguished responsibilities: the data component (Subject) is purely concerned with internal data management, whilst the view component (Observer) is purely concerned with presentation of the data. The pattern improves the adaptability and extensibility of the system by using inheritance: new forms of data and new kinds of view can be added to the system without changing the observer mechanism, provided that the data and view classes conform to the Subject and Observer interfaces. On the other hand, the pattern has potentially negative implications for efficiency, because all interaction between the data and views has to take place via method calls. This is a common problem with many design patterns: improvements in the logical structure of a system may reduce efficiency. However it is generally considered that the gains are more significant for software quality—and therefore long-term reductions in software maintenance costs—than the loss of optimal performance.

Fig. 2 Front controller
pattern

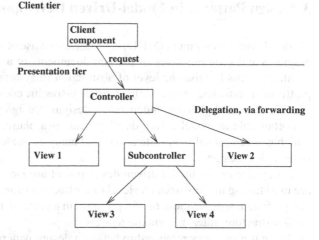

Patterns are distinguished from *idioms*: small-scale repetitive structures of code, such as the standard for-loop header in C. They are also distinguished from *refactorings* of programs or models: small-scale and incremental structural transformations of systems, eg.: pulling up attributes from a subclass to a superclass. However, in some cases refactorings can be used as steps by which a pattern can be introduced [10].

2 Specialised Design Patterns

Following the identification and formulation of a large collection of general purpose software patterns, work began on the identification of patterns specialised for particular domains. For example, in [13], a collection of patterns aimed at improving the design of enterprise information systems (EIS) is described. The patterns serve an educational purpose, transferring some expertise in this complex domain from experienced developers to those unfamiliar with its particular problems and solutions. EIS patterns include Front Controller (Fig. 2), Intercepting Filter, Value Object, Data Access Object, etc.

These patterns are in some cases specialisations of classical patterns (e.g.: Intercepting Filter can be regarded as a special case of Chain of Responsibility, and Front Controller as a version of Facade), or they may be specific to the domain (e.g.: Value Object).

Likewise, in the domain of service-oriented architectures (SOA), patterns for services, such as Broker, Router, etc. have been formulated, and for security concerns there are patterns such as Access Proxy [9]. Patterns have also been recognised at the specification and analysis stages, e.g.: the Scenario pattern of [5]. More recently, patterns have been defined for model transformations, such as Auxiliary Metamodel, Phased Construction, etc. [15].

3 Design Patterns in Model-Driven Development

Model-driven development (MDD) emphasises the use of models such as UML class diagrams and state machines as the key documents of a software system development, and aims to raise the level of abstraction in system development away from platform-specific and programming language-specific coding towards business-level specifications and platform-independent designs. Design patterns certainly have an important role in model-driven development, as a platform-independent technique which can be applied to specifications and analysis models as well as to language-independent designs.

A key element of model-driven development are *model transformations*, which are used to map models from one level of abstraction to another (e.g.: generation of a design from a specification, or of a program in a particular language from a design), or to restructure, filter or combine models.

There is a two-way relationship between design patterns and model transformations: a design pattern can be seen as a kind of model or program transformation, defining how a system can be rewritten from an initial structure that is deficient or of poor quality in some sense, to an improved version. Such a transformation is termed a restructuring or refactoring transformation. On the other hand, transformations themselves can be the subject of patterns.

In the first case, patterns have been used in semi-automated MDD to guide development by identifying good design choices [11]. Patterns have also been incorporated into programming languages and frameworks, such as the use of Iterator within Java, C# and C++ libraries, and of Observer/Model-View-Controller in internet application frameworks.

Model transformation patterns, together with quality measures of transformations, have been used to guide model transformation development, eg., to define modular designs, and to optimise transformations [15].

An example of a model transformation design pattern is the Phased Construction pattern of [15], shown in Fig. 3.

This pattern defines a particular style of organisation for a transformation specification, where successive layers of the structure of the target model are constructed by successive rules of the transformation. This contrasts with a recursive style of specification in which a rule may carry out the mapping of all layers of structure navigable from a particular object. The phased construction pattern improves the modularity of the specification.

4 Design Pattern Formalisation and Verification

Design patterns are usually described using text, diagrams such as UML class or interaction diagrams, and code. A standard form of pattern descriptions has evolved from the Gamma et al. book onwards, and usually involves a description of the

Fig. 3 Phased construction
pattern

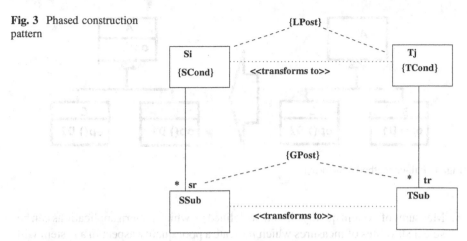

problem that the pattern is designed to solve, positive and negative indicators for using the pattern, and a description of how to introduce the pattern, together with a rationale for using it.

While such informal descriptions are useful to communicate the concepts and purpose of the pattern, they are insufficient to support automated selection and application of the pattern, or to support verification that the introduction of the pattern preserves desirable properties of the system, or that it actually improves some measure of quality such as modularity.

Approaches for pattern formalisation include [3, 4], which characterises pattern instances using a first-order predicate over the UML metamodel. For example, to specify that there is an instance of Template Method in a system, the predicate asserts that there is an abstract class in the set *classes* of classes of the system, that it has a finalised (leaf) template method which calls non-leaf operations, etc. This approach enables checking of a model for conformance to a pattern, but does not represent the process of introducing a pattern as a design improvement. A related approach using metamodelling to represent patterns and their applications is [11]. In [12] we characterise design patterns as model transformations, based on a modal logic semantics for UML.

Patterns are difficult to formalise because they often have considerable variability: the Template Method pattern for example could apply to any number of classes in the initial system model which have the same operation, and the factoring out of common code from these classes could be carried out in many alternative ways.

However, despite these limitations, we consider that it is of benefit to try to formalise patterns as far as possible, and to do so in a manner which supports their automated selection and application, and which supports their verification. We suggest that:

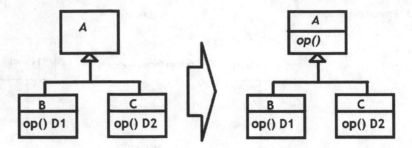

Fig. 4 Pull-up method refactoring

1. Measures of system quality should be defined by which pattern applications can be selected: values of measures which indicate a poor quality aspect in a system will identify that particular patterns should be applied to improve this measure; if there are several possible alternative pattern applications, then one which maximally improves the measure should be chosen.
2. Pattern applications should be formalised as model transformations, usually as update-in-place restructuring transformations.

This approach models both the *purpose* of a design pattern (improvement in particular quality measures) and the *process* of introducing a pattern, as a model transformation.

A range of quality measures could be defined, which characterise the modularity, complexity, degree of code duplication, data dependency and operation dependency structure of the system.

For example, two measures of a design-level UML class diagram which could be formulated are:

1. The number of classes A which have two or more subclasses, and where all these subclasses have a common operation $op(T1) : T2$ (possibly with different definitions, but with the same signature), but A does not have this operation defined.
2. The sum of all syntactic complexities of method definitions, e.g.: the sum of the number of features, operators and statements in their code, if expressed in a pseudocode programming language.

Non-zero values for measure 1 will identify cases where commonalities of subclasses have been incompletely recognised (e.g.: the LHS of Fig. 4), and indicate the application of the 'Pull up method' refactoring [6], to produce a system with an improved measure (RHS of Fig. 4).

If the definitions $D1$ and $D2$ have no common subcode, then measure 2 cannot be improved. However, if they share some small segment $D0$ of code, then a single definition of this code can be factored out and placed in A, reducing measure 2 by $complexity(D0)$, in the case of two subclasses, and by $(n - 1) * complexity(D0)$ if there are n subclasses with the duplicated code. Finally, if the majority of the code of $D1$ and $D2$ is in common, then the factorisation can be inverted, which leads

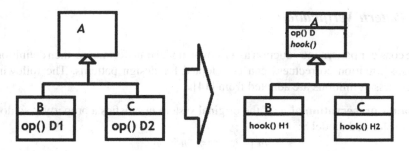

Fig. 5 Template method pattern application

to application of the Template Method pattern (Fig. 5), and a reduction in overall complexity of *complexity(D)* or $(n - 1) * complexity(D)$.

The introduction of a pattern can be considered as the application of a transformation rule, of the general form:

if pattern applicable to model part $\Longrightarrow$

rewrite model part according to pattern

In the case of Template Method, the pattern is recognised as applicable if there is a situation shown on the LHS of Fig. 5 where the common parts of $D1$ and $D2$ have a larger complexity than the distinct parts. The application of the pattern should factor out the maximum common part D of $D1$ and $D2$ in order to maximise the reduction in measure 2. Likewise, Front Controller should be introduced if there is duplicated request checking code in two or more presentation tier request target components. The duplicated code should be factored out of the maximal number of such components possible.

In [15] we give a set of measures and design patterns for transformation specifications, and give rules for selection of patterns based on the measures. For example, an alternation of quantifiers value greater than 0 in a constraint conclusion suggests applying the "Phased construction" pattern to the constraint, in order to remove this alternation, which complicates analysis, adaption and verification of the constraint. Similarly, if an expression of more than a given critical complexity occurs in two or more separate places in a specification, it should be factored out as a called operation: the larger the expression complexity and the higher the number of occurrences, the higher is the priority for application of this refactoring.

4.1 Pattern Verification

If we consider pattern introduction as a form of model transformation, then definitions of transformation correctness can be adopted for design patterns. The following correctness definitions are adapted from [14]:

Semantic preservation of φ: if the original system m satisfies a property φ so does the transformed model n:

$$m \models \varphi \implies n \models \varphi$$

For example, factoring out code of an operation by applying Template Method does not change the pre-post semantics of the operation.

Syntactic correctness: the transformed model satisfies necessary restrictions of the modelling/programming language. For example, that Template Method cannot introduce name conflicts of features into classes: in order to ensure this, names of hook methods should be chosen appropriately to avoid any existing method names.

Termination: that an automated series of pattern applications will eventually terminate.

In fact the use of measures will help to ensure termination: if each pattern application definitely reduces one measure and does not increase any other, then eventually the process will terminate with no pattern being applicable (assuming that measure values are always non-negative integers).

Confluence is also important in some cases, i.e.: a guarantee of the uniqueness of models resulting from a transformation process is required. One technique to ensure this is to show that the quality measures attain their minimal (best) values in an essentially unique situation, amongst those which can be reached by applying the rules. This holds for Pull up Methods and measure 1, for example.

5 Conclusions

Patterns have been a very productive area of research in software engineering, with many practical applications and benefits. The use of patterns is consistent with Model-driven development in raising the level of abstraction in software development from low-level coding to the level of concepts and ideas.

It is still an open-ended issue of how best to describe and formalise design patterns, and how to automate/semi-automate the selection and application of patterns. In addition, the general verification of the correctness of pattern applications is not solved.

In this chapter we have surveyed the research into these issues, and we have proposed that design patterns should be treated as model transformations for the purpose of formalisation and verification, and that measures should be defined to support the detection and selection of patterns, and to provide evidence of improvements obtained by introducing a pattern.

References

1. Alexander C. A Pattern language: towns, buildings, construction. New York: Oxford University Press; 1977.
2. Alexander C. The timeless way of building, New York: Oxford University Press; 1979.
3. Bayley I, Zhu H. Formalising design patterns in predicate logic, SEFM '07. Taiwan: IEEE Press; 2007.
4. Bayley I, Zhu H. Specifying behavioural features of design patterns in first order logic COMP-SAC '08. Washington: IEEE Press; 2008.
5. Fowler M. Analysis patterns: reusable object models. Boston: Addison-Wesley; 1997.
6. Fowler M. Refactoring: improving the design of existing code. Boston: Addison-Wesley; 2000.
7. Gamma E, Helm R, Johnson R, Vlissides J. Design patterns: Elements of reusable object-oriented software. Reading: Addison-Wesley; 1994.
8. Grand M. Patterns in Java. New York: John Wiley & Sons, Inc; 1998.
9. Hafiz M. Security pattern catalog. http://www.munawarhafiz.com/securitypatterncatalog/index.php 2013.
10. Kerievsky J. Refactoring to patterns. Reading: Addison Wesley; 2004.
11. Kim D. Software quality improvement via pattern-based model refactoring, 11th IEEE high assurance systems engineering symposium. Washington: IEEE Press; 2008.
12. Lano K. Formalising design patterns as model transformations. In: Taibi T. editor. Design pattern formalisation techniques. Hershey, PA: IGI Press; 2007.
13. Lano K. Model-driven software development with UML and Java. London: Cengage Learning; 2009.
14. Lano K, Kolahdouz-Rahimi S, Clark T. Comparing verification techniques for model transformations. MODELS: Modevva workshop; 2012.
15. Lano K. Kolahdouz-Rahimi S. Optimising model-transformations using design patterns. MODELSWARD: 2013.
16. Massoni T, Gheyi R., Borba P. Formal refactoring for UML class diagrams, 19th Brazilian symposium on software engineering. Uberlandia: 2005.

Chapter 4
Challenges for a Formal Framework for Patterns

Ian Bayley

Abstract To arrive at such a common framework we propose to leverage the existing work on design patterns, which are specified as predicates on the static and dynamic models of software systems. By reviewing the techniques for reasoning about design patterns, and what these techniques can achieve, we can propose a suitable way of structuring all patterns. This method of structuring is also informed by a detailed comparison between the headings used to structure each of design, attack and security patterns. The difficulties in producing a common framework for all types of pattern are also briefly considered, before a suitable method of structuring patterns is described in detail as a conclusion.

1 Introduction

Patterns are general, reusable solutions to commonly occurring problems within a given sphere of computer science. They originated in architecture, were transferred to software design as design patterns, in the so-called Gang of Four (GoF) book [1], and from there, by analogy, they entered the realm of cybersecurity, as attack patterns and security patterns. In all three cases, patterns are presented informally, as natural language text organised under headings. Although even informal documentation has done much to enhance the exchange of knowledge between practitioners, the software engineering community has found that software tools can be written that use formal definitions of design patterns to diagnose patterns instances. They could also assist in the implementation of patterns by "reminding" the user of the necessary rules. So

I. Bayley (✉)
Department of Computing and Communication Technologies, Oxford Brookes University,
Wheatley Campus, Wheatley, Oxford OX33 1HX, UK
e-mail: ibayley@brookes.ac.uk

C. Blackwell and H. Zhu (eds.), *Cyberpatterns*, DOI: 10.1007/978-3-319-04447-7_4,   47
© Springer International Publishing Switzerland 2014

it is natural to ask whether formality in the definition of attack patterns and security patterns can likewise benefit the cybersecurity community. If so, it may even be possible for tools to be kept updated by communicating newly discovered patterns in this way.

We begin by reviewing the concept of software design patterns. We explain one approach to formalisation and then extend it to express the intent of a pattern. We then review the headings of design, attack and security patterns with a view to proposing a common set of headings with a common approach to formalisation.

2 Design Patterns

First we consider the concept of design patterns as applied to object-orientated software design.

2.1 Design Patterns as Solutions

The Strategy Pattern, shown in Fig. 1, is used to select an algorithm at runtime.

Each separate implementation of operation *algInt* is a separate algorithm. To change the algorithm, we just need to create an object of a different subclass of *Strategy* and replace the existing object. We can formalise this as a schema, the declaration part of which identifies the components of the diagram and the predicate part of which specifies the constraints on those components. Let $\mathbb{C}$ denote the type of classes and let $\mathbb{O}$ denote the type of operations.

Strategy

$Context, Strategy : \mathbb{C}$
$conInt, algInt : \mathbb{O}$
$ConcreteStrategies : \mathbb{P}(\mathbb{C})$

$Context \diamond\!\!\rightarrow Strategy$
$conInt \in Context.opers$
$\{algInt\} = Strategy.opers$
$algInt.isAbstract$
$\forall CS \in ConcreteStrategies.CS \rightarrow\!\!\!\triangleright Strategy \land \neg CS.isAbstract$
$calls(conInt, algInt)$

Above, we use the relations between elements of $\mathbb{C}$ and $\mathbb{O}$ given in Table 1.

A software system conforms to the pattern if there exist bindings for the variables in the declaration part that make the statements in the predicate part true. Given such a formal definition, a tool can indicate whether a pattern appears in a software system and if so, where it does, in the sense of which variable bindings make the statement

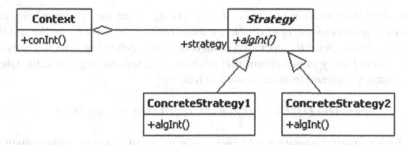

Fig. 1 Class diagram of the strategy pattern

Table 1 Predicates used to define patterns

Symbol	Meaning
$C \leftrightarrow C'$	class C contains an instance of C'
$C.opers$	the operations of class C
$C.isAbstract$	class C is abstract
$o.isAbstract$	operation o is abstract
$C \rightarrow C'$	class C inherits from class C'
$calls(o, o')$	operation o calls operation o'

true. Here, we have presented design patterns as concrete *instantiations* of a general *solution* to software problems.

2.2 Further Benefits of Formality

It is also possible to *infer consequences* from a design. For example, [2] shows how to prove that the abstract methods in the Template Method pattern must be defined in a subclass if that subclass is concrete, and the same argument applies to the similar Strategy pattern shown here. Similarly, it is possible to state formally and prove correct the proposition that one pattern is a *generalisation* of another eg that the Composite pattern is a generalisation of the Interpreter pattern. Although there are relatively few examples of generalisation within the Gang of Four catalog, it is noteworthy that the concept completely pervades the presentation of attack patterns and so a formal definition may well prove to be useful.

2.3 The Intent of Design Patterns

In the above, we have captured the concept of patterns being *general* solutions, with the concept of instantiation, without expressing the problems for which they are general solutions. Turning back to the diagram of the Strategy pattern, we can see that although the operation $Strategy.algInt$ is being called, the operation being run is one of $\{ConcreteStrategy_1.algInt, ConcreteStrategy_2.algInt\}$. (We use the notation $C.o$ to indicate the operation of an operation o defined in class C.) This set represents the family of algorithms that might be selected. So in general, the intent of the Strategy pattern can be expressed as follows:

$$runsOneOf(Context.conInt, imps(Strategy.algInt)) \qquad (1)$$

Here, for any abstract operation o, let $imps(o)$ be the set of concrete implementations of that operation; since $algInt$ is the only operation in the strategy class there is one for each concrete strategy if we assume that implemented operations are not overidden.

The expression $imps(o)$ can formally be defined as

$$\{C'.o \mid C \neq C' \wedge C' \twoheadrightarrow C \wedge \neg C'.isAbstract\} \qquad (2)$$

The tool can be used in a concrete situation as follows. The user defines the intent (s)he wants in the language introduced in the table above augmented with predicates such as $runsOneOf$. After supplying the relevant operations os in some way, the method call can be added by the tool automatically, together with the relevant classes with those operations distributed among them, by unifying os with $imps(o)$, providing a valuable conceptual shortcut, and enabling the user to think usefully at a more abstract level than that given by the UML.

3 Design Versus Attack and Security Patterns

Although it is very much an open problem whether or not attack and security patterns can be formalised in this way, we are working towards a common framework. Such a framework would involve logic expressions of the sort seen above interspersed with headings like those seen in the informal definitions. So there is a need to identify a common set of headings that can be used for all three types of pattern; at the moment different headings are used for each.

3.1 Design Patterns

Design patterns are general reusable solutions to commonly occurring *software design* problems. Each pattern is given a name and some aliases; the same is true for attack patterns and security patterns.

The problem to be solved, what we call the intent, is described by several headings. The main such heading is Intent, which is a one-or-two-sentence summary short enough to be used for selecting candidate patterns to read in a given situation.

However, other headings that describe the problem are Applicability and the first half of Motivation.

Likewise, the solution is described by several headings. The main heading is Structure which consists of a UML-like class diagram. This diagram is generic in its identifer names and intended to be representative of several such solutions. For example, if an inheritance hierarchy is drawn with two subclasses, it is generally understood that three, four or even one subclasses would be acceptable. This is apparent in the diagram for Strategy pattern given above.

Two other headings are Participants and Collaborations, which mostly contain information directly readable or inferrable from the diagram. We discussed the possibilities of inferring information from the diagram in the previous section. The information in Consequences is less directly inferrable or not inferrable at all and some of it restates the intent. Another two important headings are Sample Code and Motivation (again) which give illustrative concrete instances of the pattern defined by the generic diagram in Structure. The heading Known Uses does this too but with less detail.

Clearly, the relation of instantiation, between patterns and pattern instances, is an extremely important one for understanding patterns, since that is necessary for patterns to be identified in existing code and to be used to create new code. The relationship between the problem and the solution also appears to be important. We discussed both in the previous section. Finally, Implementation gives optional suggestions, and Related Patterns, in spite of its name, recommends different ways of composing the pattern with other patterns to give new patterns.

3.2 Security Patterns

Security patterns [3] are like design patterns except that the recurring problems being solved are in the sphere of information security. We focus on the 16 patterns categorised as structural patterns, rather than procedural patterns. These tend to focus on matters such as passwords, privileges, and sessions. The Abstract heading is similar to the Intent heading of design patterns. The Problem heading does not give a single concrete example like the Motivation heading of design patterns. Instead it describes various subtypes of the pattern. There is an Examples heading too and it performs a similar role, at a similar level of detail, to the Known Uses heading of design patterns.

The Solution heading has block diagrams, which are intended perhaps more for pictorial illustration than detailed analysis. Components can be deployment nodes (eg client or server), files (eg web pages), data items (eg session key), code modules (eg filter or encryption module). All are related by only one form of connection. Crucially, the diagrams are in any case optional. For some patterns, such as Network Address Blacklist, the heading contains a list of components. For others, such as Password Authentication, it contains a step-by-step recipe.

Unlike with design patterns, the Related Patterns heading describes similar alternative patterns, as opposed to possible combinations of patterns. The Issues and Trade-Offs heading taken together correspond to the Implementation heading of design patterns, though Trade-Offs is more structured.

3.3 Attack Patterns

Attack patterns [4], in contrast, solve the problems of those wishing to compromise information security. The problem to be solved is given by the Attacker Intent and Motivation sections. The solution is given by the Attack Execution Flow, which presents algorithms using sequence and selection constructs. Examples are given under the Examples-Instances heading. The Related Patterns heading includes specialisations and generalisations of the pattern being documented. Another heading is Attack Pre-requisites, the essential pre-conditions required for the attack to take place.

4 Commonalities Between Patterns

It seems likely therefore that the following commonalities between patterns will need to be part of a general theory of patterns.

- Patterns must be *instantiatable*. It should be possible to produce a clear unambiguous list of actions for a concrete instance given a description of a pattern and it should be possible to easily identify to which pattern a concrete instance belongs.
- There should be a *generalisation relationship* between patterns such that one pattern is a subclass or superclass of the other.
- It should be possible to *infer consequences* from a pattern solution.
- In particular, it should be possible to *state the problem* that the pattern is intended to solve and prove that the *pattern solves the problem*. In the case of the intent of Strategy above, the concept $runs\,One\,Of$ is defined informally, but perhaps an independent more formal definition is possible.
- It should be possible to *compose* two patterns to form a new pattern that solves a greater problem than either of the two constituent patterns. Much work has already been done on defining compositions of design patterns, and it is possible that the same might be done for attack and security patterns.
- Finally, although this is only implicit in each type of pattern, each pattern can be seen as a *modification of an existing system* to achieve a certain result, be it attacking a system with an attack pattern, defending a system with a security pattern, or augmenting a software system with access to a particular class or method, as with design patterns. We see this with the extra classes added to get from the intent of the Strategy pattern to the solution.

4.1 Formalisation of Design Patterns

Aspects of such a general theory of patterns have already been realised for design patterns as already discussed. However, three further ideas are of possible interest.

Work by Jason Smith [5] has demonstrated that some design patterns can be thought of as being composed of more elementary patterns. For example, Decorator is shown to consist solely of three more elementary patterns chained together. This echoes the original architectural patterns by Alexander, which as [6] points out, are documented in terms of both the smaller (in terms of physical space) subpatterns which the pattern is made up of, and the larger patterns of which it can form a part.

Also, Amnon Eden [7] describes design patterns in terms of recurring concepts such as tribes of related classes sharing the same methods all in the same hierarchy. It would be very useful to identify such similar recurring concepts in attack and security patterns, and then to work on formalising them or make them atomic concepts in a new theory. Candidates in the case of security patterns would include passwords, the data resources they are needed to access, the hardware resources on which they reside etc.

Finally, there appears to be some counterbalancing relationship between some security patterns and some attack patterns. For example, the security pattern of Password Lock Out would appear to counterbalance (or in other words, defeat) an attack pattern in which a password is broken by exhaustively trying all possible combinations.

4.2 Potential Benefits of Formalisation

It seems possible that the activities listed above that are supported by tools for design patterns (or can be supported where the tools have not yet been produced) could also be supported for attack and security patterns. For example, penetration testing could be assisted if attacks could be automated from a generic description in the form of a formalised attack pattern. Conversely, attacks could be recognised in real-time given a library of attack patterns, and patterns could be exchanged more easily given a common formalisation. Furthermore, composite attack patterns could be composed more easily to generate an attack, or decomposed to detect a complex attack. Analogues of all these are currently possible for design patterns.

Furthermore, although this can be achieved without formality, a formalisation of generalisation could assist in "tidying up" existing knowledge. All three types of patterns document variants but they do so in different ways. Attack patterns are most explicit, with headings for generalisation and specialisation. Security patterns achieve this with a combination of the Issues, Trade-offs and Related Patterns headings. Design patterns do this with the Implementation headings.

4.3 Barriers to Successful Formalisation

Design patterns are formalised as characteristic predicates on a model of a software system. In other words, the predicate is true of the model if and only if the design pattern is to be found in the system. A single model of software systems can be used for all design patterns in the GoF book. Typically this predicate, asserts the existence of classes and methods with certain properties. Usually the definitions of methods are not constrained except to dictate that one method must call another method. In a sense, formalisation of design patterns works because it is possible to produce a single model of software systems with a suitable level of abstraction.

Somehow, a similar model, containing all relevant information but not too much fine detail, should be devised for attack patterns and security patterns. It may be possible to start with different piecemeal models for each of the different categories of attack patterns but only a unified model will allow arbitrary attack patterns to be composed.

5 Conclusion

A unified model of design, attack and security patterns facilitating formal reasoning and tool support in the manner proposed above will need to have the following elements:

1. a definition of patterns as a modification of a system, together with definitions of

   a. composition
   b. instantiation
   c. intent satisfaction

2. for each of attack, security and design patterns:

   a. a single model suitable for expressing all solutions for that class of patterns
   b. a single model similarly suitable for expressing all problems for that class of patterns; this could be an extension of the model for solutions, as proposed above for design patterns
   c. a set of base patterns that do not derive from (ie do not specialise) any other patterns
   d. a set of patterns derived from the base patterns

3. each pattern should be listed without alternatives since these should be factored out into different patterns, and each pattern should consist of:

   a. name and aliases
   b. a list of the patterns from which they derive
   c. a list of the patterns that derive from it (for convenience of reference)

d. a problem defined in predicate logic, stated in terms of the problems of patterns from which the pattern derives, if it is a base pattern
e. the condition, defined in predicate logic, in which the pattern is applicable
f. a solution defined in predicate logic, stated in terms of the solutions of patterns from which the pattern derives, if it is base pattern
g. a proof that the solution solves the problem
h. a list of examples, written as instantiations of any variables in the formalisations
i. a list of pattern compositions involving that pattern that have been found to be useful.

Also, ideally the pattern should be defined in terms of a modification of the existing system. Although this representation may seem too abstract for human readers, tools can transform it into representations more suitable for human readers by, for example, flattening the inheritance hierarchy and instantiating the solutions and problems to illustrative examples.

This work can then perhaps be extended to procedural security patterns, and HCI patterns.

References

1. Gamma E, Helm R, Johnson R, Vlissides J. Design patterns: elements of reusable object-oriented software. Addison Wesley, Reading; 1994.
2. Bayley I, Zhu H. Formalising design patterns in predicate logic. In: Fifth IEEE International Conference on Software Engineering and Formal Methods (SEFM 2007), pp. 25–36.
3. Security Patterns Repository. http://www.scrypt.net/~celer/securitypatterns/. Accessed 9 Sept 2013.
4. Common Attack Pattern Enumeration and Classification. capec.mitre.org. Accessed 9 Sept 2013.
5. Smith J. Elemental design patterns. Addison Wesley, Upper Saddle River; 2012.
6. Price J. Christopher Alexander's pattern language. IEEE Trans Prof Commu. 1999;42(2):21–27.
7. Eden A. Codecharts: roadmaps and blueprints for object-oriented programs. John Wiley & Sons, Hoboken; 2011.

Chapter 5
Towards a General Theory of Patterns

Hong Zhu

Abstract As knowledge of solutions to recurring design problems, a large number of software design patterns (DP) has been identified, catalogued and formalized in the past decades. Tools have been developed to support the application and recognition of patterns. However, although the notions of pattern in different subject domains carry a great deal of similarity, we are in lack of a general theory that applies to all types of design patterns. This paper is based on our previous work on formalization of OO DPs and an algebra of pattern compositions. We propose a generalization of the approach so that it can be applied to other types of DPs. In particular, a pattern is defined as a set of points in a design space that satisfy certain conditions. Each condition specifies a property of the instances of the pattern in a certain view of the design space. The patterns can then be composed and instantiated through applications of operators defined on patterns. The paper demonstrates the feasibility of the proposed approach by examples of patterns of enterprise security architecture.

1 Introduction

Since 1980s, much work has been reported in the literature on the patterns of OO software designs. Here, a design pattern (DP) is a piece of codified knowledge of design solutions to recurring design problems. A pattern-oriented design methodology has been advanced by the identification and catalogue of patterns, the formalization of them and the development of techniques and tools for formal reasoning about patterns and automating pattern oriented design and code recovery. Its success in improving OO design has also fostered research on patterns of other aspects of software design, such as interface, architecture and fault tolerant designs. The notion of patterns has

H. Zhu (✉)
Department of Computing and Communication Technologies, Oxford Brookes University,
Wheatley Campus, Wheatley, Oxford OX33 1HX, UK
e-mail: hzhu@brookes.ac.uk

C. Blackwell and H. Zhu (eds.), *Cyberpatterns*, DOI: 10.1007/978-3-319-04447-7_5,
© Springer International Publishing Switzerland 2014

also been extended to other phases of software lifecycle, such as analysis patterns in requirements analysis, architectural patterns in software architectural design, process patterns in software process modelling, test patterns in software testing, etc.

In a more general context, the notion of pattern has been investigated in many subject areas of computer science. In particular, security patterns [1, 2] and attack patterns have been identified and catalogued in the study of computer security. However, although the notions of patterns in different subject areas carry a great deal of similarity, we are in lack of a general theory that applies to all types of patterns.

In this chapter, we propose an approach to generalize our previous work on the formalization of OO DPs and algebra of pattern compositions and instantiations. We will also explore the applicability of the general theory to security and identify the new problems in the study of security patterns.

2 Related Works

2.1 OO Design Patterns

In the past decade, several formalisms for formally specifying OO DPs have been advanced [3]. In spite of differences in these formalisms, the basic underlying ideas are quite similar. That is, patterns are specified by constraints on what are its valid instances via defining their structural features and sometimes their behavioural features too. The structural constraints are typically assertions that certain types of components exist and have a certain configuration of the structure. The behavioural constraints, on the other hand, detail the temporal order of messages exchanged between the components.

Therefore, in general, a DP P can be defined abstractly as a tuple $\langle V, Pr_S, Pr_D \rangle$, where $V = \{v_1 : T_1, \ldots, v_n : T_n\}$ declares the components in the pattern, while Pr_S and Pr_D are predicates that specify the structural and behavioural features of the pattern, respectively. Here, v_i's in V are variables that range over the type T_i of software elements, such as class, method, and attribute. The predicates are constructed from primitive predicates either manually defined, or systematically induced from the meta-model of software design models [4]. The semantics of a specification is the ground formula $\exists V_1.(Pr_S \wedge Pr_D)$.

The notion of *pattern conformation*, i.e, a concrete design D *conforms* to a pattern P, or D *is an instance of* P, can be formally defined as logic entailment $D| = \exists V \cdot Pr$ (i.e. the statement $\exists V \cdot Pr$ is true on D), where $Pr = Pr_S \wedge Pr_D$ and we write $D| = P$. Consequently, for patterns $P_i, i = 1, 2, \exists V_1 \cdot Pr_1 \Rightarrow \exists V_2 \cdot Pr_2$ means pattern P_1 is a specialization of pattern P_2 and we have that for all designs $D, D| = P_1$ implies that $D| = P_2$. In other words, reasoning about the specialization relation between patterns and the conformation of designs to patterns can be performed in formal logics.

In [5], we have proposed the following operators on DPs for pattern composition and instantiation.

- *Restriction P*[*C*]: to impose an additional constraint *C* to pattern *P*;
- *Superposition P₁* * *P₂*: to require the design to conform to both pattern P_1 and P_2;
- Generalisation *P* ⇑x: to allow an element x in pattern P become a set of elements of the same type of x.
- *Flatten P⇓x*: to enforce the set *x* of elements in the pattern *P* to be a singleton.
- *Lift P↑x*: to duplicate the number of instances of pattern ψ in such a way that the set of components in each copy satisfies the relationship as in *P* and the copies are configured in the way that element *x* serves as the primary key as in a relational database.
- *Extension P*#(*V●C*): to add components in *V* into *P* and connect them to the existing components of *P* as specified by predicate *C*.

Using these operators, pattern oriented design decisions can be formally represented [6]. A complete set of algebraic laws that these operators obey has also been established so that the result of design decisions can be worked out formally and automatically. Moreover, with the algebraic laws, the equivalence between different pattern expressions can be proven formally and automatically through a normalization process. For example, we can prove that the equation $P[\|X\| = 1] = P \Downarrow X$ holds for all patterns P.

2.2 Design Space

Generally speaking, a design space for a particular subject area is a space in which design decisions can be made. Each concrete design in the domain is a point in this space. Understanding the structure of a design space of a particular domain plays a significant role in software design [7]. Three approaches to represent design spaces have been advanced in software engineering research:

- *Multi-dimensional discrete Cartesian space*, where each dimension represents a design decision and its values are the choices of the decision.
- *Hierarchical structure*: where nodes in a tree represent a design decision and alternative values of the decision are the branches, which could also be dependent design sub-decisions [8].
- *Instance list*: where a number of representative instances are listed with their design decisions.

In the General Design Theory (GDT) proposed by Yoshikawa [9, 10], a design space is divided into two views: one for the observable (structural) features of the artefacts, and the other for functional properties. These two views are linked together by the instances in the domain. These instances show how combinations of structural properties are associated to the combinations of functional properties. These two views are regarded as topological spaces and the links as continuous mappings between them. By doing so, two types of design problems can be solved automatically.

- *Synthesis problem* is to find a set of the structural features as a solution that has certain functional features that are given as design requirements.
- *Analysis problem* is to find out the functional properties from an object's structural properties.

The existing work on OO DPs can be understood in the GDT very well, which also provides a theoretical foundation for the approach proposed in this paper. However, existing approaches to the representation of design spaces cannot deal with the complexity of software design satisfactorily. Thus, we propose to use meta-modelling.

2.3 Meta-Modelling

Meta-modelling is to define a set of models that have certain structural and/or behavioural features by means of modelling. It is the approach that OMG defines UML and model-driven architecture [11]. A meta-model can be in a graphic notation such as UML's class diagram, or in text format, such as GEBNF, which stands for graphic extension of BNF [12].

In GEBNF approach, meta-modelling is performed by defining the abstract syntax of a modelling language in BNF-like meta-notation and formally specifying the constraints on models in a formal logic language induced from the syntax definition. Formal reasoning about meta-models can be supported by automatic or interactive inference engines. Transformation of models can be specified as mappings and relations between GEBNF syntax definitions together with translations between the predicate logic formulas.

In GEBNF, the abstract syntax of a modelling language is a 4-tuple $\langle R, N, T, S \rangle$, where N is a finite set of non-terminal symbols, and T is a finite set of terminal symbols. Each terminal symbol, such as String, represents a set of atomic elements that may occur in a model. $R \in N$ is the root symbol and S is a finite set of syntax rules. Each syntax rule can be in one of the following two forms.

$$Y :: = X_1 | X_2 | \cdot \quad \cdot \quad \cdot | X_n \tag{1}$$

$$Y :: = f_1 : E_1, f_2 : E_2, \cdot \quad \cdot \quad \cdot, f_n : E_n (2) \tag{2}$$

where $Y \in N$, $X_i \in T \cup N$, $f_i's$ are field names, and $E_i's$ are syntax expressions, which are inductively defined as follows.

- C is a basic syntax expression, if C is a literal instance of a terminal symbol, such as a string.
- X is a basic syntax expression, if $X \in T \cup N$.

Table 1 Meanings of GEBNF notation

Notation	Meaning
$X*$	A set of elements of type X
$X+$	A non-empty set of elements of type X
$[X]$	An optional element of type X
$\underline{X@Z.f}$	A reference to an existing element of type X in field f of an element of type Z

- $\underline{X@Z.f}$ is a basic syntax expression, if $X, Z \in N$, and f is a field name in the definition of Z, and X is the type of f field in Z's definition. The non-terminal symbol X is called a referential occurrence.
- $E*$, $E+$ and $[E]$ are syntax expressions, if E is a basic syntax expression.

The meaning of the above meta-notation is informally explained in Table 1.

Informally, each terminal and non-terminal symbol denotes a type of elements that may occur in a model. Each terminal symbol denotes a set of predefined basic elements. For example, the terminal symbol String denotes the set of strings of characters. Non-terminal symbols denote the constructs of the modelling language. The elements of the root symbol are the models of the language.

If a non-terminal symbol Y is defined in the form (1), it means that an element of type Y can be an element of type X_i, where $1 \leq i \leq n$.

If a non-terminal symbol Y is defined in the form (2), then, Y denotes a type of elements that each consists of n elements of type $X_1, \ldots, X_n$, respectively. The k'th element in the tuple can be accessed through the field name f_k, which is a function symbol of type $Y \rightarrow X_k$. That is, if a is an element of type Y, we write $a.f_k$ for the k'th element of a.

Given a well-defined GEBNF syntax $G = \langle R, N, T, S \rangle$ of a modelling language L, we write $Fun(G)$ to denote the set of function symbols derived from the syntax rules. From $Fun(G)$, a predicate logic language can be defined as usual (C.f. [13]) using variables, relations and operators on sets, relations and operators on types denoted by terminal and non-terminal symbols, equality and logic connectives *or* $\vee$, *and* $\wedge$, *not* $\neg$, *implication* $\Rightarrow$ and *equivalent* $\equiv$, and quantifiers *for all* $\forall$ and *exists* $\exists$.

3 The Proposed Approach

3.1 Overview

The proposed approach consists of the following aspects.

- *Definition of design space.*

We will use GEBNF-like meta-notation to define a meta-model as the design space. The meta-model will defines a number of views. In each view, the meta-model will define a number of types of component elements in the subject domain and relations and properties of the elements.

From a GEBNF-like meta-model, a predicate logic language will be induced as in [12]. In this language, the sorts of the elements are the types defined in the meta-model. The primitive relation symbols, function symbols and predicate symbols are the functions, relations and properties defined for the design space.

- *Specification of patterns in a design space.*
  The patterns in a design space can then be specified formally using the induced predicate logic in the same way as we define OO DPs. That is, each pattern is defined by a predicate in the induced predicate logic language.

  Patterns can also be defined as compositions and instantiations of existing patterns by applying the operators on patterns defined in [5]. We believe that the algebraic laws proved in [6] should also hold for such design spaces. Therefore, the proofs of properties of patterns can be performed in the same way as in OO design patterns.

3.2 Definition of Design Spaces

We represent a design space in the following form.

DESIGN SPACE <Name>;
    <Element type definitions>;
    <View definitions>
END <Name>

An element type definition is in the form of GEBNF formula (1). For example, the following is the definition of elements in an object oriented design.

DESIGN SPACE OODesign;
    TYPE
        Class : := name: String, attrs: Property*, ops: Operation*;
        Property : := name: String, type:Type;
        Operation : := name: String, params: Parameter*;
        Parameter : := name: String, type: Type;
    VIEW …
END OODesign.

A view defines a set of properties of the element types and relationships between them together with some constraints. For example, the following is the structural view of OO designs at class level. The constraint states that inheritance is not allowed to be in cycles.

VIEW Structure;
BEGIN
    PROPERTY
     Features:
      {Class | Operation | Property}->
       {Abstract, Leaf, Public, Private, Static, Query, New}*;
     Direction:
      Parameter -> {In, Out, InOot, Return};
RELATION
    association, inherits, composite, aggregate: Class x Class;
CONSTRAINT
    FOR ALL c, d : Class THAT
     NOT (inherits(c,d) AND inherits(d,c)).
END Structure;

A view may also contain additional element types. For example, the behavioural view of OO design contains new types of elements such as *messages*, *lifelines*, and *execution occurrences*, *frameworks*.

VIEW Behaviour;
    TYPE
     Message: := OpId:string, params: ActuralParameter*;
     Life-line: := ObjName:string, ClassName:string, Finish: [INT];
     ExecutionOcc::= lifeline: Life-line, start, finish: INT; ...
    PROPERYTY
     Type: Message ->{synchronous, asynchronous, return};
    RELATION
     Message: Lifeline x Lifeline;
     ActiveExec: ExecutionOcc x Lifeline;
     Trigs: Message x ExecutionOcc;
END Behaviour;

3.3 Specification of Patterns

A pattern can be defined in two ways. The first is to define a pattern as a set of points in a design space in the following form.

PATTERN <Name> OF <Design space name>;
    COMPONENT {<Var> : <TypeExp>}+
    CONSTRAINT {IN<View name>VIEW : <Predicate>}*
END <Name>

For example, the *Composite* pattern in the Gang-of-Four catalogue can be defined as follows.

```
PATTERN Composite OF OODesign;
    COMPONENT
        leaves: SET OF Class;
        component, composite: Class;
    CONSTRAINT
        IN Structure VIEW
            inherits(composite, component);
            composite(component, composite);
            FOR ALL c IN leaves THAT inherits(c, components);
            component.features = {abstract};
        IN Behaviour VIEW ...
END Composite.
```

The second way is to define a pattern as a composition or instance of other patterns by applying the pattern composition operators to existing ones. For example, the following defines a generalised version of the *Composite* pattern.

```
PATTERN G-Composite OF OODesign;
    COMPONENT
        components: SET OF Class;
    EQUALS
        Composite ⇑ (component / components)
END G-Composite.
```

4 Application to Security Design Patterns

In this section, we apply the proposed approach to security design patterns to demonstrate the style of design space definition and pattern specification in the proposed approach.

4.1 The Design Space of Security Systems

Computer and network security replies on a wide range of issues and various levels. Here, as an example, we focus on the logic and context level of enterprise architecture. In this case, we can model security systems in box diagrams [14]. A box diagram consists of a number of boxes and arrows. Each box represents a subsystem or entity of the system. Each arrow represents a channel of information flow or interaction between subsystems. For the sake of space, we will only define the structural view of the design space. The dynamic view of system's behaviour will be omitted.

```
DESIGN SPACE SecuritySystems;
    TYPE
```

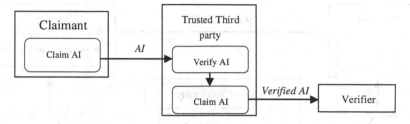

Fig. 1 Indirect in-line authentication architecture

Subsystem:
    name: STRING, content: [Value], description: [STRING];
InfoFlow:
    name: STRING, from, to: Subsystem, type: [STRING];
VIEW Structure;
    PROPERTY
        type: Subsystem -> {aataStore, computation};
        mode: Subsystem -> {active, passive};
    RELATION
        Is-a-part-of: Subsystem x Subsystem;
    END structure;
END SecuritySystems

4.2 Security System Design Patterns

Now, we demonstrate that security system design patterns can be design with a number of special components that fully fill various security specific functions, such as encryption and decryption.

Figure 1 shows the architecture of an indirect in-line authentication architecture, where *AI* stands for authentication information.

This architecture can be represented as follows.

PATTERN Indirect-In-Line-Authentication IN SecuritySystem;
    COMPONENT
        Claimant, TrustedThirdParty, Verifier: Subsystem;
        ClaimAI1, VerifyAI, ClaimAI2: Subsystem
        ClaimAI12VerifyAI, VerifyAI2ClaimAI2: InfoFlow;
        ClaimAI22Verifier: Infoflow;
    CONSTRAINT
        ClaimAI is-a-part-of Claimant;
        VerifyAI is-a-part-of TrustedThirdParty;
        ClaimAI2 is-a-part-of TrustedThirdParty;

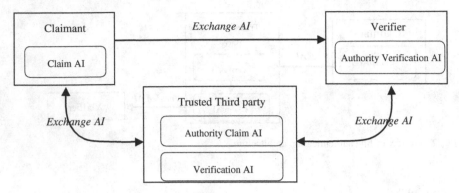

Fig. 2 Online authentication architecture

       ClaimAI12VerifyAI.from = ClaimAI1;
       ClaimAI12VerifyAI.to = VerifyAI;
       VerifyAI2ClaimAI2.from= VerifyAI;
       VerifyAI2ClaimAI2.to = VerifyAI;
       ClaimAI22Verifier.from = ClaimAI2;
       ClaimAI22Verifier.to = Verifier;
END

An alternative authentication pattern is online authentication shown in Figure 2.

PATTERN Online-Authentication IN SecuritySystem;
   COMPONENT
      Claimant, TrustedTP, Verifier: Subsystem;
      ClaimAI, AuthorityClaimAI, VerifAI: Subsystem;
      AuthorityVerifAI: Subsystem;
      ClaimantTrustedTP, VerifierTrustedTP: InfoFlow;
      ClaimantVerifier: InfoFlow;
   CONSTRAINT
      ClaimAI is-a-part-of Claimant;
      AuthorityClaimAI is-a-part-of TrustedTP;
      VerifAI is-a-part-of TrustedTP;
      AuthorityVerifAI is-a-part-of Verifier;
      … (* Some *constraints are omitted for the sake of space* *)
END

Another set of examples of security design patterns are encryption and decryption techniques, as shown in Fig. 3.

PATTERN EncryptDecrypt IN SecuritySystem;
   COMPONENT
     encrypt, decrypt, source, ciphered, recovered,
       key1, key2: Subsystem;

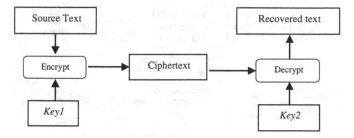

Fig. 3 Encryption and decryption

    source2encrypt, encrypt2ciphered, ciphered2decrypt,
    decrypt2recovered, key12encript, key22decrypt: InfoFlow;
CONSTRAINT
    encrypt.type=computation; decrypt.type=computation;
    source.type=dataStore; ciphered. type=dataStore;
    recovered. type=dataStore;
    key1.type=dataStore; Key2.type=dataStore;
    source2encrypt.from=source; source2encrypt.to= encrypt;
    encrypt2ciphered.from= encrypt;
    encrypt2ciphered.to= ciphered;
    ciphered2decrypt.from= ciphered;
    ciphered2decrypt.to= decrypt;
    decrypt2recovered.from= decrypt;
    decrypt2recovered.to= recovered;
    ...
END

There are two types of encryption/decryption techniques: symmetric and asymmetric. The former uses the same key in encryption and decryption, while the later uses different keys. Thus, we have two specialisations of the patterns.

PATTERN SymetricEnDEcryppt in SecuritySystem EQUALS
    EncryptDecrypt [key1.content =key2.content] END
PATTERN AsymetricEnDEcryppt in SecuritySystem EQUALS
    EncryptDecrypt [not (key1.content = key2.content)] END

Figure 4 shows a conceptual model of access control sub-system [14]. It is in fact a design pattern for access control in enterprise systems.

PATTERN AccessControl IN SecuritySystem
    COMPONENT
    Subject, EnforcementFun, DecisionFun, Object,
    AuditLogs, AccessControlList, SubjectReg: Subsystem;
    AccessReq, ApprovedAccessReq, DecisionReq,
    DecisionResp, WriteAuditRecord, SubjectInfo,

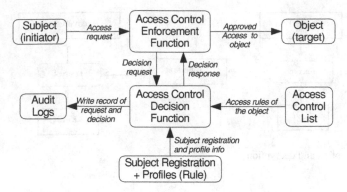

Fig. 4 Conceptual model of access control system

        AccessRule: InfoFlow;
     CONSTRAINT …
END.

5 Conclusion

In this paper we have proposed an approach to define design spaces so that design patterns in various subject domains can be defined in the same way as we define OO design patterns. We demonstrated the applicability of the proposed approach by examples of security design patterns. However, the structures of security systems have been simplified by representing them in box diagram models. Their dynamic features are omitted. The examples given in this paper are only skeletons. Many obvious constraints have been omitted for the sake of space. Further details must be worked out. There are also a number of other security design patterns can be identified. A case study of them and their composition is worth trying.

Existing research on relationships between DPs has limited to those within the same design space. However, to study patterns in cyberspaces, we need relationships between patterns across different design spaces. In particular, a security DP may be designated to against an attack pattern. They are in different design spaces. Hence, we have the following research questions:

- How to formally define the 'against' relationship between such pairs of patterns? And, how to prove a security pattern can successfully prevent all attacks (i.e. instances) of a certain attack pattern?
- Assume that the composition of security DPs (and attack patterns as well) be expressed in the same way as composition of OO DPs. Then, a question is: if a number of security patterns are composed together to enforce the security for an information system, can they prevent attacks of the target attack patterns and their all possible compositions?

Acknowledgments The work reported in this paper is funded by the Oxford Brookes University. The author would like to thank Prof. David Duce, Dr. Ian Bayley and Mr. Clive Blackwell for discussions on related topics.

References

1. Blakley B, Heath C et al. The open group: Security design patterns. Technical Guide; 2004.
2. Yoshioka N, Washizaki H, Maruyama K. A survey on security patterns. Prog Inform. 2008;5:35–47.
3. Taibi T, editors. Design patterns formalization techniques. Hershey: IGI Publication; 2007.
4. Bayley I, Zhu H. Formal specification of the variants and behavioural features of design patterns. J Syst Softw. 2010;83(2):209–21.
5. Bayley I, Zhu H. A formal language for the expression of pattern compositions. Int J Adv Softw. 2011; 4(3, 4):354– 366.
6. Zhu H, Bayley I. An algebra of design patterns. ACM Trans Softw Eng Methodol. 2013; 22(3):23.
7. Shaw M. The role of design spaces. IEEE Softw. 2012;29(1):46–50.
8. Brooks FP Jr. The design of design: Essays from a computer scientist. Boston: Addison-Wesley; 2010.
9. Yoshikawa H. General design theory and a CAD system. Proceedings of the IFIP WG5.2-5.3 1980 working conference on man–machine communication in CAD/ CAM, p. 35–57, North-Holland; 1981.
10. Kakuda Y, Kikuchi M. Abstract design theory. Annals of Japan Association for Philosophy of Science; 2001.
11. OMG. MDA Specification. Object management group, USA (2010). http://www.omg.org/mda/specs.htm
12. Zhu H. An institution theory of formal meta-modelling in graphically extended BNF. Front Comput Sci. 2012;6(1):40–56.
13. Chiswell I, Hodges W. Mathematical Logic, volume 3 of Oxford Texts in Logic. Oxford: Oxford University Press; 2007.
14. Sherwood J, Clark A, Lynas D. Enterprise security architecture: A business-driven approach. CA: CMP Books; 2005.

Part III
Introduction to Security Patterns

Clive Blackwell

Security patterns are based on design patterns, made famous in the software engineering community by the 'Gang of Four' (GoF) Design Patterns book. Security patterns have been widely studied and are the most mature domain within cyberpatterns, but many questions remain unanswered regarding their scope, contents and use. There have been many efforts at cataloguing security patterns, but the latest and most comprehensive with nearly 100 patterns is curated by Munawar Hafiz who worked with the Microsoft Patterns and Practices group to classify all known good security patterns and organise them into a pattern language [1]. This section suggests some novel uses of security patterns and related concepts for cyber security and resilience.

Chapter 6, *Extending AOP Principles for the Description of Network Security Patterns* by Llewellyn-Jones, Qi Shi and Madjid Merabti, discusses Aspect Oriented Programming [2], which is increasingly used for addressing crosscutting concerns that apply to multiple components but are largely independent of other issues. Security features give archetypal examples of crosscutting concerns, along with other system properties such as redundancy and Quality of Service (QoS). Security concerns present particular challenges when components are distributed across a network with the need to apply different aspects depending on the roles that components play within the overall system. The authors establish a suitably expressive language for reasoning across multiple heterogeneous components to allow aspects to be applied in different locations without inadvertently introducing new security weaknesses. The method is based on templates that match properties within the code allowing patterns to be identified and suitable aspects applied to the different components. They demonstrate the techniques using scenarios for secure data forwarding, end-to-end security and separation of duty.

Chapter 7, *Management Patterns for Network Resilience: Design and Verification of Policy Configurations*, by Schaeffer-Filho, Smith, Mauthe and Hutchison, aims to specify management patterns that describe the dynamic intrusion tolerance of networks. Much of the existing work on security patterns has focused only on static defence, but analysis of dynamic behaviour is also crucial for network management. The knowledge gained from resilience strategies and mechanisms, along with the best practices and experience is crystallised into reusable management patterns for addressing different types of network issue. They used architectural styles, similar in intent to software design patterns, for specifying the structure and interaction of the mechanisms within a pattern. The aim is to define a catalogue of management patterns to meet the challenges in providing dynamic network resilience. Their approach is framed within a two-phase strategy called $D^2R^2 + DR$ (Defend, Detect, Remediate, Recover + Diagnose, Refine) [3] that first deals with the immediate issue and subsequently uses feedback to improve the system. The plan is to generate management patterns from high-level specifications using goal refinement into specific sub-goals that independently realise the operational phases of the $D^2R^2 + DR$ strategy. They may also refine pre-existing patterns as part of the feedback control loop in the diagnose and refine stages of $D^2R^2 + DR$. They give an example scenario of a pattern to combat high-volume traffic challenges, such as from distributed denial of service (DDoS) attacks.

Chapter 8, *A Heuristic Approach for Secure Service Composition Adaptation*, by Zhou, Llewellyn-Jones, Lamb, Muhammad Asim, Qi Shi and Merabti, discusses techniques to help achieve secure composition for service-oriented applications. A service-oriented architecture (SOA) provides interfaces for services from different providers to work together to offer new applications by composition. However, security is an important concern with the possibility of inconsistent security policies and configurations, which need continuous monitoring and adaptation to find and overcome anomalies by using new services or arrangements. This chapter presents an approach to composition adaptation with systematic substitution of faulty services for various common modes of failure, using a simple heuristic strategy since exact solutions are NP-hard. In order to compare services directly, a quantification method is proposed using numerical measures for each security property of Confidentiality, Authenticity, Availability and Privacy. The measures are combined using suitable weights depending on the importance of each security concern to determine which services give the greatest security. The paper did not specifically use security patterns, but the level of abstraction would seem to suggest that security patterns might be suitable for modelling services and their compositions.

References

1. Hafiz M. Security pattern catalog. M Hafiz. 2013. www.munawarhafiz.com/securitypatterncatalog. Accessed 30 Oct 2013.
2. Kiczales G, Lamping J, Mendhekar A, Maeda C, Lopes C, Loingtier J.-M, Irwin J. Aspect-oriented programming. New York: Springer; 1997.
3. Sterbenz JP, Hutchison D, Çetinkaya EK, Jabbar A, Rohrer JP, Schöller M, P Smith. Resilience and survivability in communication networks: Strategies, principles, and survey of disciplines. Comput Netw. 2010; 54(8):1245–1265 (Elsevier).

Chapter 6
Extending AOP Principles for the Description of Network Security Patterns

David Llewellyn-Jones, Qi Shi and Madjid Merabti

Abstract Aspect Oriented Programming is increasingly being used for the practical coding of cross-cutting concerns woven throughout an application. However, most existing AOP point-cut definition languages don't distinguish in their application between different systems across a network. For network security there is a need to apply different aspects depending on the role a piece of code has within the larger networked system, and a new approach for this is therefore required. In this chapter we present a formalism for how this might be approached, proposing a way to capture distributed point-cuts for applying different aspects in different parts of the network. The method is based on templates that match properties within the code, and a set of flexible relationships that can be defined between them.

1 Introduction

While the majority of modern, mainstream programming languages have adopted object-oriented programming (OOP) approaches, it's nonetheless widely acknowledged that the OOP paradigm fails to adequately reflect the full breadth of structural features applicable to software development. In particular, while objects are a great way to compartmentalise functionality into reusable components, they can make it difficult to introduce functionality spanning multiple components. Aspect-oriented programming (AOP) has become established as an effective way for addressing this.

D. Llewellyn-Jones (✉) · Q. Shi · M. Merabti
School of Computing and Mathematical Sciences, Liverpool John Moores University,
Liverpool, UK
e-mail: D.Llewellyn-Jones@ljmu.ac.uk

Q. Shi
e-mail: Q.Shi@ljmu.ac.uk

M. Merabti
e-mail: M.Merabti@ljmu.ac.uk

C. Blackwell and H. Zhu (eds.), *Cyberpatterns*, DOI: 10.1007/978-3-319-04447-7_6,   73
© Springer International Publishing Switzerland 2014

Although AOP can be achieved statically at compile-time, the most successful AOP technologies have drawn upon the reflective (introspection and introcession) capabilities of modern languages (e.g. those built using virtual machine abstractions, such as Java, .Net, etc.) to provide dynamic aspects that can be introduced and removed at run-time.

From a security perspective, AOP techniques are an exciting development that offer considerable promise. Along with logging, redundancy and Quality of Service (QoS), security features are invariably considered as canonical examples of cross-cutting concerns particularly amenable to AOP approaches. However, security concerns present particular challenges, not least because the most pressing and relevant cases occur when components are distributed across a network. In contrast, most AOP approaches still focus on individual pieces of software, with aspects woven into the code in multiple places, but without considering how concerns cut across multiple interacting networked systems.

While security features should therefore be ideal AOP candidates, the need to introduce them across distributed networked systems creates both conceptual and practical challenges. For example, how can we *describe* concerns to allow reasoning across multiple heterogeneous components? Having established a suitably expressive language, how can aspects be applied simultaneously and so as not to inadvertently introduce new security vulnerabilities?

In this chapter we focus on the question of describing suitable patterns for applying security concerns. We focus particularly on ensuring that patterns can be identified, and solutions applied, even where this must take place across multiple distributed systems. While a number of AOP methodologies have been developed with distributed systems in mind, including several that consider security in particular, we believe there is still scope for improvements in terms of their expressiveness, and that these improvements are needed to allow the wider variety of security requirements found in networked systems to be adequately described.

The remainder of this chapter is structured as follows. In the next section we will consider a selection of the existing proposed AOP approaches applicable to distributed systems. We build on this in Sect. 3 by considering examples of issues that these systems do not yet address, but which are needed for security patterns in networked systems. Section 4 turns these into a set of requirements we aim to fulfil, with the resulting point-cut definition language described in Sect. 5. Section 6 considers application of the language to the aforementioned examples. Finally we conclude and suggest future work in Sect. 7.

2 Related Work

Broadly speaking, AOP involves the introduction of aspects into a piece of software. These aspects represent cross-cutting concerns, so that the same (or similar) functionality can be added in the same way across multiple components (e.g. objects or methods) within the same piece of software.

There are already a number of well-established AOP platforms, including AspectJ [3], PROSE [6], JAsCo [10], LOOM.Net [9] and DSAW [7]. One of the important characteristics that distinguishes these different platforms is the selection of *join-points* each supports. A join-point represents the possible types of location where aspects can be introduced into an existing body of code. Common examples of join-points include before, after or around a method call (where the latter potentially allows the call to be replaced entirely). In addition, some platforms will allow new attributes to be added to objects, or alteration of attributes through changes to the relevant getter or setter methods. Other language features, such as operator overloading, ensure even a relatively restricted set of join-points can nonetheless offer powerful and flexible program extensions.

Join-points provide a set of *potentials* which are turned into *actuals* through the use of point-cuts and advice. A *point-cut* is a description of a precise set of join-points, restricted for example by method name (often using wildcards) or parameter types. Each is associated with an *advice*, which constitutes the code to be injected at each of the join-points satisfying the point-cut description. For a more complete explanation about the fundamentals of AOP, see for example Ortín and Vinuesa's paper on the subject [7].

These existing techniques are well-suited to individual pieces of software, but require extension in order to be applied in distributed environments. For example, Pawlak et al. [8] developed A-TOS, a "general purpose aspect-oriented reflective middleware" to introduce such extensions. In A-TOS aspects are encapsulated in *aspect components*, which describe both wrappers that are applied to—and respond to events from—the existing distributed objects, and centralised code that provides a global state and semantics available to all the individual wrappers.

This provides a clean way for describing distributed aspects, and the authors also apply it to security in particular, demonstrating how Kerberos-like authentication can be achieved using the technique. However, while the system utilises the network to offer a global state to the aspect code spread across multiple components, it provides limited means for reasoning about how the wrappers should be applied (e.g. refining the choice of join-points based on the nature of the components).

A different approach is taken by Duzan et al. [1], by focussing on the boundary between a component and the middleware used to abstract the network functionality (e.g. CORBA). This work allows advice to be added across client-server connections, for example to allow different data to be sent from the server depending on the network conditions at the client end. The work introduces the concept of *regions*, which allow different code to be executed depending on dynamic properties such as QoS parameters defined using a contract. The work focusses tightly on QoS, but the use of contracts to define dynamic behaviour dependent on external conditions could potentially be adapted for security properties.

The DiaAspect Architecture Description Language [5] also focusses on distributed middleware, but in this case as an extension of existing modelling languages such as UML. The DiaAspect models can be translated into more specific implementations based on technologies such as RMI or Web Services. A carefully tailored join-point model allows point-cuts to be defined based on a variety of messaging patterns that include commands, publish/subscribe events, network sessions, component registration/discovery, and so on. Advice is injected at both the message emitter and receiver ends. As a modelling language DiaAspect is potentially well-suited to the abstraction of patterns, and the authors demonstrate its use for both SSL certificate management and access control.

At the implementation end, Horie et al. [4] take synchronisation of advice injection as a cross-cutting concern itself. They show how aspects can be used to bootstrap the synchronisation of other aspects by first injecting code to separate deployment from activation, before using this to simultaneously activate further aspects. A method is proposed for dynamically introducing encryption/decryption that avoids the packet loss that would occur if the encryption code were to be activated before the decryption code.

In previous work with García and Ortín we have also considered the application of dynamic AOP for implementing security measures. The work looked at practical implementations of aspects for applying access control and encryption to real-world software, in this case using the DSAW platform [2]. While this demonstrates the practicality of using AOP in distributed environments for security, the existing point-cut definition language of DSAW—concentrating on single systems—was used. Thus it was necessary to apply separate point-cut definitions to separate systems simultaneously in order to effectively apply the aspects. This chapter can therefore be seen as an attempt to understand better how the application of aspects across multiple systems can be appropriately described.

3 AOP Security Challenges

While all of these techniques tackle important issues related to applying distributed aspects, one area which is left open is that of reasoning about how aspects should be applied across multiple distributed components. Invariably a binary client/server-style relationship is assumed. While in many cases aspects can be easily introduced across connections (i.e. different coordinated code at the client and server ends of a connection) there is no coordination across multiple components.

We therefore explore how patterns can be defined to allow aspects to be woven into multiple components straddling multiple network connections. To understand the requirements of this approach we first consider a number of example scenarios.

3.1 Secure Data Forwarding

A very simple example of a security requirement is where data should be accessible by one system but not another. A simple example is shown in Fig. 1a, where different systems managing data classified at different security levels (High and Low) can communicate only with those systems certified to handle data of the same

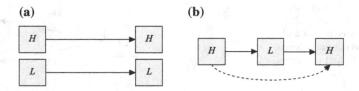

Fig. 1 Enforcing sensitivity levels to ensure high and low sensitivity data do not mix. In case **a** the requirement is met by ensuring high sensitivity systems cannot communicate with low sensitivity systems and *vice versa*. In case **b**, high sensitivity data can pass *through* low sensitivity systems, as long as the data isn't decrypted *en-route*

Fig. 2 End-to-end data flow security. In initiating and finalising the security process, the systems labelled *A* apply security measures that are different from the intermediate systems labelled *B*

classification level. This can be enforced using AOP at network endpoints in several ways. For example, by applying aspects that introduce an access-control negotiation step on initiation of any network connections. By using aspects this can be achieved transparently from the main functionality of the software by designing aspects to add metadata and encryption at one end of a network connection, then check the metadata and decrypt it at the other end. This scenario can be captured using aspects applied to pairs of atomic services and can already be represented using existing (e.g. client-server) methods.

However, this scenario can be extended to offer a more flexible approach. For example data might be allowed to travel through a system not entitled to access it, as long as decryption doesn't take place at the intermediate systems, as shown in Fig. 1b. An implementation of this approach using aspects was demonstrated in collaboration with García et al. [2]. However, this requires a more complex pattern description than a simple binary relation. Defining a point-cut language that can identify the various cases that might arise and apply the correct advice appropriately is therefore more challenging.

3.2 End-to-End Security

Extending the example in Sect. 3.1, we might consider a case where endpoint security must be applied using aspects at the source and destination node, but tackled differently at intermediate nodes. Such a scenario often arises where end-to-end security is required in a more complex networked arrangement of systems, as shown for example in Fig. 2.

In this case, in order to describe the arrangement a more flexible pattern is required. It must capture the chain of nodes, but with the length of the chain being

Fig. 3 Separation of duty.
Component *A* is entitled to
access component *B* if and
only if it has not yet accessed
component *C*, and *vice versa*

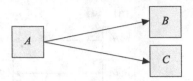

indeterminate. The set of instances satisfying the pattern is therefore infinite, although nonetheless clearly defined. Current methods have difficulty capturing this case adequately.

3.3 Separation of Duty

Not all patterns involve linear chains and it may be necessary to match different branch-types within a network graph. For example, a separation of duty requirement might allow component *A* in Fig. 3 to access *B* only if it had not yet accessed *C* (or *vice versa*). Aspects could be woven into *A*, *B* and *C* to enforce this, but would need to be applied only where such a split occurs. Moreover this represents another case where aspects cannot be applied uniformly: a different aspect must be applied to *A* as compared to that for *B* and *C*.

4 Requirements

In order to allow the above concepts to be formalised through pattern descriptions, we formulate a number of requirements that we believe a distributed point-cut definition language must fulfil.

1. Patterns must be capable of capturing sequences of more than two systems.
2. Patterns may match multiple (potentially infinite) sets of networked system. Flexibility is needed in both the depth (length of sequences) and breadth (number of links entering/leaving a system) in the network.
3. Patterns must not be indeterminate. That is, while there may be multiple arrangements that satisfy a pattern, the question of whether a particular pattern matches a particular set of systems should be decidable.
4. Pattern matches should be based on both the contents of the system code (obtained through introspection) and the relationship between systems (the structure).
5. It should be possible to relate the aspect code with the distributed point-cut and associated code. For example a different aspect is needed at either end of an asymmetric encrypt-decrypt network link.

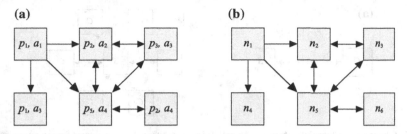

Fig. 4 Template graphs and actual graphs. The template **a** defining properties p_i and aspects a_i can be matched against the actual graph **b** comprised of nodes n_i

In the remainder of this chapter we aim to define a point-cut definition language which satisfies these requirements. The resulting language combines a pattern language with existing point-cut definition approaches, but leaves open the interesting question of whether a language that integrates the two more tightly could offer additional advantages.

5 Point-cut Definition Language

In order to fulfil the above requirements we define a formalism for specifying patterns that allows system properties to be combined with network interactions. Our intention is to allow a language to be developed from this for the flexible definition of distributed AOP point-cuts and advice.

In essence, we aim to specify a graph, where each node in the graph represents an atomic system (a piece of code to which an aspect can be applied), and where the links between nodes represent possible interactions between code across the network.

However, we must generalise this, so that the nodes represent *sets* of atomic systems (defined by a set of properties that a system must match). Consequently we distinguish between an *actual* graph of interacting systems and a *template* graph. The actual graph represents a set of networked systems. If each atomic system (nodes in the actual graph) fits the properties of a respective node in the template graph, and if the interactions also match, then the template matches the actual. Figure 4a shows an example of a template, with various properties $p_1, \ldots, p_5$. Figure 4b suggests an actual graph that might match it with actual systems $n_1, \ldots, n_6$. In order for the template to hold, the systems n_1, n_2, n_3, n_4, n_5 and n_6 would have to fulfil the properties p_1, p_2, p_3, p_1, p_5 and p_2 respectively.

A suitably generalised language would allow us to test templates against actual graphs, but doesn't tell us how to apply any aspects. For each node in the template graph we therefore assign a point-cut template and advice to apply to that system. These are represented by the point-cuts and advice $a_1, \ldots, a_4$ in Fig. 4a. In this case, the same nodes would have the aspects a_1, a_2, a_3, a_3, a_4 and a_4 applied to them respectively.

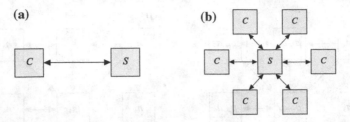

Fig. 5 Client-server template. A template satisfying a traditional client-server arrangement must apply equally whether **a** only a single client C is connected to the server S or **b** multiple clients are connected to the server S

Unfortunately such a system is still too restrictive. In many cases we want to apply advice to networked systems without being so prescriptive about the interactions between them. For example, in a client-server setting, we may want to specify advice to apply to the client and server separately. We can capture this with the graph shown in Fig. 5a (where C represents client code and S represents server code), but this will then fail to match if the server is managing multiple connections as in Fig. 5b. Flexibility is therefore needed to define which connections are relevant for a template, which can be ignored and which are prohibited (i.e. result in a template that doesn't match).

In order to fulfil Requirement 2 we must therefore allow flexibility in the way the input and output patterns are defined. Presenting this diagrammatically is difficult: how should we represent a set of—potentially infinite—distinct input and output patterns on a single diagram? We therefore consider a more formal description.

First we establish some definitions. Let N be the set of actual services in the scope of consideration, with $n_1, \ldots, n_j \in N$ being actual systems as above. Let P be a set of property descriptions and A be the set of point-cut advice definitions with $p_1, \ldots, p_k \in P$ and $a_1, \ldots, a_l \in A$. The a_i can be written in any existing AOP point-cut specification language such as that provided by DSAW [7]. We leave the choice of language for both the property definition and aspects open at this stage.

Let S be a set of states; for simplicity we can assume $S = \mathbb{N}$ (the natural numbers) using some kind of encoding. In practice it may be convenient to give S a more defined structure.

It will be convenient for us to define sets of properties, as well as sets of properties with associated actions (advice and point-cuts). We therefore note that these can be defined as any member from the sets 2^P and $2^{P \times A}$ respectively, where 2^X represents the power set of X. A member $x \in 2^P$ can be any subset of P, so takes the form

$$x = \{p_1, \ldots, p_j\}$$

for some $j \in N$ and $p_i \in P$. A member $y \in 2^{P \times A}$ takes the form

$$y = \{(p_1, a_1), \ldots, (p_k, a_k)\}$$

for some $k \in \mathbb{N}$, $p_i \in P$ and $a_i \in A$.

For a given node satisfying a given set of properties $p \in P$ we want to define a set of possible templates to match it against. A single template is defined as follows.

$$(a, x_I, x_O, \bar{x}_I, \bar{x}_O) \in A \times 2^{P \times A} \times 2^{P \times A} \times 2^P \times 2^P.$$

We call this an *atomic template* since it allows a specific set of input and output properties to be specified as a template for a single atomic system. We set T to be the set of all atomic templates:

$$T = A \times 2^{P \times A} \times 2^{P \times A} \times 2^P \times 2^P.$$

Suppose we have a node n satisfying the properties of p. Then in the atomic template for p the set x_I represents the set of properties that any node with inputs to n must satisfy; x_O represents the set of properties that must be satisfied by any node n connects to; $\bar{x}_I$ represents the set of properties that any node with inputs to n must *not* satisfy; $\bar{x}_O$ represents the set of properties that any node n connects to must *not* satisfy. Note also that each property in x_I and x_O has an advice associated with it. In case the complete template holds, this advice will be applied to the related actual node satisfying the property, which we will discuss in more detail shortly.

The above defines a template for only one property. We must extend this to allow templates for graphs of properties (that will then be matched against actual systems). We do this by specifying a function f of the following form.

$$f : P \times S \to 2^{T \times S}.$$

The function f defines a single general template and can be used to match against sets of actual systems. Note that as well as the atomic template, the function also maps to and from an input and output state S. This is to allow the same atomic template to apply at different places in the graph in different ways. We will assume that the initial state s_1 for any general template must be zero.

So for example, consider the arrangement from Fig. 4b again. The system n_1 satisfies the property p_1, hence we first apply the function to $(p_1, 0)$. The function will return a set of associated atomic templates $t_1, \ldots, t_j$ and an updated state s_2. We can then test the inputs and outputs of n_1 against the properties in each of the t_i to establish whether any of these hold. If they do, the process is repeated recursively, applying the function to each of the atomic systems that n_1 connects to/from, along with the updated state s_j. Note that at any point it may be possible for multiple of the t_i to match. In this case, each is tested separately. The process completes if either every recursive branch fails to match at some level, or one of the templates matches in full.

In the event that the template matches in full, the aspects defined in the template should then be applied to their respective systems.

To understand this better, in the next section we will return to our examples from Sect. 3 to see how such functions can be defined.

6 Application

In order to demonstrate further the application of the pattern descriptions, we consider how they might apply to the examples from Sect. 3. For secure data forwarding the key is to apply four different aspects at different points across the sequence of systems. We can do this by defining the function f to contain the following mappings.[1]

$$(H, 0) \mapsto (\emptyset, \emptyset, \{(L, a_O^H)\}, \emptyset, \emptyset, 0),$$

$$(L, 0) \mapsto (\emptyset, \{(H, a_I^L)\}, \{(H, a_O^H)\}, \emptyset, \emptyset, 0),$$

$$(H, 0) \mapsto (\emptyset, \{(L, a_I^H)\}, \emptyset, \emptyset, \emptyset, 0),$$

with all other inputs mapping to the empty atomic template. This matches only sequences of the form $H \longrightarrow L \longrightarrow H$. Note that for the above template any other inputs or outputs are ignored, but we could set it to fail if there are any other inputs or outputs by setting the $\bar{x}_I$ and $\bar{x}_O$ sets accordingly.

For the case of end-to-end security we require a slightly more flexible function. In this case we define the following mappings (with all others mapping to the empty template).

$$(A, 0) \mapsto (\emptyset, \emptyset, \{(B, a_O^A)\}, \emptyset, \emptyset, 1),$$

$$(B, 1) \mapsto (\emptyset, \{(X_1, a_I^{Y_1})\}, \{(X_2, a_O^{Y_2})\}, \emptyset, \emptyset, 1),$$

$$(A, 1) \mapsto (\emptyset, \{(B, a_I^A)\}, \emptyset, \emptyset, \emptyset, 2),$$

where X_1, X_2 are one of A, B and Y_1, Y_2 are one of B, A respectively. This generates a total of six templates. The first requires a sequence $A \longrightarrow B$. We then have four mappings that allow any sequence of the form $A \longrightarrow B, B \longrightarrow B, B \longrightarrow A$ or $A \longrightarrow A$. Note that the last of these could be left out if we required at least one connection through B. The last template stipulates the input requirement of the final A node. This is needed in order to ensure the sequence of templates matches through to the end.

Finally, the separation of duty requirement could be specified using a function f with the following mappings.

$$(A, 0) \mapsto (\emptyset, \emptyset, \{(B, a_O^A), (C, a_O^A)\}, \emptyset, \emptyset, 1),$$

$$(X, 1) \mapsto (\emptyset, \{(A, a_I^X)\}, \emptyset, \emptyset, \emptyset, 1),$$

where $X \in \{B, C\}$, generating three rules in total.

This case is slightly different, since we have two tuples in the x_O set of A: one for B and another for C. However, note that the rules for B and C have only a single input, since the template only sees the limited view of the world from the perspective

---

[1] The authors are indebted to Eduardo Pena Viña of Télécom Bretagne for identifying an error that appeared in the original version of this example.

of *B* or *C* respectively. Any interactions requiring a larger world-view must capture this through the state variable.

7 Conclusion

In this chapter we have briefly outlined a formalism for applying aspects to networked systems which extends existing techniques in a novel way, thereby providing greater flexibility. The approach allows complex structures to be defined across multiple networked systems using mappings between properties and atomic templates to which actual systems can be matched. While this provides the high-level mechanisms, there are a number of significant gaps in the work. For example, we did not present the point-cut language or explain how properties can be specified. Although an existing point-cut and advice language could be used, a more complete solution would also integrate state values into the advice.

Our approach as presented here is also theoretical, and doesn't explain how a template function would be specified in practice. All of the examples given here require only a finite set of possibilities for the inputs and outputs from any given system, which allows us to specify them as a finite list of atomic templates. The reason we use a function rather than a list is to allow more flexibility than this, and in general it wouldn't be possible to represent f using a finite list. In our future work, we therefore aim to demonstrate how these issues can be overcome in practice, using a practical implementation for applying distributed AOP security techniques.

Nonetheless we feel this serves as a foundation to demonstrate that richer point-cut definition languages are viable. In particular, the ability to apply appropriate advice flexibly depending on both the structure of the code and the structure of the network is an important capability. This is especially the case for security. While the cross-cutting nature of security makes it an important target for AOP approaches, many security concerns relate to interactions between systems. The ability to define how aspects should be applied to multiple systems simultaneously is therefore key to allowing AOP to be viably used to enforce security measures.

Acknowledgments The research leading to these results has received funding from the European Union Seventh Framework Programme (FP7/2007–2013) under grant no 257930 (Aniketos). The authors are especially grateful to Francisco Ortín and Miguel García at the University of Oviedo in Spain for their contributions to this work. We would also like to thank Eduardo Pena Viña of Télécom Bretagne for interesting correspondence on the topic that led to improvements in the text.

References

1. Duzan G, Loyall J, Schantz R, Shapiro R, Zinky J. Building adaptive distributed applications with middleware and aspects. In: Proceedings of the 3rd international conference on aspect-oriented software development, AOSD 04. ACM Press; 2004. pp. 66–73. doi:10.1145/976270. 976280.
2. García M, Llewellyn-Jones D, Ortín F, Merabti M. Applying dynamic separation of aspects to distributed systems security: a case study. Softw IET. 2012;6(3):231–48. doi:10.1049/iet-sen. 2010.0160.
3. Hilsdale E, Hugunin J. Advice weaving in AspectJ. In: Proceedings of AOSD 2004: 3rd international conference on aspect-oriented software development, Lancaster, UK; 2004. pp. 26–35. doi:10.1145/976270.976276.
4. Horie M, Morita S, Chiba S. Distributed dynamic weaving is a crosscutting concern. In: Proceedings of the 2011 ACM symposium on applied computing—SAC 11. ACM Press; 2011. p. 1353. doi:10.1145/1982185.1982479.
5. Jakob H, Loriant N, Consel C. An aspect-oriented approach to securing distributed systems. In: Proceedings of the 2009 international conference on pervasive services. 2009. pp. 21–30. doi:10.1145/1568199.1568204.
6. Nicoara A, Alonso G, Roscoe T. Controlled, systematic, and efficient code replacement for running Java programs. SIGOPS Oper Syst Rev. 2008;42(4):233–246. doi:10.1145/1357010. 1352617.
7. Ortín Soler F, Vinuesa Martínez LA, Félix Rodríguez JM. The DSAW aspect-oriented software development platform. Int J Softw Eng Knowl Eng. 2011;21:891–929. doi:10.1142/S0218194011005554.
8. Pawlak R, Duchien L, Florin G, Martelli L, Seinturier L. Distributed separation of concerns with aspect components. IEEE Comput Soc. 2000;276–287. doi:10.1109/TOOLS.2000.848768.
9. Rasche A, Schult W, Polze A. Self-adaptive multithreaded applications: a case for dynamic aspect weaving. In: Proceedings of the 4th workshop on reflective and adaptive middleware systems, ARM '05. New York: ACM; 2005. doi:10.1145/1101516.1101526.
10. Vanderperren W, Suvée D, Verheecke B, Cibrán MA, Jonckers V. Adaptive programming in JAsCo. In: Proceedings of the 4th international conference on aspect-oriented software development, AOSD '05. New York: ACM; 2005. pp. 75–86. doi:10.1145/1052898.1052905.

Chapter 7
Management Patterns for Network Resilience: Design and Verification of Policy Configurations

Alberto Schaeffer-Filho, Paul Smith, Andreas Mauthe and David Hutchison

Abstract Computer and communication networks are becoming increasingly critical in supporting business, leisure and daily life in general. Thus, there is a compelling need for resilience to be a key property of networks. The approach we present in this paper is intended to enable the specification of management patterns that describe the dynamic intrusion tolerant behaviour of resilient networks. A management pattern describes a policy-based collaboration between a set of resilience mechanisms used to address a specific type of challenge. Much of the existing work on security patterns has focused only on the static defence aspect of a network. However, dynamic behaviour adds a great deal of complexity to network management, thus making the specification of patterns for this activity very desirable.

1 Introduction

Computer and communication networks are becoming increasingly critical in supporting business, leisure and daily life in general. There is also an evident increase in the number of cyber attacks and security threats to networked systems. Thus, there is a compelling need for resilience to be a key property of networks. Resilience is the ability of the network to maintain acceptable levels of operation in the face of

A. Schaeffer-Filho (✉)
Institute of Informatics, Federal University of Rio Grande do Sul, Porto Alegre, Brazil
e-mail: alberto@inf.ufrgs.br

P. Smith
Safety and Security Department, AIT Austrian Institute of Technology, Seibersdorf, Austria
e-mail: paul.smith@ait.ac.at

A. Mauthe · D. Hutchison
School of Computing and Communications, Lancaster University, Lancaster, UK
e-mail: a.mauthe@lancaster.ac.uk

D. Hutchison
e-mail: d.hutchison@lancaster.ac.uk

C. Blackwell and H. Zhu (eds.), *Cyberpatterns*, DOI: 10.1007/978-3-319-04447-7_7,
© Springer International Publishing Switzerland 2014

challenges, such as malicious attacks, operational overload, mis-configurations, or equipment failures [17]. The study of network resilience deals with the dependability aspects of networked systems, but also involves other disciplines more related to network security and Quality of Service (QoS). In this context, the term *resilience management* encompasses and perhaps supplants some elements of the traditional FCAPS (fault, configuration, accounting, performance, and security) network management functionalities.

The nature of network attacks and challenges in general typically requires the coordinated use of a range of resilience mechanisms across various layers of the protocol stack, across a number of administrative domains, and across heterogeneous infrastructures. Our approach to the resilience problem is framed in the context of a two-phase high-level strategy, called $D^2R^2 + DR$: *Defend, Detect, Remediate, Recover + Diagnose, Refine* [17]. The strategy deals not only with the installation and configuration of various defence mechanisms, such as firewalls, but also with the dynamic adaptation of the configuration of a network in response to detected challenges—in effect implementing *intrusion tolerance*, an aspect of security that is increasingly being understood to be vital.

In order to ensure the resilience of a network, we advocate the systematic design and evaluation of resilience strategies, the careful coordination of various resilience mechanisms for monitoring and control, and also the capture of best practices and the experience of network operators into reusable *management patterns* [14]. Management patterns define an implementable policy-based collaboration between a set of resilience mechanisms used to address a specific type of challenge. Thus, a set of management patterns can describe the dynamic intrusion tolerant behaviour of resilient networks. Much of the existing work on security patterns has focused only on the static defence aspect of a network [9, 12]. However, dynamic behaviour adds a great deal of complexity to network management, thus making the specification of patterns for this activity very desirable. Management patterns can promote the systematic design and reuse of tested solutions for a range of potential challenges when building network resilience configurations.

The remainder of the paper is structured as follows: Sect. 2 describes the background and related work relevant to this paper. Section 3 outlines the idea of reusable patterns for the specification of resilience strategies and presents an example of a pattern to combat a high-volume traffic challenge. Section 4 discusses a number of research issues related to management patterns, namely: the specification of a catalogue of attack- and challenge-specific management patterns, conflict analysis and resolution, and pattern and policy refinement. Finally, Sect. 5 presents the concluding remarks.

2 Background and Related Work

We previously defined a management pattern as an abstract resilience configuration for addressing a particular type of network challenge [14]. During run-time, when challenges are observed in the live network, one or more management patterns can be automatically selected and instantiated, in conjunction with specific devices, based on the current availability and capability of resources. The aim is to support the systematic design and reuse of solutions for a range of challenges when building dynamic network resilience configurations. Policy-based management [16] is used to control the operation of mechanisms within a pattern, and how they should be reconfigured in the face of new types of challenges or changes in their operational context.

In [13], a number of application-independent structural constructs were presented for specifying the systematic federation of policy-based systems. These constructs, named *architectural styles*, are similar in intent to software *design patterns* [5], in the sense that they provide a set of standard solutions for recurring problems. Design patterns and software architectures can be seen as a set of principal design decisions made during the conceptualisation and development of a system [18]. Software architecture-based approaches typically separate computation (*components*) from interactions (*connectors*) to design and specify the overall structure of a system. The benefits brought by this distinction have been widely recognised as a means of structuring software development for distributed systems [8].

Configuring policy-enabled resilience mechanisms can present difficulties, especially when one considers the interaction between mechanisms for detection and remediation. Therefore, we propose the use of software engineering principles and management patterns to assist in the design of network resilience strategies. Although components and connectors do not cater for the adaptive behaviour of policy-based systems, similar principles can be applied for designing and reusing these systems.

3 Reusable Patterns for Resilience Strategies

A management pattern is a policy-based configuration for a set of resilience mechanisms and their relationships. Patterns are used to address a particular type of network challenge. Different challenge types will demand specific sets of mechanisms to monitor features in the network (e.g., current traffic load or alarms generated by an anomaly detection mechanism), and initiate remediation actions to combat anomalous behaviour (e.g., blocking malicious flows or selectively dropping packets). This assumes the existence of policy-driven mechanisms supporting a range of resilience functions in the network.

3.1 Pattern Specification

Patterns are abstractly specified in terms of *roles*, to which management functions and policies are associated. Roles in a given pattern represent the types of mechanism that are required to combat a specific challenge, and a given pattern may require roles with specific capabilities in terms of their ability to, e.g., monitor links, capture flows or classify traffic. Thus, a pattern specification consists of:

(a) Types of required mechanisms (represented by *roles*);
(b) How these mechanisms must interact with each other.

For example, a pattern for handling a flash crowd challenge may include roles such as *VMReplicator* and *WebServerMonitor*, to replicate virtual machines and monitor Web service activity, respectively, whereas a pattern for combating a *Distributed Denial of Service* (DDoS) attack may include roles such as *TrafficClassifier* and *RateLimiter*. To these roles, specific mechanism instances are assigned when a pattern is instantiated. Note, the same mechanism instance may be assigned to more than one role. For example, an enhanced router [20] may perform the generation of netflow records and also filter malicious flows. Role assignment provides a way of *type-checking* [13] mechanism instances in order to verify their suitability for the respective roles.

In addition to roles, a pattern also defines the management relationships between these roles, in terms of the policies that should be loaded and the events that should be exchanged. These relationships are expressed in terms of more primitive *architectural styles*, which are used as building blocks to connect the roles in the pattern. A catalogue of styles defining common management relationships for federating policy-based systems, such as *p2p*, *event diffusion*, *hierarchical management*, has been presented in [13]. The manner in which roles are connected using such architectural styles prescribes the relationships between the mechanisms used in a pattern.

3.2 Example Scenario: High-Volume Traffic Challenge

Figure 1 illustrates part of the *textual specification*[1] of a pattern to combat high-volume traffic challenges, e.g., a DDoS attack. The pattern is parameterised with four roles, which are described in Table 1. The relationships between the roles are defined in terms of the policies that must be loaded and the events that must be exchanged. In lines 6–14, styles are used to establish these relationships. In particular, we are setting an event diffusion between `IPFlowExporter` and `Classifier` (lines 6–8), another event diffusion between `AnomalyDetection` and `RateLimiter` (lines 9–11), and a hierarchical policy loading to be enforced between `AnomalyDetection` and `RateLimiter` (line 12–14).

A set of policies that can be loaded into another system is called a *mission* [7]. Figure 1 defines two missions, `throttling` in lines 16–19 (to be loaded into `RateLimiter`) and `detection` in lines 21–30 (loaded into `Anomaly Detection`). The former specifies a simple rate limiting policy when a specific

---

[1] We use a succinct pseudo syntax but in the current implementation patterns are written in *PonderTalk* [19] which is more verbose. We also limit the example to the configuration of a small set of mechanisms.

```
1   type pattern HighVolumeTraffic (role AnomalyDetection,
2                                    role IPFlowExporter,
3                                    role RateLimiter,
4                                    role Classifier)
5   {
6     bind style diffusion (target Classifier,
7                    source IPFlowExporter)
8                    event: notify_new_record(flow);
9     bind style diffusion (target RateLimiter,
10                   source AnomalyDetection)
11                   event: notify_detection(IPAddress);
12    bind style hierarchical (manager AnomalyDetection,
13                   managed RateLimiter)
14                   mission: throttling;
15
16    mission throttling {          //loaded into RateLimiter
17      on notify_detection(IPAddress)
18         do limit(IPAddress, %x);
19    }
20
21    mission detection {      //loaded into AnomalyDetection
22      on notify_load(name, rate, link)
23        if ((process(link, IPAddress) > %y) &&
24              anomalyList notContain(IPAddress))
25        do {
26            anomalyList add(link, IPAddress));
27            Classifier setAlgorithm(KNearestNeighbors, %z);
28            generateAlarm notify_detection(IPAddress);
29        }
30    }
31  }
```

Fig. 1 Management pattern specification for a high-traffic volume challenge

Table 1 Roles contained in a pattern to combat high-volume traffic challenges, such as a DDoS attack

AnomalyDetection	Performs online analysis to identify anomalies in network traffic, for example, anomalous changes in the entropy distribution of ports, IP addresses, or other statistical features
IPFlowExporter	Responsible for generating IP flow records using a specific sampling rate, which are truncated and sent at specific time out period, e.g., 60 s or 180 s, to other mechanisms to process the records
RateLimiter	Selectively throttles network traffic in specific links when anomalous activity is detected but not yet determined (suspicious but not necessarily malicious)
TrafficClassifier	Receives IP flow records and applies machine learning algorithms to identify the precise nature of the flow information, e.g., a flow is benign or part of a TCP SYN attack

IP address is deemed suspicious, and the latter defines what should occur when an anomaly is detected with a certain confidence level ($\%y$), in particular flag the anomaly, configure `Classifier` to use a specific algorithm, and generate an alarm.

When instantiated, a pattern will deploy the policy-based configurations across the mechanisms assigned to its roles in order to implement the prescribed interactions. Note, a pattern is instantiated only if the available mechanism instances satisfy the requirements for their roles [14]. This ensures that the policies inside the pattern can be executed by these mechanisms. Patterns facilitate the systematic building of policy-driven configurations, and can also be reused to cater for similar challenges that manifest at different parts of the network, or variations of an attack.

4 Research Issues

This section discusses a number of research issues related to the notion of reusable management patterns for resilience strategies.

4.1 Attack- and Challenge-Specific Management Patterns

A key research issue is to be able to define a catalogue of management patterns that are effective against different types of challenges. An attack- or challenge-specific management pattern can be seen as a *"recipe"* for addressing a particular type of network challenge. For example, Distributed Denial of Service (DDoS) attacks [11] aim to saturate a target resource, such as a set of network links or servers, with unusually high demands for service. A key challenge for service providers is to be able to determine automatically when such a situation (manifested as large volumes of network traffic) can be attributed to a DDoS attack, with nefarious ends, or a legitimate flash crowd event. This is important because the best means to mitigate these two challenges can be quite different. Related to DDoS attacks are computer worms that automatically propagate malicious programs over a network [6]. Despite this type of malware being studied for a number of years, they still constituted approximately 9 % of the successful malware infections in 2011 [10].

Regarding detection and remediation of these challenges, a number of candidate resilience mechanisms can be applied. For example, monitoring sensors, anomaly detection systems, and traffic classifiers can be used to detect and characterise a challenge, and determine whether unusually high volumes of traffic are being observed, e.g., caused by a DDoS attack. Complementary to anomaly detection systems are signature-based intrusion detection systems (IDSes) that attempt to match observed traffic against sets of rules or signatures, which describe attacks. With respect to remediating a DDoS attack, various forms of traffic shaping can be used, from blocking traffic to probabilistic throttling, which can be applied at different protocol levels and to individual network device ports, for example. Moreover, other techniques such as load balancing and virtual service migration could be used to remediate a flash crowd event.

Apart from statically configuring (or deploying) these mechanisms, it is also necessary to describe their relationships to orchestrate dynamic behaviour, e.g., based on output from a classifier, replicate a service because of a flash crowd rather than perform traffic shaping. It is our aim to understand how different malicious attacks and other network challenges manifest and how they can be optimally addressed. This knowledge can then be used to build a catalogue of implementable management patterns that capture best practices on how to configure the necessary resilience mechanisms.

To support the development of a catalogue of management patterns, we have developed a *resilience simulator* [15] that couples the OMNeT++ network simulator[2] and the Ponder2 policy management framework.[3] The purpose of the simulator is to evaluate the effectiveness of policy-driven resilience strategies that address a given challenge. Strategies that prove to be effective in the simulator can subsequently be promoted to management patterns. At the moment, the promotion of policy-driven strategies to patterns is carried out manually; future work will investigate tools to support this process.

4.2 Conflict Analysis and Resolution

In complex multi-service networks, determining the existence of conflicting config-urations is of critical importance. One of the key aspects that need to be addressed is the formal analysis of these configurations to prevent collateral effects, such as *policy conflicts* [1]. Formal analysis is necessary to assist in the design of policy-based systems and allow the verification of the correctness of anticipated interactions before these are implemented or policies are deployed.

The categorisation of policy conflicts presented in [1] is particularly relevant. The authors identify a set of primitives that can be used for policy ratification, namely: *dominance checks*, for determining when a policy is dominated by another, and therefore does not effect the behaviour of the system; *potential conflict checks*, where two or more policies cannot be applied simultaneously; *coverage checks*, which can be used to identify if policies have been defined for a certain range of possible cases; and *consistent priority assignment*, to prioritise which policies should be executed. Whilst [1] presents the theoretical foundations for this type of analysis, it explicitly leaves domain-specific information outside the scope of study.

However, domain-specific information is arguably necessary to detect conflicts. It is our intention to build on these general techniques for policy analysis and include domain specific expertise. For example, consider a scenario with two concurrent challenges—a DDoS attack targeted at a server farm and a flash crowd event directed towards another resource. Because of the DDoS attack, some remediation policies may lead to rate limiting being invoked on access routers; a network-level mechanism. However, a different set of policies may indicate that in the presence of a flash crowd event, we could reasonably decide to replicate a virtual service to another server farm; a service-level mechanism. This is indicated as a *vertical conflict* in Fig. 2. In this particular example, because of the naïve rate limiting that is operating as a consequence of the DDoS attack, trying to replicate a service can make the resource starvation situation worse. Also, it is necessary to guarantee the correct

---

[2] http://www.omnetpp.org/
[3] http://ponder2.net/

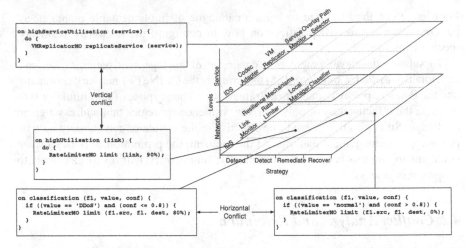

Fig. 2 Defining configurations for resilience is a multi-level problem, with *vertical* configuration conflicts across levels, and *horizontal* conflicts along the $D^2R^2 + DR$ strategy

enforcement of the interaction during run-time in which, for example, a device may fail and the interaction may have to be re-checked. Thus we intend to investigate how management patterns can be pre-verified for conflicts, possibly extending existing solutions and tools for policy analysis [3, 4].

4.3 Pattern and Policy Refinement

A given management pattern and its policies are expected to realise a high-level requirement to ensure network resilience, e.g., defined in terms of the availability of a server farm and the services that it provides. Whilst management patterns provide the means for establishing policy-based interactions, resilience strategies still have to be *pre-specified* manually. Although for a small case study it is relatively straightforward to specify the policies, more complex scenarios, for instance, that require cooperation across different autonomous domains, would make creating concrete policies by hand difficult. For this reason, toolsets are required to aid this process.

We will thus seek to (semi-) automatically derive implementable pattern and policy configurations from high-level specifications and requirements, with minimum human involvement. Considerable research has been directed to address the problem of policy and goal refinement [2]. One of the reasons for the lack of success so far is the difficulty of defining general-purpose goal refinement techniques. In contrast, by relying on application-specific domain knowledge we intend to provide support for the generation of management patterns from higher-level specifications, through the use of goal refinement and planning techniques. For example, by decomposing specific sub-goals that independently realise the different phases of the $D^2R^2 + DR$ strategy, each phase can thus be refined into more concrete sub-goals, until it consists only of concrete implementable operations (Fig. 3). Furthermore, this also includes

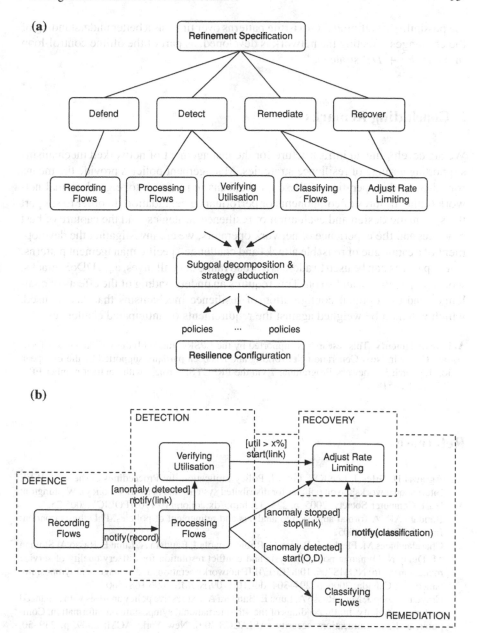

Fig. 3 **a** Goal decomposition of a resilience specification and refinement into low-level configuration policies, and **b** resilience strategy for the scenario (intermediary step)

the possibility of refining pre-existing patterns over time, as a better understanding of the challenges affecting the network is developed, as part of the offline control-loop in the $D^2 R^2 + DR$ strategy.

5 Concluding Remarks

We are developing an infrastructure for the management of networked mechanisms supporting a range of resilience strategies. Management policies provide the means for adapting the operation of these mechanisms in response to, e.g., abnormal network traffic, failures of components or performance degradation. In order to support the systematic design and evaluation of resilience strategies, and the capture of best practices and the experience of network operators, we are investigating the development of a catalogue of reusable attack- and challenge-specific management patterns. These patterns can be used to address a broad range of challenges, e.g., DDoS attacks, worm propagations, and so on. This requires an understanding of the effects of challenges and the optimal configuration of resilience mechanisms that can be used, which will then be weighed against the requirements of anticipated challenges.

Acknowledgments This research is supported by the EPSRC funded India-UK Advanced Technology Centre in Next Generation Networking and has been partially supported by the European Union Research Framework Programme 7 via the PRECYSE project with contract number FP7-SEC-2012-1-285181.

References

1. Agrawal D, Giles J, Lee KW, Lobo J. Policy ratification. In: Proceedings of the sixth IEEE International workshop on policies for distributed systems and networks (Policy). Washington: IEEE Computer Society; 2005. p. 223–32. http://dx.doi.org/10.1109/POLICY.2005.25.
2. Bandara AK. A formal approach to analysis and refinement of policies. PhD thesis,London: Imperial College; 2005.
3. Charalambides M, Flegkas P, Pavlou G, Rubio-Loyola J, Bandara A, Lupu E, Russo A, Sloman M, Dulay N. Dynamic policy analysis and conflict resolution for diffserv quality of service management. In: NOMS '06: 10th IEEE/IFIP network operations and management symposium, vancouver. Canada; 2006. p. 294–304. doi:10.1109/NOMS.2006.1687560.
4. Craven R, Lobo J, Ma J, Russo A, Lupu E, Bandara A. Expressive policy analysis with enhanced system dynamicity. In: Proceedings of the 4th International symposium on information, Computer, and communications security (ASIACCS '09). New York: ACM; 2009. p. 239–50. doi:10.1145/1533057.1533091.
5. Gamma E, Helm R, Johnson R, Vlissides J. Design patterns: elements of reusable object-oriented software. Boston: Addison-Wesley Longman Publishing Co. Inc; 1995.
6. Li P, Salour M, Su X. A survey of internet worm detection and containment. Commun Surv Tutor IEEE. 2008; 10(1):20–35. doi:10.1109/COMST.2008.4483668.
7. Lupu E, Dulay N, Sloman M, Sventek J, Heeps S, Strowes S, Twidle K, Keoh SL, Schaeffer-Filho A. AMUSE: autonomic management of ubiquitous e-health systems. Concurrency and computation: Pract Experience. 2008; 20(3):277–95. doi:10.1002/cpe.v20:3.

8. Medvidovic N, Taylor R. A classification and comparison framework for software architecture description languages. IEEE Trans Softw Eng. 2000; 26(1):70–93. doi:10.1109/32.825767.
9. OSA. The open security architecture. Available at. http://www.opensecurityarchitecture.org. Last accessed Sep 2013.
10. PandaLabs. PandaLabs Annual Report 2011 Summary. Tech. rep. Panda Security. 2011. http://press.pandasecurity.com/wp-content/uploads/2012/01/Annual-Report-PandaLabs-2011.pdf.
11. Peng T, Leckie C, Ramamohanarao K. Survey of network-based defense mechanisms countering the DoS and DDoS problems. ACM Comput Surv. 2007; 39(1):3. doi:http://doi.acm.org/10.1145/1216370.1216373.
12. Rosado DG, Fernandez-Medina E, Piattini M, Gutierrez C. A study of security architectural patterns. In: Proceedings of the first International conference on availability, reliability and security (ARES '06). Washington: IEEE Computer Society; 2006. p. 358–65. doi:10.1109/ARES.2006.18.
13. Schaeffer-Filho A. Supporting management interaction and composition of self-managed cells. PhD thesis. London: Imperial College London; 2009.
14. Schaeffer-Filho A, Smith P, Mauthe A, Hutchison D, Yu Y, Fry M. A framework for the design and evaluation of network resilience management. In: Network operations and management symposium (NOMS), IEEE. 2012. p. 401–08. doi:10.1109/NOMS.2012.6211924.
15. Schaeffer-Filho A, Mauthe A, Hutchison D, Smith P, Yu Y, Fry M. PReSET: a toolset for the evaluation of network resilience strategies. In: Proceedings of the IFIP/IEEE integrated network management symposium (IM 2013). Ghent, Belgium: IEEE Computer Society; 2013. p. 202–9.
16. Sloman M, Lupu E. Security and management policy specification. Network, IEEE. 2002;16(2):10–19. doi:10.1109/65.993218.
17. Sterbenz JPG, Hutchison D, Çetinkaya EK, Jabbar A, Rohrer JP, Schöller M, Smith P. Resilience and survivability in communication networks: strategies, principles, and survey of disciplines. Comput Netw. 2010;54(8):1245–1265. doi:10.1016/j.comnet.2010.03.005.
18. Taylor RN, Medvidovic N, Dashofy EM. Software architecture: foundations, theory, and practice. New Jersey: Wiley Publishing; 2009.
19. Twidle K, Lupu E, Dulay N, Sloman M. Ponder2 - a policy environment for autonomous pervasive systems. In: POLICY '08: IEEE workshop on policies for distributed systems and networks. Palisades, New York: IEEE Computer Society; 2008. p. 245–46. http://dx.doi.org/10.1109/POLICY.2008.10.
20. Yu Y, Fry M, Schaeffer-Filho A, Smith P, Hutchison D. An adaptive approach to network resilience: evolving challenge detection and mitigation. In: proceedings of the 8th International workshop on the Design of reliable communication networks (DRCN). 2011. p. 172–179. doi:10.1109/DRCN.2011.6076900.

Chapter 8
A Heuristic Approach for Secure Service Composition Adaptation

Bo Zhou, David Llewellyn-Jones, David Lamb, Muhammad Asim, Qi Shi
and Madjid Merabti

Abstract Secure adaptation of service composition is crucial for service-oriented applications. An effective adaptation method must improve a composition's adherence to specified behaviour, performance and security guarantees at reasonable cost in terms of computing complexity and time consumption. This chapter discusses current techniques that have been developed to help achieve secure service composition. Based on security verification results, which have been categorised into four patterns in this chapter, a simple heuristics-based adaptation strategy is proposed. This proposal aims at more accurate yet relatively fast secure service adaptation strategy. In order to make direct comparisons of different services, a simple quantification method is also introduced.

B. Zhou (✉) · D. Llewellyn-Jones · D. Lamb · M. Asim · Q. Shi · M. Merabti
School of Computing and Mathematical Sciences, Liverpool John Moores University,
Byrom Street, Liverpool L3 3AF, UK
e-mail: B.Zhou@ljmu.ac.uk

D. Llewellyn-Jones
e-mail: D.Llewellyn-Jones@ljmu.ac.uk

D. Lamb
e-mail: D.J.Lamb@ljmu.ac.uk

M. Asim
e-mail: M.Asim@ljmu.ac.uk

Q. Shi
e-mail: Q.Shi@ljmu.ac.uk

M. Merabti
e-mail: M.Merabti@ljmu.ac.uk

C. Blackwell and H. Zhu (eds.), *Cyberpatterns*, DOI: 10.1007/978-3-319-04447-7_8,   97
© Springer International Publishing Switzerland 2014

1 Introduction

A service-oriented architecture (SOA) provides the opportunity for services from different providers to work together. SOAs offer new applications via composition of services; facilitated by standardised interoperations among services. An important issue that shadows SOA platform and application development is security. Concerns around inconsistent security policies and configurations must be continually monitored and addressed. One way to overcome this issue is by adapting current compositions with new services or configurations.

As part of the work undertaken for the Aniketos project [1], we carried out a study on existing techniques relevant to secure service composition. The result reveals that while many efforts have been made in different areas to support SOAs, a practical solution is still missing for composition adaptation, which plays a crucial part in the secure service composition process.

In this chapter we consider this issue in more detail and present an initial approach for composition adaptation. Instead of a random substitution of services, we try to make the adaptation process is more accurate and fast. It targets component service in a composition based on formal verification result. In order to compare services directly, a quantification method is also proposed to support the adaptation strategy. The rest of this chapter is organised as follows. The next section presents an analysis of existing techniques in the area of service composition and verification adaptation. A heuristics based process is proposed in Sect. 3 towards secure composition adaptation. In order to support the heuristic method, Sect. 4 discusses a novel algorithm that quantifies services in terms of security. The chapter concludes with a brief review in Sect. 5.

2 Service Composition and Verification

2.1 Service Composition

SOA platforms provide a foundation for modeling, planning, searching for and composing services. They specify the architectures required, as well as providing tools and support for service composition standards. Enterprise servers such as Glassfish or Microsoft IIS do offer security parameterisations, yet these are typically domain or platform-specific [2].

Therefore, in order to facilitate service composition across platforms; service modeling languages are used to describe a) the business requirements of a system, and b) system resources. By expressing behavior processes and system organisation in agreed formats, compositions can be validated against desired criteria and modified to suit required changes in operation.

A number of languages relevant to service composition already exist. Business Process Model and Notation (BPMN) can be used to model relationships of composed services within a business model or process workflow [3]. Web Services

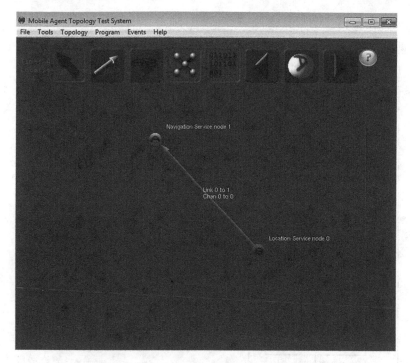

Fig. 1 User interface indicates an information flow relationship between two services

Description Language (WSDL) is widely used for describing a web service interface [4]; subsequent standards augment the basic description to add semantic, behavioral, and to a limited extent, authentication and security data [5]. Other such property-based extensions, including United Service Description Language (USDL) [6], constitute standards that target trust and security, to bridge the previously-identified vendor divide. Some work tries to look at the issue from the point of view of quality of services, i.e. achieve high productivity and low cost while producing new application [7]. Security-domain-specific modeling languages are also used to specify security requirements and policies. For example, $S \times C$ [8] is able to support programmable negotiation and monitoring of services with regard to agreed contracts.

Despite all these efforts, selecting the most suitable service from a service pool still can be problematic, especially when services are previously unknown. In such cases, trust plays an important role in service selection. $S \times C \times T$ extends $S \times C$, supporting maintenance of trust based on recommendations and penalties [9]. Trust calculation relies heavily on consideration of which parameters affect the trust value. The chosen parameters must be monitored closely to provide an accurate indication. In paper [10], the authors proposed a formal specification-based testing approach towards accurate service selection.

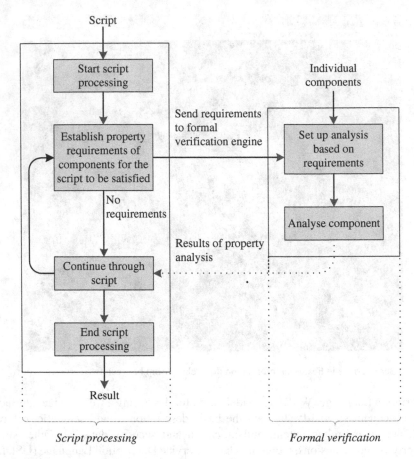

Fig. 2 The property analysis process

2.2 Composition Verification Techniques

Once services are selected for composition, verification can occur to ensure selected services comply with security policy at both design-time and runtime. At design-time, formal analysis and proof-based techniques can establish that stated service behavior is compliant with security policy. AVANTSSAR [11] is a tool for reasoning on service compositions. The Deploy tool supports formal analysis of security properties [12].

The Mobile Agent Topology Test System (MATTS) is a platform that has been designed primarily to allow modeling of system-of-systems scenarios and testing of secure service composition analysis techniques at runtime [13]. It is designed to support analysis and verification of various security-associated risks for the composite services.

In MATTS there is a graphical user interface that allows creating different scenarios. A user can construct a scenario by specifying the used services and their relationships. The term 'relationship' here can be considered in general terms to be abstract, with different relationships annotated using different properties. However, in this particular case the relationship represents the information flow between services. For example, if a navigation service A requires the input from a location service B, their relationship is simply represented as shown in Fig. 1. The arrow represents the flow direction of the location information. In addition, the user can also specify the security properties of an individual service through the interface. These properties will be used to determine the overall security features of the composition.

Behind the user interface, there is a backend engine that analyses the scenario and its properties at run-time. Figure 2 provides a very brief overview of the security property analysis process. This is based on a special scripting language that allows the incorporation of both service properties and the interactions between services to be considered. For example, a script file can specify what kind of encryption algorithm a service should adopt, or which particular service is allowed to make connections. Each script file specifies a set of rules that determines whether the composition satisfies a particular security property. Once a script is loaded, the engine will measure the scenario against its rules. If the measurement result indicates a violation of a rule, the engine will notify the user. This process repeats every time when the scenario evolves.

As scenarios in MATTS allow evolution and change at runtime, the properties and connections between services are dynamically analysed to determine the security properties of the overall service composition.

3 Heuristics-Based Composition Adaptation

Composition Adaptation aims to mitigate issues identified during verification and monitoring. Available actions normally include the followings:

- Rearranging components.
- Adding or removing components.
- Enclosing components in a wrapper.
- Reconfiguring components (e.g. changing on parameters).
- Direct code adaptation (e.g. using aspect weaving).

Although adaptation options seem adequate, deciding the best action is complex. For example, adaptation can often be presented as an optimisation problem with constraints; however in certain security cases this has been demonstrated to be a NP-complete [14, 15]. Consequently heuristic methods are likely to offer the only practical way to address these cases.

Heuristic algorithms solve problems based on experiences, where exhaustive search for a solution is impractical. Adaptation of a composition falls into this category. Even though the verification process can tell a problem has been identified, it can nonetheless be computationally complex to give immediate suggestions as to how to correct the issue. For example a brute force approach to composition adaptation might simply cycle through and verify each of the possible solutions until a composition with adequate security characteristics is found. However, with the number of services getting large, this process quickly becomes unmanageable. In contrast, heuristic methods select compositions 'intelligently', attempting to find increasingly successful adaptations until an adequate solution is found.

For our initial approach we present a pragmatic technique that improves the composition based on the level of detail returned by the verification process. In future work we aim to use methods such as genetic algorithms, swarm intelligence or simulated annealing to improve the optimisation process.

As discussed in the last section, verification techniques are available to establish whether a composition satisfies the security policy. The verification result may just be a boolean value which is either true or false. Nonetheless, it is also not unusual for the verification result to include two other elements or any one of them: the violating service S and the violated security property P.

Based on this, we propose an initial process for composition adaption that replaces the violating service with a preferable alternative and verifies the adapted composition again. The strategy used depends on the pattern of the verification results:

- If the verification result indicates both the violating service S_1 and its property P, we simply replace S_1 with another service S_2 that has stronger property P with the same functionality. The strength of P depends on the nature of the property.
- If the verification result only identifies the violating service S_1 without knowing the exact cause P, service S_2 will be selected to replace S_1, where S_2 is chosen based on an overall assessment value of the services.
- If the verification result only specifies the violated property P without identifying the violating service, the service that has the weakest security property P in the composition will be replaced.
- If the verification result specifies neither S nor P, the service that has the lowest overall assessment score in the composition will be replaced. An assessment methodology will be introduced in the next section.

As an enhanced solution, if the new composition still cannot pass the verification after adaptation and the result remains the same (i.e. the verification result indicates the same S and P), the adaptation process will be extended to a wider range that involves services either having the second weakest property P or one hop away from the previously replaced service S.

4 Service Quantification

Security is a broad concept that includes many aspects such as confidentiality and privacy. One service may be stronger than another in terms of confidentiality; while it is also possible that the very same service has weaker protection for privacy. To tell if a service is better than another, we have to find a way to determine the security value of services.

The key to a quick and accurate analysis of service is to formalise the security property descriptions. A service description can cover various features about the service. For example, one feature may state 'Communication with others is secured', while the other one may state 'My estimated availability ratio is 90 %'. Semantically the features can be described in very different ways. Although some policy languages have been proposed to formalise service descriptions [16], the content of the actual description is still very open. Due to this lack of confinement, the comparison of different services and their compositions can be very difficult. It is necessary to have a dictionary that can define the description of services, both semantically and quantitatively. For example, in the above cases the text descriptions can be translated to statements like 'secured communication = true; (optional: encryption algorithm = 3DES)' and 'availability = 0.9'. The subjects at the left hand of the equations, i.e. 'secured communication', 'encryption algorithm' and 'availability' in this case, should be items from the dictionary, and their format/data type should have been determined in advance. This will allow a platform to be built that can measure and compare different services and their compositions without human intervention.

To judge if a service composition is more secure than another, we propose the concept of **security impact factors** to standardise security properties such as those mentioned above. For example, 'secured communication = true' could contribute 0.5 to Confidentiality and 0.3 to Privacy; 'encryption algorithm = 3DES' could contribute another extra 0.1 to Confidentiality. A security property could have impact on more than one key security aspect such as Confidentiality and Privacy. The security impact factors are predetermined based on expertise. With the dictionary that defines the security properties to be checked, the process of calculating security impact factors can be fairly fast. Moreover, in situations where new threats are identified or there is a breakthrough in the security protection techniques, the dictionary can help allow the security impact factors to be updated and maintained easily. At the end of the evaluation process the services will be quantitatively estimated in four key areas, namely Confidentiality, Authenticity, Availability and Privacy. These are also the main properties that are likely to be specified in a user's security policy.

Once the four security impact factors have been calculated we can give users the flexibility to adjust the weights of these four properties. This is important since in different scenarios the user's priorities may change. The weight could be any number between 0 and 1. Now assume a user sets the weights to 0.4, 0.2, 0.1 and 0.3 respectively for the aforementioned four properties, the overall security value I for the service will be:

$$I = 0.4 \times C + 0.2 \times U + 0.1 \times V + 0.3 \times P \tag{1}$$

where C represents the value of Confidentiality, U represents Authenticity, V represents Availability and P represents Privacy.

5 Future Work and Conclusions

Based on our study, secure adaptation of service composition is an area that demands significant effort for a feasible and practical solution. In this chapter, we proposed a rather intuitive method that making adaptation of service compositions based on verification result. A supporting algorithm is used to quantify services in respect to their security properties.

There are many other factors that could affect the adaptation strategy. Nonetheless, we aim for the proposed method to serve as a starting point for achieving more effective secure adaptation of service compositions in the future.

The proposed adaptation strategy will be assessed in the Aniketos project, together with other strategies such as simulated annealing based approach. Their effectiveness will be tested based on adaptation speed and accuracy.

Acknowledgments The research leading to these results has received funding from the European Union Seventh Framework Programme (FP7/2007-2013) under grant no. 257930 (http://www.aniketos.eu/).

References

1. Aniketos website. http://www.aniketos.eu/. Accessed 12 Sept 2013.
2. Chan SW. Security annotations and authorization in GlassFish and the Java EE 5 SDK. http://www.oracle.com/technetwork/articles/javaee/security-annotation-142276.html (2006). Accessed 12 Sept 2013.
3. OMG. Business process model and notation 2 specification. http://www.omg.org/spec/BPMN/2.0/PDF (2011). Accessed 12 Sept 2013.
4. Christensen E, Curbera F, Meredith G, Weerawarana S. Web services description language (WSDL) 1.1. http://www.w3.org/TR/2001/NOTE-wsdl-20010315 (2001). Accessed 12 Sept 2013.
5. Akkiraju IR, et al. Web Service Semantics—WSDL-S. http://www.w3.org/Submission/2005/SUBM-WSDL-S-20051107/ (2005). Accessed 12 Sept 2013.
6. Kadner K, Oberle D, et al. Unified service description language XG final report. http://www.w3.org/2005/Incubator/usdl/XGR-usdl-20111027/ (2011). Accessed 12 Sept 2013.
7. Miao W, Liu S. Service-oriented modeling using the SOFL formal engineering method. IEEE Asia-Pacific services computing conference. IEEE CS press, Jeju; 7–11 Dec 2009. doi:10.1109/APSCC.2009.5394123. p. 187–192
8. Dragoni N, et al. Security-by-contract (SxC) for software and services of mobile systems. In: Di Nitto et al., editors. At your service: service-oriented computing from an EU perspective. Cambridge: MIT Press; 2009. p. 429–454.
9. Costa G, et al. Security-by-contract-with-trust for mobile devices. J Wirel Mob Netw Ubiquitous Comput Dependable Appl. 2010;1:75–91.
10. Miao W, Liu S. A formal specification-based testing approach to accurate web service selection. IEEE Asia Pacific Services Computing Conference. IEEE CS Press, Jeju, Korea; 12–15 Dec 2011. p. 259–266. doi:10.1109/APSCC.2011.34.
11. AVANTSSAR website. 2013. http://www.avantssar.eu/. Accessed 12 Sept 2013.
12. SAP Product Page: Netweaver Composition Environment. 2013 http://scn.sap.com/community/netweaver. Accessed 12 Sept 2013.

13. Zhou B, Drew O, Arabo A, Llewellyn-Jones D, Kifayat K, Merabti M, Shi Q, Craddock R, Waller A, Jones G. System-of-systems boundary check in a public event scenario. 5th international conference on systems of systems engineering, winner of the conference best paper award, Loughborough, UK; June 2010. doi:10.1109/SYSOSE.2010.5544013.
14. Gritzalis S, Spinellis D. The cascade vulnerability problem: the detection problem and a simulated annealing approach to its correction. Microprocess Microsyst. 1998;21(10):621–8.
15. Zhou B, Llewellyn-Jones D, Shi Q, Asim M, Merabti M, Lamb D. Secure service composition adaptation based on simulated annealing. Proceedings of the 6th layered assurance workshop, annual computer security applications conference (ACSAC 2012), Orlando, Florida, USA; Dec 2012. p. 49–55.
16. Aktug I, Naliuka K. ConSpec—a formal language for policy specification. Electron Notes Theoret Comput Sci (ENTCS). 2008;197(1):45–58.

Part IV
Introduction to Attack Patterns

Clive Blackwell

An attack pattern is analogous to a design pattern, as it describes how a particular type of attack is implemented as a conceptual pattern. Attack patterns are classified using a common definition and schema in the Common Attack Pattern Enumeration and Classification (CAPEC) schema [1]. The repository of attack patterns has greatly increased since their inception in 2007 to reach 400 today in 15 different categories, from the expected data leakage, resource depletion and spoofing categories to include broader emerging classes such as physical, social engineering and supply chain attacks. Attack patterns are specified from the attacker's viewpoint and they therefore describe undesirable, unintentional and unexpected behaviour. Current techniques for design patterns need to be modified and extended for attack patterns as they are used descriptively to help understand and counter malicious behaviour rather than for implementing systems and software. It would also be beneficial to structure and formalise the description of attack patterns to aid better understanding and machine automation, going beyond textual depiction to using UML diagrams and clearly defined languages.

Chapter 9, "A Strategy for Structuring and Formalising Attack Patterns" by Clive Blackwell, discusses a systematic framework for modelling security incidents. The scheme classifies computer attacks into different stages of access, use and effect, and utilises a three-layer model to describe incidents within the social, logical and physical domains. The author also links the six questions of the Zachman Framework [2] (who, what, where, when, why and how) to entities involved in the attack and maps them to sections within the attack pattern template. The proposed semantics for attack patterns helps to overcome the current informal descriptions of incidents leading to more systematic and comprehensive accounts of attacks. The plan is to adapt existing work on formalising design patterns to attack patterns, with a roadmap outlined for formulating attack patterns using his ontology and then translating them in logic. The attack patterns then form a logical specification, which can be intersected with the model of the defensive system to determine corresponding defensive observations and actions that counter the specific attack instances. This would allow convincing reasoning about possible defensive response measures, and holds out the possibility of proving security against certain types of attacks.

Chapter 10, "Attack Pattern Recognition through Correlating Cyber Situational Awareness in Computer Networks" by Shirazi, Schaeffer-Filho and Hutchison, aims to provide cyber resilience by combining data from multiple sources to achieve better situational awareness. They gather and correlate evidence from multiple locations, vertically across protocol levels and horizontally along network paths, in order to identify patterns of correlated events originating from particular attacks. The authors provide a model to select attack features from different datasets, then use clustering to discover meaningful relationships, before finally aggregating and refining the results from all the datasets to update the knowledge base of attack data profiles and patterns. This bottom-up approach to the detection of attack patterns complements the top-down approach of the CAPEC taxonomy [1]. They propose further research using a comparative study of clustering and classification techniques to evaluate their performance in discovering attack patterns. Unsupervised classification techniques will be the focus, because of the uncertainty and lack of information about attack indicators. Unsupervised learning attempts to find inherent patterns in the data without manual labelling of training data with the correct output values. They indicate the use of their model with a simple denial of service scenario.

Chapter 11, "Towards a Penetration Testing Framework using Attack Patterns" by Clive Blackwell, attempts to improve the validity of penetration testing by using structured tests based on attack patterns. The problems of system security are well known, but no satisfactory methods to resolve them have ever been discovered. One heuristic method is to use penetration tests with the rationale of finding system flaws before malicious attackers. However, this is a craft-based discipline without an adequate theoretical or empirical basis for justifying its activities and results. For example, many pen tests are tool-driven, where automated tools are executed to find exploitable weaknesses, leading to the production of extensive reports detailing all discovered low-level system and application flaws, but without adequate consideration of the broader organisational context. The author uses attack patterns to help develop a pen-testing framework to help avoid the limitations of these current approaches. An attack pattern template adapted from the CAPEC schema [1] gives extensive information about attack types thereby helping pen testers to develop appropriate test cases for simulating attacks more realistically. The attack pattern sections include detailed information about the context of the attack, such as the purpose and meaning of targeted data and the possible effects from exposure or destruction. Finally, attack patterns aid documentation and reporting by providing information about the wider situation beyond the low-level technical details provided by tools.

Chapter 12, "A Method for Resolving Security Vulnerabilities Through the Use of Design Patterns" by Walker, Coull, Ferguson and Milne, creates a small pattern language for memory corruption vulnerabilities. Memory corruption occurs when the contents of a memory location are modified unintentionally or maliciously (typically by writing outside a fixed size space such as in buffer overflow), or by incorrect system calls to free memory. Memory corruption vulnerabilities are very common, difficult to detect and can be very dangerous. They are hard to locate during testing, especially because the source of an error and its manifestation to crash the programme or gain unauthorised access may be far apart in code. Their basic pattern template contains five fields for the vulnerability's origin, behaviour, prerequisites for use, impact and countermeasures. It appears sensible to refine the taxonomy further by using MITRE's Common Weakness Enumeration (CWE) dictionary of software weaknesses [3].

Chapter 13, "'Weird Machine' Patterns", by Bratus, Bangert, Gabrovsky, Shubina, Locasto and Bilar, discusses patterns in the context of weird machines. The term 'weird machine' [4] refers to a computational environment within a target system that consists of a subset of possible system states that allows the exploit programmer to take over and control the system to execute malicious computation. It uses low low-level machine language execution artefacts to construct a powerful (often Turing-complete) language within the runtime environment using sequences of machine-level memory reads and writes, rather than the usual programmer-visible function calls operating on abstract data types in a high-level language. They characterise exploit engineering as a systematic process using an invented programming language operating on these low-level automata, rather than as ad hoc attacks exploiting isolated weaknesses that are ubiquitous today. Developers use abstractions to decrease implementation effort, increase code safety and avoid unnecessary detail. However, exploit engineers distil abstractions into new implementation primitives and synthesize low-level attack patterns from them. They posit the need for developers to understand the underlying machine languages better in order to anticipate how they might be misused, and that a useful way to understand this possible unwelcome behaviour is to familiarise themselves with these low-level attack patterns.

References

1. Mitre Corporation. Common Attack Pattern Enumeration and Classification (CAPEC). Mitre Corporation. http://capec.mitre.org. Accessed 15 November 2013.
2. Zachman J. A framework for information systems architecture. IBM Syst J. 1987;26(3):276–292.
3. Mitre Corporation. Common Weakness Enumeration (CWE). Mitre Corporation. http://cwe.mitre.org. Accessed 15 November 2013.
4. Bratus S, Michael E. Locasto, Meredith L. Patterson, Len Sassaman, Anna Shubina. Exploit programming: from buffer overflows to weird machines and theory of computation. Usenix; login 2011;36(6):13–21.

Chapter 9
A Strategy for Structuring and Formalising Attack Patterns

Clive Blackwell

Abstract We have created a framework for modelling security that divides computer incidents into their stages of access, use and effect. In addition, we have developed a three-layer architectural model to examine incidents with the social, logical and physical levels. Our ontology that combines the architectural and incident models provides the basis for a suitable semantics for attack patterns, where the entities and relationships between them can be precisely defined. The current informality of these patterns means that their utility is limited to manual use, so we plan to adapt existing work on formalising design patterns to attack patterns, to aid the detection of attack patterns leading to the possible creation of effective defensive controls. A specification in logic, which is progressively refined into code, is a common method of developing high integrity and secure software, but there are additional issues in system protection, as the system is a diverse set of components housing different and unrelated functionality rather than a single program. The attack patterns form a logical specification, which can be intersected with the model of the defence to determine the corresponding defensive observations and actions to counter the attacks. This would allow convincing reasoning about possible defensive response measures, and holds out the possibility of proving security against certain types of attacks. We outline a roadmap for formulating attack patterns in our ontology and then translating them in logic.

1 Introduction

We have created a framework for modelling both security [1] and forensics [2] that divides computer incidents into their various stages of access, use and effect. This enables us to consider prevention, detection and response at different stages and locations to provide coherent and comprehensive defence-in-depth.

C. Blackwell(✉)
Department of Computing and Communication Technologies, Oxford Brookes University,
Wheatley Campus, Wheatley, Oxford OX33 1HX, UK
e-mail: CBlackwell@brookes.ac.uk

C. Blackwell and H. Zhu (eds.), *Cyberpatterns*, DOI: 10.1007/978-3-319-04447-7_9,   111
© Springer International Publishing Switzerland 2014

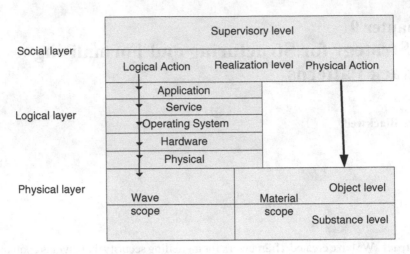

Fig. 1 The multilevel architectural model

In addition, we have developed a three-layer architectural model to model systems, which enables us to consider comprehensive attack surfaces [3] at all levels to defend against all modes of attack, whether logical, physical or social. The three aspects of vertical level, spatial scope and temporal progression are fundamental aspects of our security ontology [1] that enable modelling incidents and their effects on systems in their entirety. We also indicate how our ontology can be represented in logic, which will enable the translation of attack patterns precisely into logic to help enable their detection by the defence.

Evidently, our architectural three-layer model shown in Fig. 1 is inspired by the OSI model, but we explicitly model people at the social level rather than their logical user accounts, and the physical world that is underneath the purely logical OSI network model. In addition, our logical layers are also more abstract and general, as they incorporate all computational aspects, including storage, processing and control, not only networking. More details on these and other design issues, such as discussion of sublevels, are described elsewhere [4].

We focus on the logical level with our investigation of attack patterns, but the other two layers are also important. The social layer at the top includes people and organisations along with their goals and intentions, which are necessary for understanding attacks in their totality, and have their own sections within attack patterns.

The logical layer in the middle contains computers, networks, software and data, and has five sublevels to help with detailed analysis. Each level has it own semantics and different conception of location and time, which is important to consider, as attacks must be recognised, understood and reacted to by different defensive measures using varying observational and control abilities. We note that any logical event ultimately has a physical existence that may be used indirectly to recognise attacks, and could therefore be part of comprehensive defensive response, but we do not discuss the physical level further [2].

Howard and Longstaff invented a classification for network security incidents [5, 6] that shows the different types of entity involved in attacks, with some discussion of their characteristics and the relationships between them. We extended the model, inter alia, to divide attacks into individual stages within our incident classification scheme, where each stage has a particular purpose in supporting the incident goals, and is possibly performed by different actors with differing motivations and abilities. The three main active stages in an incident are system access, target use and incident outcome, along with the incident prologue stage before, and epilogue stage after the active attack to make five stages in total.

In an active incident *stage*, the *actor* uses a *method* to perform an *action* that executes a *threat* to exploit a *vulnerability* with an *immediate effect* on a *target*. The incident has a social-level goal that is met by the *ultimate effect,* whereas the immediate stage effect is only a means to an end and may have no direct impact. This recognises that attacks involve multiple actions that can possibly be recognised by the defence, which is important to consider, as the main attack step may be impossible to stop directly. The consideration of the wider incident scenario and system environment is an advantage of attack patterns over attack trees [7] that only model the main incident steps and not the wider context.

The kill chain [8] is an integrated, end-to-end process of several stages used to describe and analyse intrusions systematically, by recognising that an intrusion first breaches a system boundary and then possibly moves to the target before finally launching a payload to achieve its goals. The kill chain stages are reconnaissance, weaponisation, delivery, exploitation, installation, command and control (C2), and actions on objectives. We plan to investigate how our more systematic and detailed incident model can be informed by incorporation of more stages as in the kill chain.

Whittaker et al. [9] proposed semi-structured documents to describe how to break software with what appeared to be rudimentary attack patterns. Each 'attack pattern' is informally described by a name or concise description, followed by sections starting with the keyword *when, what*, or *how*. A *when* section explains a situation where the attack might be successful, which shows the properties of the system that may be vulnerable. A *what* section indicates faults (implementation bugs or design flaws) that can be exploited in a successful attack, and therefore must be removed from or otherwise addressed by the system. A *how* section explains the methods used to conduct the attack, and corresponding defensive controls to determine whether the system is compromised.

Whittaker's idea of using questions to describe attack patterns has been discovered and extended independently by two authors inspired by the Zachman Framework. The Zachman Framework [10] is a complex metamodel for designing enterprise computing architecture using a two-dimensional grid, where six questions (who, what, where, when, why and how) are posed to describe the different system perspectives, which are answered for each of five conceptual levels. The SABSA (Sherwood Applied Business Security Architecture) model invented by Sherwood [11] is based closely on the Zachman framework, but is specifically adapted for

Table 1 Relationship between incident entities and questions

Question	Incident entity
Who	Perpetrator
Why	Motivation
Know how	Ability
Know what	Knowledge
With what	Resources
How	Action
Where	Path
When	Stage
To what	Target
What	Effect

security architecture. More relevantly, Zachman's questions were used by Hafiz et al. [12] in their classification of security patterns, although they ware dropped from their later work [13], presumably because most of the patterns fell into only two classes representing the functional and data viewpoints answered by the *how* and *what* questions respectively.

We use the six Zachman questions, extended with additional questions, to help analysis of attack patterns by aligning the different conceptual viewpoints posed by the questions to different sections of the attack pattern template. Therefore, we use the full range of questions for each pattern, analogous to the original Zachman vision, except that we are analysing operational systems rather than designing proposed new systems.

We use these questions to describe the components within our incident framework to guide systematic analysis of attack patterns. We extend Zachman's framework with two questions for passive participants involved in the attack, using *with what* for resources used during the attack, and *to what* for the target.

Furthermore, we can use the social level of our architectural model to conceptualise the attacker's goals, motivation, planning, knowledge and perception. We identify the class of attacker using the question *who* and their possible motivations using the *why* question. It is common in epistemology to distinguish between procedural and propositional knowledge [14]. Procedural knowledge or 'knowledge-how' is the ability to perform practical activities, which we express using the question *know how*. There is also the kind of knowledge about the state of the world called propositional knowledge or 'knowledge that', which we refer to as *know what* rather than *know that* for consistency with the other questions in our framework.

The full set of questions is answered for the entire incident and each stage to help comprehensive analysis. Each question has a relationship with an incident or stage entity as shown in Table 1. These questions are used to decompose and investigate the attack patterns, and are fundamental in their logical analysis. Further research will investigate if additional questions will help understand and analyse incidents better.

2 Attack Patterns

Attack patterns [15] are based on design patterns, made famous in the software engineering community by the 'Gang of Four' Design Patterns book [16], which were themselves originally based on Christopher Alexander's architectural patterns for designing buildings [17]. A design pattern is a general reusable solution to a commonly occurring problem in software design, and therefore represents desirable, intentional and expected system behaviour.

Attack patterns apparently appeared around 2001 in the community, and originated in the literature by Moore et al. [18], followed by Hoglund et al. [19], but these gained inspiration from attack trees and a staged model similar to the kill chain respectively, and did not fully represent the notion of design pattern. Both attack trees [7] and the kill chain have narrow scope in being restricted to malicious actions alone rather than the complete attack context modelled by attack patterns.

Finally, Barnum and Sethi [20] systematised what is now understood as an attack pattern with a comprehensive template consistent with design patterns. Fernandez et al. [21] also created attack patterns by adapting design patterns, adding some additional fields to aid digital forensic investigation and incident response. Subsequently, attack patterns were classified using a common definition and schema in the Common Attack Pattern Enumeration and Classification (CAPEC) taxonomy [22] that has subsequently become the de facto standard for attack patterns. The CAPEC repository has greatly increased since its inception in 2007 to reach nearly 500 attack patterns today in 15 different categories.

An attack pattern is analogous to a design pattern, as it describes how a particular type of attack is performed as an abstract pattern. However, attack patterns are specified from the attacker's viewpoint and they therefore represent undesirable, unintentional and unexpected operational behaviour. Although attack patterns were inspired by design patterns, attack patterns have become adorned with several additional sections to give further contextual information and provide advice for the defence. We consign the sections representing the defensive concerns, such as countermeasures, to a separate defensive concept for clarity, and we also recognise that the meaning of some fields have been amended, such as intent to represent the attacker's viewpoint rather than the intent for the pattern designer. The number of patterns together with their lack of unity (by incorporating unrelated concepts) leads to a pressing need to characterise attack patterns more circumspectly and methodically.

We take the sections of our attack pattern template from Fernandez et al. [21] and CAPEC [22] along with our previous work [23]. We clearly distinguish between attack and defence, as the attacker's activities may be difficult to find or attribute even if all attacks could be completely characterised (which they clearly cannot). The information available to the defence may be inadequate, as the incident may not be observed rapidly enough or it may be indistinguishable from legitimate activities. We separate out the possible protective observation and response measures into a separate defensive concept containing, inter alia, the countermeasures and evidence sections in Fernandez's template [21].

We incorporate the concepts from our incident and architectural models, especially the extended Zachman questions, to help organise attack patterns. We describe how to trace and remediate incidents that instantiate particular attack patterns with corresponding defensive controls, using our incident progression model to analyse possible defences at each stage with proactive avoidance, timely detection or subsequent response countermeasures. In addition, we use the semantics of entities at different levels and locations from our architectural three-layer model to help recognise the different types of observable incident information and control measures.

We indicate how our existing incident ontology helps to structure attack patterns making them more amenable to analysis and ultimately helping their formalisation. We link the attack pattern template to the ten incident questions (shown in brackets) in Table 2, to illustrate how attack patterns help us to understand the surrounding incident context to gain a broader view of incidents. The answers to the ten incident questions extend attack trees [7], which only model observable events (how) as nodes within the tree to achieve the goal (what) at the root node.

The attack patterns contain generic fields or slots that are instantiated with particular values when a matching attack is executed. Unlike typical design patterns where all the sections are relevant to design, attack patterns lack unity, as they do not solely focus on attack concerns, but also generally give recommended defensive remedial measures. We omit several sections of the attack pattern relating to the defence along with others that are not relevant to our current discussion. We separate out the unrelated sections into new coherent entities having a single clear purpose. These new entities form intermediary links between attack patterns and corresponding security or defence patterns that contain sections removed from the attack pattern such as countermeasures.

3 Modelling Attack Patterns

3.1 Informal Modelling Advantages

Attack patterns attempt to provide some clarity, consistency and completeness in planning and implementing security solutions. They highlight the essential characteristics of the attack and therefore help to indicate possible defensive requirements. The attack pattern shows the undesirable activities, which aids the discovery of opposing defence techniques to mitigate the attack and its deleterious effects.

We have attempted to provide a greater degree of structure to attack patterns to aid their understanding and systematic analysis. Our security ontology provides a stronger basis for an adequate semantics for attack patterns where the entities and relationships between them are suitably defined and understood. An ontology [25] represents knowledge as a set of concepts, their properties and the relationships between them within a domain of interest. The definition and description of the

Table 2 Conceptual attack pattern template (abridged)

Section (Question)	Description of Contents
Name	Generic name for attack
Classifier	Each pattern should have a unique identifier, as the same pattern may be known by different names
Description	Textual description summarising the type of attack
Perpetrator (who)	We add the general class of perpetrator to the attack pattern template, as it is important for considering their motivation, abilities and methods
Motivation (why)	The purpose of the attack, which is different from intent that describes the desired effect that satisfies the goal
Resources (with what)	The resources required by the attacker. Resources are part of the static object model. Resources include subjects when they are used as means to an end, as the victims are in social engineering attacks
Attacker skill (know how)	The skills needed to execute the attack, which are internal abilities involving attacker's own minds and bodies (eg in social engineering or physical attacks) or enabling them to use external resources (eg hacking techniques)
Attacker knowledge (know what)	The knowledge needed to execute the attack, including both general knowledge about the world and specific information about the targeted system
Context or prerequisites (when)	Description of the conditions needed for the attack to succeed. Includes the required structure, behaviour and characteristics of the targeted system
Activation zone (where)	Location within the system where the offensive activities occur. Our incident model aids the determination of possible logical paths followed by the attack. An annotated class or object diagram may help establish possible locations
Execution (how)	Known as solution in design patterns. Describes how the attack is performed to achieve its anticipated results. Our incident model aids the determination of the logical progression through the different attack stages. An attack tree or sequence diagram showing the logical sequencing of attack activities is useful
Target (to what)	We include the type of target as a separate field in the attack pattern. The desired result can only occur if the system hosts a suitable target instance and it is accessible to the attacker
Security or immediate impact	CAPEC calls this field CIA impact referring to possible breaches involving Confidentiality, Integrity and Availability, but we takes a wider perspective based on Microsoft's STRIDE model [24] considering violations of access control, authentication and accountability as well
System or ultimate impact	A new field containing the effects typically caused by the attack to the targeted system and people reliant on it. Our ontology separates out different types of impact into ends and means by distinguishing the direct security breach from ultimate incident effects. The wider service, financial and reputational effects are impacts that meet the attacker's goal, not security breaches

(continued)

Table 2 (continued)

Section (Question)	Description of Contents
Instances	Description of known scenarios where the type of attack occurred
Object diagrams	Diagrams that visually show the participants involved in the attack and their relationships. Class and object diagrams are common
Process diagrams	Diagrams that visually show the attack execution and path. Sequence and activity diagrams are common. We can also use our comprehensive incident diagram to show the entire attack pattern in operation [4]
References	Pointers to further sources of information about the attack such as CAPEC

entities enables collective consistent understanding using the shared vocabulary, and may be used to reason about problems in the domain.

We have seen that attack patterns suitably embellished with aspects of our security ontology, especially the incident questions, can enable broader incident modelling. Conversely, attack trees [7] only indicate the incident actions and goals, whereas attack patterns also contain several other aspects such as motivation and surrounding context, enabling a wider analysis of defensive protection measures including deterring the attacker and constraining system functionality.

3.2 Strategy for Formalisation

The current informality of these patterns means that their utility is limited to manual use, with little work in formalisation to aid automation in creating effective defensive measures. We can use our security ontology together with Zhu and Bayley's existing work on formalising design patterns [26, 27] to model attack patterns and corresponding defences in logic, which would aid better understanding and reasoning about the effectiveness of different defensive measures.

The attack pattern contains the attacker's behaviour and goals that must be recognised, understood and countered by the defence, using various defensive controls in the networks, computers, applications and people within the system. A key issue is that the attacker's activities cannot always be directly recognised, but must be inferred from indirect evidence, and so we separate attack patterns from their possible defensive observation and control.

The attack patterns can be described in logic as specifications of possible states and behaviour, aided by our linkage to the ten incident questions. A specification in logic that can be progressively refined into code is a common method of developing high integrity software. For example, a logical specification using the logic-based B method [28] can be progressively refined into executable code whilst maintaining correctness at each stage.

Our attack pattern forms a logical specification whose range of implementation possibilities can be intersected with the defensive system model and its various elements. This may allow us to determine the abilities of the system components depending on their specific functionality and housed at different locations and levels to observe and control instances of the attack.

We intend to formalise the attack patterns from the Common Attack Pattern Enumeration and Classification (CAPEC) [22] taxonomy overseen by MITRE. Other possibilities are to take possible defensive flaws categorised by the Common Vulnerabilities and Exposures (CVE) [29] or Common Weakness Enumeration (CWE) [30] schemata, and directly create suitable security or defence patterns.

The reader may ask here why we do not simply create the required defensive patterns to model possible protection measures directly. This is certainly plausible and finds expression already in the concept of security patterns [31]. However, there is no direct linkage to possible incidents and so the security patterns may be hard to validate against fielded attacks. Conversely, attack patterns model deployed attacks and so their formalisation holds out the possibility of proving that some classes of attack must fail (assuming the defensive controls are operating correctly), or at least discover the conditions under which they can succeed to determine where additional defensive controls will be required.

3.3 Formalisation

We describe the difference between logical proof and model-theoretic semantics [32, pp 247-250], as it is relevant to proofs of security. Proofs refer to logical entailment between sentences in logic, whereas semantics deal with possible worlds of individuals and their relationships. The link between the two is that the arguments (constants like Alice and variables x like x ∈ Employees) of logical clauses refer to individuals in these hypothetical worlds, and therefore logical proofs should make true statements in these domains. There should be a sound and complete correspondence between the two views, where a statement can be proved in logic if and only if it holds in the domain of individuals under discussion.

In mathematical logic, the identity or even existence of these individuals is irrelevant, and any model satisfying the soundness and completeness condition above will suffice. However, we wish these individuals and their characteristics and relationships to refer to real entities, which is why we use our security ontology. The bottom line, if the above paragraph is unclear, is that our ontology includes the relevant entities, properties and relationships; therefore, logical proofs about the patterns prove the required security properties hold for the real entities in the system under discussion. This is why the sections in the attack pattern are represented using our security ontology, including the level, location, purpose, behaviour and state of entities, rather than simply as a set of textual fields without adequate semantics.

The attack patterns form a specification, which is intersected with the model of the defence to determine the corresponding defensive observations and controls to counter the attacks. This would allow well-founded reasoning about possible defensive measures with the possibility of proving security against certain attacks. The scope of the attack patterns provide suitable threat models, rather than using abstract and unrealistic threat models to give all-encompassing proofs of security.

We can view attack patterns as templates, with slots to instantiate the variables for particular attacks. One way to prove an attack pattern cannot succeed is to use the logic programming language Prolog to represent the pattern. The goal of the attack is then posed as a query to the program, which attempts to discover the circumstances where the goal will succeed. The query will fail if there is no possible attack with that pattern against the system under discussion, and will instantiate the variables if it succeeds to show all the scenarios where the attack is possible.

The formalisation of attack patterns thus aids translation into realisable behaviour, but there are some differences from existing work on transforming logical system specifications into executable code. The corresponding defensive implementation that mitigates the attack pattern will usually be divided into controls at different locations and levels with particular limited recognition and response abilities.

We indicate how our existing ontology helps to overcome the issues:

- Network devices, computers and applications do not have complete visibility of incidents or all the necessary powers to respond → our architectural model contains *location* that helps to determine what attack activities can be observed by each system component, and *level* helps to determine what the entities can understand
- Defensive controls may not see incident activities when required → our incident progression model divides incidents into stages that help to decide when the defence must be deployed
- The protection measures may give indirect protection at a different level, location or time if the main attack vector cannot be detected or countered → the architectural and incident models together help to determine the spread of observable attack activities through space and time

An adequate classification criteria for an attack pattern needs to determine the particular fields and field contents in the template that characterise the type of attack. We must determine the essential attributes of the attack compared to optional or correlated aspects. There is an established philosophical theory called essentialism [33] that could be useful here, as it characterises the distinction between an essential property of an entity that it must have compared to an accidental property that it could lack. This characterisation can be formalised in modal logic [34] using the operators □ for Necessarily and ◇ for Possibly.

4 Conclusions and Further Work

We outlined a roadmap for formulating attack patterns in our security ontology, which is useful for understanding and analysing attack patterns. We then indicated our strategy for formalising attack patterns in logic, which can possibly aid automated translation into executable behaviour. We are modelling some of the CAPEC attack patterns, and plan to use the Web Ontology Language (OWL) [35] to give them a well-defined semantics using our ontology. Then, we can use the description logic associated with OWL to model the patterns formally.

Existing 'proofs of security' often make a number of assumptions using unrealistic system models, where many systems that have been proved secure have subsequently been found to have serious flaws. We cannot prove any system is secure without considering its surrounding context. We need to consider the disposition of the system, its organisation, critical assets, weaknesses, goals and adversarial threats, which are all included in our security ontology.

Our formalisation of attack patterns leads to the idea of secure-by-construction systems, where it may be possible to prove that certain attacks must fail, rather than give an unrealistic and all embracing proof of system security. Attack patterns provides an adequate threat model against particular types of attacks, rather than using unrealistic threat models such as Dolev-Yao [36] that give all-encompassing proofs of security. Dolev-Yao models threats to communication over an insecure medium such as the Internet, but only considers attacks against cryptographically protected messages in the communication channel, without considering the security of the endpoints, which accounts for nearly all deployed attacks using malware and social engineering.

A more pragmatic goal is to systematise attack patterns using UML diagrams [37]. Class or object diagrams are commonly used for visually depicting participants in design patterns and their relationships. Unlike design patterns, attack patterns are usually only described textually and the participants in the attack and their behaviour need greater clarification. The attack participants include components in the targeted system under the control of the attacker. Suitably annotated UML diagrams can help establish the full range of participants, including unwilling contributors, and help to resolve the locus of control of the attack activities.

Similarly, process diagrams that visually show the attack execution such as sequence and activity diagrams are often used to illustrate design patterns, but not attack patterns. We can also use our comprehensive incident diagrams to show the entire scope of the attack pattern [4]. These diagrams can show the various stages in the attack and therefore help to develop more holistic mitigation measures, rather than focusing simply on limiting access to the system and its potential targets. Broader protection measures include deterring the attacker aided by our explicit attacker modelling, and backup and restore to maintain essential system services aided by considering the entire system rather than just narrow security measures.

We focused on security in this paper, but similar ideas also apply to the creation of forensic patterns to determine the evidence that may be collected to hold the perpetrator responsible and repair damaged systems after a successful incident.

References

1. Blackwell C. A security ontology for incident analysis. In: 6th Cyber security and information intelligence research workshop. New York: ACM press; 2010.
2. Blackwell C. A Framework for investigative questioning in incident analysis and response. In: 7th IFIP WG 11.9 International conference on digital forensics. Springer Advances in Digital Forensics VII; 2011.
3. Howard M. Attack surface: mitigate security risks by minimizing the code you expose to untrusted users. MSDN magazine; 2004. http://msdn.microsoft.com/en-us/magazine/cc163882.aspx. Accessed 23 Sept 2013.
4. Blackwell C. A forensic framework for incident analysis applied to the insider threat. In: 3rd ICST international conference on digital forensics and cyber crime. Berlin: Springer; 2011.
5. Howard JD. An analysis of security incidents on the internet, 1989–1995. PhD thesis. Carnegie-Mellon University. 1997. www.cert.org/archive/pdf/JHThesis.pdfy. Accessed 23 Sept 2013.
6. Howard JD, Longstaff TA. A common language for computer security incidents. Sandia National Laboratories; 1998. http://www.cert.org/research/taxonomy_988667.pdf.Accessed 23 Sept 2013.
7. Schneier B. Attack trees: modeling security threats. Dr. Dobb's J; 1999.
8. Hutchins EM, Cloppert MJ, Amin RM. Intelligence-driven computer network defense informed by analysis of adversary campaigns and intrusion kill chains. In: 6th Annual international conference on information warfare and security, Washington, DC; 2011. www.lockheedmartin.com/content/dam/lockheed/data/corporate/documents/LM-White-Paper-Intel-Driven-Defense.pdf. Accessed 23 Sept 2013.
9. Whittaker JA, Thompson HH. How to break software security. Boston, MA: Addison Wesley; 2001.
10. Zachman J. A framework for information systems architecture. IBM Syst J. 1987;26(3).
11. Sherwood J, Clark A, Lynas D. Enterprise security architecture, a business driven approach. San Francisco: CMP Books; 2005.
12. Hafiz M, Adamczyk P, Johnson RE. Organising security patterns. IEEE Softw. 2007;24(4): 52–60.
13. Hafiz M, Adamczyk P, Johnson RE. Growing a pattern language (For Security). In: Proceedings of the 27th object-oriented programming, systems, languages and applications. OOPSLA; 2012.
14. Fantl J. Knowledge how. In: EN Zalta editor. The stanford encyclopedia of philosophy (Winter 2012 Edition). http://plato.stanford.edu/archives/win2012/entries/knowledge-how. Accessed 23 Sept 2013
15. Barnum S, Sethi A. Attack patterns as a knowledge resource for building secure software. Cigital Inc. 2007. http://capec.mitre.org/documents/Attack_Patterns-Knowing_Your_Enemies_in_Order_to_Defeat_Them-Paper.pdf. Accessed 23 Sept 2013.
16. Gamma E, Helm R, Johnson R, Vlissides J. Design patterns: elements of reusable object-oriented software. Reading, MA: Addison-Wesley; 1995.
17. Alexander C, Ishikawa S, Silverstein M. A pattern language: towns, buildings. Construction, New York: Oxford University Press; 1977.
18. Moore AP, Ellison RJ, Linger RC. Attack modeling for information security and survivability. No. CMU-SEI-2001-TN-001. Software Engineering Institute, Carnegie Mellon University, Pittsburgh PA; 2001.

19. Hoglund G, McGraw G. Exploiting software: how to break code. Addison-Wesley; 2004.
20. Barnum S, Sethi A. Introduction to attack patterns. Cigital Inc. 2006 (revised 14 May 2013). https://buildsecurityin.us-cert.gov/bsi/articles/knowledge/attack/585-BSI.html. Accessed 23 Sept 2013.
21. Fernandez EB, Pelaez JC, Larrondo-Petrie MM. Attack patterns: a new forensic and design tool. In: 3rd Annual IFIP WG 11.9 international conference on digital forensics. Berlin: Springer. 2007.
22. Mitre Corporation. Common attack pattern enumeration and classification (CAPEC). Mitre Corporation. http://www.capec.mitre.org. Accessed 23 Sept 2013.
23. Blackwell C. Formally modelling attack patterns for forensic analysis. In: 5th International conference on cybercrime forensics education and training. Canterbury; 2011.
24. Swiderski F, Snyder W. Threat modeling. Redmond, WA: Microsoft Press; 2004.
25. Noy NF, McGuinness DL. Ontology development 101: a guide to creating your first ontology. Technical Report KSL-01-05. Stanford Knowledge Systems Laboratory; 2001.
26. Bayley I, Zhu H. Formalising design patterns in predicate logic. In: 5th IEEE international conference on software engineering and formal, methods; 2007. pp. 25–36.
27. Bayley I, Zhu H. Specifying behavioural features of design patterns in first order logic. In: 32nd Annual IEEE international computer software and applications conference. COMPSAC'08. IEEE; 2008. pp. 203–10.
28. Abrial J-R. The B-Book: assigning programs to meanings. Cambridge: Cambridge University Press; 1996.
29. Mitre Corporation. Common vulnerabilities and exposures (CVE). Mitre Corporation. http://www.cve.mitre.org. Accessed 23 Sept 2013.
30. Mitre Corporation. Common weaknesses enumeration (CWE). Mitre Corporation. http://www.cwe.mitre.org. Accessed 23 Sept 2013.
31. Schumacher M, Fernandez-Buglioni E, Hybertson D, Buschmann F, Sommerlad P. Security patterns: integrating security and systems engineering. Chichester, West Sussex: Wiley; 2005.
32. Kowalski R. Computational logic and human thinking: how to be artificially intelligent. Cambridge University Press; 2011.
33. Robertson T. Essential vs. Accidental Properties. In: EN Zalta editor. The stanford encyclopedia of philosophy (Fall 2008 Edition). http://plato.stanford.edu/archives/fall2008/entries/essential-accidental. Accessed 23 Sept 2013.
34. Garson J. Modal Logic. In: EN Zalta editor. The stanford encyclopedia of philosophy (Spring 2013 Edition). http://plato.stanford.edu/archives/spr2013/entries/logic-modal. Accessed 23 Sept 2013.
35. Antoniou G, van Harmelen F. A semantic web primer. 2nd ed. MA, London: MIT Press; 2008.
36. Dolev D, Yao AC. On the security of public key protocols. IEEE Trans Inf Theory. 1983;29(2):198–208.
37. Fowler M. UML distilled: a brief guide to the standard object modeling language. 3rd ed. Boston, MA: Addison-Wesley Professional; 2003.

Chapter 10
Attack Pattern Recognition Through Correlating Cyber Situational Awareness in Computer Networks

Noor-ul-hassan Shirazi, Alberto Schaeffer-Filho and David Hutchison

Abstract There is no denying that communication networks, in particular the Internet, have changed our lives in many ways. Many organizations and businesses in general benefit, but at the same time their communication networks face many challenges such as cyber-attacks, which can result in disruptions of services and huge financial losses. Therefore, resilience of these networks against cyber-attacks is a growing interest in the cyber security community. In this paper, we propose a framework for attack pattern recognition by collecting and correlating cyber situational information vertically across protocol-levels, and horizontally along the end-to-end network path. This will help to analyze cyber challenges from different viewpoints and to develop effective countermeasures.

1 Introduction

Communication networks are nowadays considered to be critical infrastructures [1]. Unfortunately, the risk of these networks failing as a result of cyber-attacks has also increased dramatically. Resilience, the subject of this paper, is the ability of the network to maintain normal levels of operation in the face of many types of challenges, including (D)DoS and other types of cyber-attacks, operational overloads, and mis-configurations [2]. Countries around the world are dedicating their resources

N. Shirazi (✉) · D. Hutchison
School of Computing and Communications, Lancaster University, Lancaster LA1 4WA, UK
e-mail: n.shirazi@lancaster.ac.uk

D. Hutchison
e-mail: d.hutchison@lancaster.ac.uk

A. Schaeffer-Filho
Institute of Informatics, Federal University of Rio Grande do Sul, Porto Alegre, Brazil
e-mail: alberto@inf.ufrgs.br

C. Blackwell and H. Zhu (eds.), *Cyberpatterns*, DOI: 10.1007/978-3-319-04447-7_10,
© Springer International Publishing Switzerland 2014

to combat cyber challenges but they all agree that it is becoming increasingly difficult [3] as cyber criminals are becoming more organized and sophisticated. One example of such an attack is *GhostNet*[1] which has infected large numbers of computers in many countries, of which close to 30 % can be considered as high-value diplomatic, political, economic, or military targets.

Moreover, network data has become more accessible to new tools and technologies that provide information about network monitoring and applications behaviour. Several research efforts have focused on the development of resilience detection and classification techniques to build cyber situational awareness based on this information. The majority of tools to monitor networks and applications, however, perform analysis on data from single sources, or datasets. Instead, we aim to make combined use of multiple datasets simultaneously, for example using information from application layer firewalls to catch attempted web application attacks, NetFlow traces for events above the data link layer, to provide multi-level cyber situation awareness.

These datasets are typically available in the form of logs, which can be normalized and correlated to extract interesting evidence about attack patterns. Patterns provide a convenient way of encapsulating and reusing knowledge. Their purpose is to communicate proven solutions in a particular domain. The use of patterns has emerged from architecture work and has been applied to software engineering by Gamma et al. [4]. Our resilience requirements suggest that a focus should be placed on the process for layered defences by collecting and correlating cyber situational information vertically across protocol levels, and horizontally along the end-to-end network path. This has led us to the following initial questions:

(a) How should we define attack patterns?
(b) What classification schemes for attack patterns can we suggest?
(c) What success criteria can we propose for evaluating attack patterns?

In working towards answers to all the above questions we intend to extract meaningful information from multiple datasets using correlation of, for example, IP addresses, timing, and behaviour (e.g., under (D)DoS attack behaviour could be the ratio of numbers of packets of server ports to total number of all service ports, flows per second per interface etc.). This makes the assumption (to be validated), that highly coordinated and sophisticated attacks are actually reflected in correlated patterns.

Correlation is used to describe the process and results of establishing important connections between various data items from multiple sources, typically from diverse and independent sensors that monitor network and application events. This meaningful information, which we expect to see in an attack patterns, is intended to highlight serious threats in real time or at least in post-event assessment for adopting and designing overall resilience controls for networks.

---

[1] Information Warfare Monitor, Tracking GhostNet: Investigation Cyber Espionage Network. March 29, 2009. http://www.infowar-monitor.net/2009/09/tracking-ghostnet-investigating-a-cyber-espionage-network/

This paper has the following structure: Section 2 presents related work. Sections 3 and 4 explain the proposed model and our approach respectively. An example scenario is illustrated in Sect. 5. Section 6 discusses briefly the future work and finally concludes the paper.

2 Background and Related Work

We aim to develop an effective and systematic method that can help to determine cyber-attacks consisting of a large number of correlated events. Attack vectors are usually largely distributed over the Internet and their lifetime varies, which can make them difficult to detect. Due to this nature, analyzing attacks is a challenging task. In our approach, we will use datasets for analysis with the assumption that high-level coordinated attacks will be reflected by the correlation of various attack events that originated from different parts of the network. Those correlations are normally not visible by using only individual datasets. We will use specific data mining and knowledge discovery algorithms, in order to assist us to find interesting attack patterns. Currently we are evaluating different clustering approaches such as Hierarchical, K-means and Graph based clustering [5–7], and comparing their performance and suitability in order to achieve objectives for our proposed model.

Traditionally, the process of attack detection and classification has been investigated by using the analysis of individual datasets, for example, NetFlow records, Server logs, and Web IDS logs etc. [8–10]. However, applying these classification techniques to a single dataset is not sufficient for identifying complete attack phenomena. Furthermore, since attacks evolve over time we believe that applying those techniques on a single dataset would not yield complete observation about specific attacks. The approach proposed in this paper is different in the sense that we aim to investigate how evidence from multiple datasets can be correlated, in order to achieve a more robust attack detection and classification.

An attack is an act of carrying out an exploit of vulnerability [11]. In [12], the authors have developed a description and classification scheme for attack pattern. This scheme includes:

(a) Name and unique ID of the attack pattern
(b) Related weakness and vulnerabilities
(c) Method of attack and attack example
(d) Describing information
(e) Related attack pattern.

The *MITRE*[2] Corporation provides a publicly available catalogue of attack patterns known as CAPECCommon Attack Pattern Enumeration and Classification. CAPEC (which was established in the year 2000) is sponsored by the U.S Department of Homeland Security and technically managed by Cigital Inc. The attack

---

[2] MITRE manages federally funded research and development centers (FFRDCs), partnering with government sponsors to support their crucial operational mission. CAPEC- CybOX is managed by MITRE http://www.mitre.org/

patternconcept from CAPEC represents a description of common attack approaches abstracted from a set of known real world exploits. The catalogue provides classification for attack patterns along with comprehensive schema and classification taxonomy. As part of CAPEC, the CybOX Cyber Observable Expression is provided which is a standardized schema and is written in XML Extensible Markup Language. CybOX is a standardized language for encoding and communicating high-fidelity information about cyber observables, whether dynamic events, or stateful measures that are observable in the operational cyber domain. CybOX provides a common structure and content mechanism for addressing cyber observables across and among different use cases for overall cyber situational awareness.

In CAPEC, attack patterns can be seen as formalized textual descriptions of high-level attacks in terms of their characteristics, such as system vulnerabilities, weaknesses, and methods for exploiting software. To some extent, CAPEC seeks to define attack patterns using a top-down approach, i.e., cataloguing attacks and identifying their key elements from the attacker's perspective. Instead, we focus on the gathering and correlation of evidence from multiple datasets in order to identify patterns of correlated events that could explain an attack. Thus, we see the two approaches as complementing each other, in the sense that we will be able to identify and extract attack features, which could be subsequently referred to as observables in CAPEC's attack patterns.

Another work similar to ours is honeynet traffic analysis, which aims to determine the occurrence of an attack by analyzing attack events using honeypot traces. Our analysis will be different from any traditional analysis of traffic traces because we will be using spatial distribution and model the behaviour of attack found in different correlated events, from multiple datasets.

Botnet tracking is another active research area relevant to our work. In [13], the author has developed a botnet detection framework based on clustering of C&C communication and activities flows to detect similarity patterns and combination of both types of patterns by cross-correlation. However, this work is different from ours as we aim to develop more general models that can be applied to the detection and classification of a range of cyber-attacks as opposed to a specialized technique that is targeted at a single type of attack.

Correlation has also become the most important technique for network management. Without applying this technique, the arrival rate of network events often becomes overwhelmingly high and limits the ability of the operator to investigate and respond to challenges [14]. However, currently, event correlation is mainly used for network management and we aim to extend this to other domains such as cyber situational awareness across multiple levels. In [15], the authors have implemented the Spice event correlation engine for detecting port scans, GrIDS [16] uses graph-based correlation for detecting intrusions, and Snort [7, 17] also applies event correlation for detecting multiple intrusions. Nevertheless, all these correlation techniques are specific to single datasets and do not provide complete insight by incorporating heterogeneous correlation across various levels.

There are several other well-known projects that are used to monitor all unsolicited traffic directed to dark subnets. Darknets are unused IP subnets, and many projects operate darknets such as the Team Cymru darknet [18] and the Internet Motion Sensor [19]. However, they are primarily used to analyze specific phenomena that are essentially related to worm propagation [20, 21]. Our approach will be different in terms of technique and objective, as we do not focus on the analysis of Internet worms alone.

Moreover, in [22], the authors have tried to characterize the non-productive network traffic. They analyzed temporal patterns and correlated activity within the unsolicited traffic. Recently, similar research has been performed by Arbor Networks [23]. Although, all this previous work provide meaningful results, at the same time they are not sufficient for complete cyber situational awareness. Therefore, we aim to apply more appropriate techniques in order to elevate the abstraction level, and to improve the insights into the behavior of global cyber situational awareness.

The approaches mentioned above are related to our work and they all provide building block techniques for analyzing threats. The model proposed in Sect. 3 intends to build on these techniques in order to support data analysis by combining collective intelligence, vertically across protocol levels and horizontally along the end-to-end network path, from different viewpoints. In summary, we note that most approaches for analyzing malicious activities are tailored to specific issues by means of particular datasets. However, these are usually only small pieces of the overall puzzle, which are only able to provide an incomplete picture of cyber activities.

3 Model

Traditional models describe how to cope with random challenges [9, 10]. However, we aim to extend these models to deal with highly sophisticated attacks across the multiple levels in networks in order to provide deterrent controls against such attacks. In today's communication network environments, events and alarms come from multiple independent sources and not all events are ordered and analyzed together, so information is lost and non-determinism is introduced [24]. This gives rise to the following further research questions:

(a) How can we identify a correlation of data that corresponds to an attack, based on the combination of all available evidence?
(b) How can we analyze the cyber-attack phenomenon from separate view-points, revealing different correlation patterns?
(c) Can we develop a model that fits multiple datasets and not just one specific dataset?

Detection technologies have matured over time, and greater depth and breadth of information is available for analysis, typically enriched with metadata and contextual information. Examples of such datasets include: attack events (honeynet logs), network traces, and web crawler logs. It is in the lack of support for identifying attacks across multiple data sources that we see the need for new research. This is because

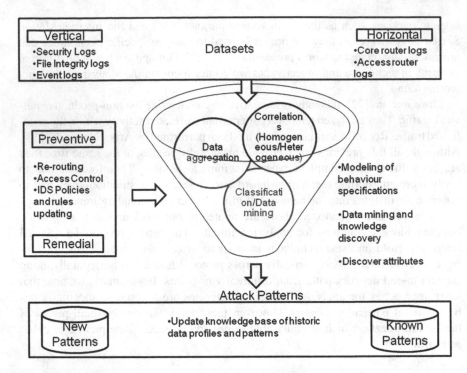

Fig. 1 High level design of the proposed model for attack pattern recognition

there is no framework to give us indicators for effectively combating cyber-attacks through combining in-formation from various data sources, which limits the opportunities for a counter-measure development process. Therefore, more comprehensive correlation awareness needs to build upon this expanded information. The high-level diagram of the proposed model for attack pattern recognition is given below: (see Fig. 1).

4 Approach

One of the primary concepts behind our approach is the recognition of attack patterns, which represent a collection of related events, with the assumption that, for a given attack, two or more viewpoints will be available. Considerable efforts have been made to apply data mining techniques to problems related to network security, and these efforts have highlighted the use of these techniques to link analysis, neural networks and other machine learning approaches for intrusion detection. However, these efforts are focused on improvements to the intrusion detection system rather than finding evidence or discovery of new insights into analyzing complete phenomena of attacks

Fig. 2 Resilience strategy
(Reproduced from [2])

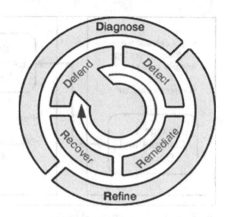

using multiple datasets. Furthermore, only few common data mining techniques such as classification algorithms, association rules have been applied to raw network data but again it aimed at improving the alert classification to enhance the performance of the intrusion detection system. In our proposed approach we will take advantage of these available datasets that contain blueprints of attacks, hence our objective of using data mining is different from has approaches that have been used previously.

Moreover, to find unknown attack patterns we propose the use of unsupervised classification, as little prior knowledge about attacks is available. In addition, to reveal patterns that may result from combining evidence extracted from different sources, we will use an aggregation process that is highlighted as one of the modules of the proposed model.

The *ResumeNet*[3] project provides a useful set of principles and design guide-lines for our model. Resilience is the ability of a network to provide and maintain accept-able level of service in the face of various faults and challenges to normal operations [25]. ResumeNet uses a general two-phase high-level network resilience strategy, called $D^2R^2 + DR$: Defend, Detect, Remediate, Recover + Diagnose, Refine [26]. The first phase comprises the use of defensive (e.g. security) measures to protect the network from foreseeable challenges, such as cyber-attacks, detection of challenges in real time and subsequently remediation of their effects before network operation is compromised, and finally recovery procedures. The second phase primarily involves improving service levels through the diagnosis and refinement of operations (see Fig. 2).

Motivated by this high-level resilience strategy, the main components of our model are the following (see Fig. 3):

(a) Stage 1: Compute and Discover: selection of attack features from a dataset
(b) Stage 2: Extraction and Selection: clustering, which aims to discover meaningful relations among patterns extracted from the dataset

---

[3] ResumeNet: http://comp.lancs.ac.uk/resilience/

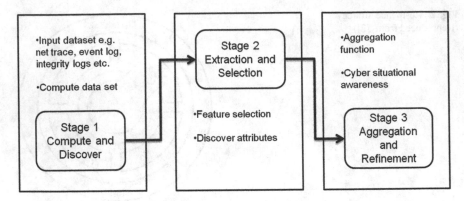

Fig. 3 Stages of the proposed model

(c) Stage 3: Aggregation and Refinement: aggregation, i.e. the use of data fusion
   and updating the knowledge base of historic data profiles and patterns

The stages of the model will be investigated using concrete examples such as the
one in Sect. 5.

5 Attack Example

A Denial-of-Service (DoS) attack is an attempt to make a computer resource unavailable to its intended users. Typically, the targets are high-profile web servers. A
Distributed Denial-of-Service (DDoS) attack occurs when multiple compromised
systems flood the bandwidth or resources of a targeted system, again usually a web
server. Attackers can use a variety of methods to compromise these systems, and
some attacks may be multi-stage. For example, e-mail spam and malware are used
first to gain control of several network nodes, then, a (D)DoS attack may be triggered
to a specified target. We aim to use application-level information to detect attempted
web server attacks. Traffic features, such as time, source IP address, and payload can
then be used to review transport and network layer logs to check if other activities
were occurring based on the same source address.

A simple way to visualize such a correlation is to imagine a series of events in
the form of logs that are generated, each looking at different aspects of a network
activity. After normalization, these logs can be placed on top of each other so that
by looking across these layers one can identify significant commonalities in terms
of the attack perspective.

6 Conclusion

In this position paper, we propose a framework for cyber situation awareness in computer networks. We believe it is possible to analyze multiple datasets with an expectation of gaining substantial insights into the diversity and types of the cyber challenges afflicting a network.

The lifetime of a cyber-attack can vary from days to months, and due to their nature, attributing different sources of events to the same attack is a challenging task. This is because the features of these attacks evolve over time, such as source or destination IP address, type of attack/exploit and so on. In addition, the fuzzy nature of attacks would make it difficult to model their behaviour.

A comparative study of clustering and classification techniques for finding security problems requires further research. Due to uncertainty and little prior knowledge of attack events, unsupervised classification techniques will be our focus.

Acknowledgments This research is partially supported by the EPSRC funded India-UK Advanced Technology Centre in Next Generation Networking.

References

1. Rinalid SM, Peerenboom JP, Kelly TK. Identifying, understanding and analyzing critical infrastructure interdependencies. IEEE Control Syst Magaz. 2001;21(6):11–25. doi:10.1109/37.969131.
2. Smith P, Hutchison D, Schöller M, Fessi A, Karaliopoulos M, Lac C, Plattner B. Network resilience: a systematic approach. IEEE Commun Magaz. 2011;49(7):88–97. doi:10.1109/MCOM.2011.5936160.
3. Computer Crime Research Center. Cybercrime is an organized and sophisticated business. 2001. http://www.crime-research.org/library/Cybercrime.htm. Accessed Sept 2013.
4. Gamma E, Helm R, Johnson R, Vlissides J. Design patterns: elements of reusable object-oriented software. Inc, Boston, MA, USA: Addison-Wesley Longman Publishing Co.; 1995.
5. Jain AK, Murty MN, Flynn PJ. Data clustering: a review. ACM Comput Surv. 1999;31(3):264–323. doi:http://doi.acm.org/10.1145/331499.331504 NULL.
6. Pavan M, Pelillo M. A new graph-theoretic approach to clustering and segmentation. In: Proceedings of the IEEE conference on computer vision and pattern recognition, Madison, Wisconsin, USA. doi:10.1109/CVPR.2003.1211348; 2003. pp. 145–152.
7. Tan P-N, Steinbach M, Kumar V. Introduction to data mining. Inc, Boston, MA, USA: Addison-Wesley Longman Publishing Co.; 2005.
8. Adrian F, Rehnhard M. Histogram matrix:Log visualization for anomaly detection. In: Proceedings of the third international conference on availability reliability and security, Barcelona, Spain; 2008. pp 610–617.
9. Kind A, Stoecklin MP, Dimitriopoulos X. Histogram based traffic anomaly detection. IEEE Trans Netw Serv Manage. 2009;6(2):110–121. doi:10.1109/TNSM.2009.090604.
10. Nousiainen S, Kilpi J, Silvonen P, HiirsalmiSami M. Anomaly detection from server log data. A Case Study. Tech. rep., VTT Research Notes. http://www.vtt.fi/inf/pdf/tiedotteet/2009/T2480.pdf (2009).
11. Barnum S, Sethi A. An introduction to attack patterns as a software assurance knowledge resource. Tech. rep., Cigital Inc. http://capec.mitre.org/documents/Attack_Patterns-Knowing_Your_Enemies_in_Order_to_Defeat_Them-Paper.pdf (2007).

12. Barnum S. Common attack pattern enumeration and classification (CAPEC) schema description. Tech. rep., Cigital Inc. http://capec.mitre.org/documents/documentation/CAPEC_Schema_Description_v1.3.pdf (2008).
13. Gu G, Perdisci R, Zhang J, Lee W. BotMiner: Clustering analysis of network traffic for protocol- and structure-independent botnet detection. In: Proceedings of the 17th USENIX security symposium. San Jose: CA, USA; 2008. pp. 139–154.
14. Varrandi R. SEC—a light weight event correlation tool. In: Proceedings of the IEEE workshop on IP operations and management. doi:10.1109/IPOM.2002.1045765; 2002. pp. 111–115.
15. Staniford S, Hoagland JA, McAlerney JA. Practical automated detection of stealthy portscans. J Comput Secur. 2002;10(1–2):105–36.
16. Staniford-Chen S, et al. GrIDS—A graph based intrusion detection system for large networks. In: Proceedings of the 19th national information systems security conference; 1996. pp. 361–370.
17. Roesch M. SNORT—Lightweight intrusion detection for networks. In: Proceedings of the USENIX technical program - 13th systems administration conference - LISA '99. Washington, USA: Seattle; 1999. p. 229–238.
18. The Team Cymru. Home page of The team Cymru darknet. http://www.team-cymru.org/Services/darknets.html. (2009). Accessed Sept 2013.
19. Bailey M, Cooke E, Jahanian F, Nazario J, Watson D. The Internet motion sensor: a distributed blackhole monitoring system. In: Proceedings of the 12th annual network and distributed system security symposium (NDSS), San Diego, CA, USA; 2005.
20. Shannon C, Moore D. The spread of the witty worm. IEEE Secur Priv. 2004;2(4):46–50. doi:10.1109/MSP.2004.59.
21. Staniford S, Moore D, Paxson V, Weaver N. The top speed of flash worms. In: Proceedings of the ACM workshop on rapid malcode, WORM 2004, Washington, DC, USA; 2004.
22. Pang R, Yegneswaran V, Barford P, Paxson V, Peterson L. Characteristics of Internet background radiation. In: Proceedings of the 4th ACM SIGCOMM, Taormina, Sicily, Italy; 2004. pp. 27–40. doi:10.1145/1028788.1028794.
23. ArborNetworks. Estonian DDoS attacks-A summary to date. Tech. rep., Arbor Networks. http://asert.arbornetworks.com/2007/05/estonian-ddos-attacks-a-summary-to-date/ (2007).
24. Pratt VR. Modeling concurrency with partial orders. Int J Parallel Prog. 1986;15(1):33–71. doi:10.1007/BF01379149.
25. Yu Y, Fry M, Schaeffer-Filho A, Smith P, Hutchison D. An adaptive approach to network resilience: evolving challenge detection and mitigation. In: 2011 8th International workshop on the design of reliable communication Networks (DRCN). doi:10.1109/DRCN.2011.6076900; 2011. pp 172–179.
26. Sterbenz JPG, Hutchison D, Çetinkaya EK, Jabbar A, Rohrer JP, Schöller M, Smith P. Resilience and survivability in communication networks: strategies, principles, and survey of disciplines. Comput Netw. 2010;54(8):1245–1265. doi:10.1016/j.comnet.2010.03.005.

Chapter 11
Towards a Penetration Testing Framework Using Attack Patterns

Clive Blackwell

Abstract The problems of system security are well known, but no satisfactory methods to resolve them have ever been discovered. One heuristic method is to use a penetration test with the rationale of finding system flaws before malicious attackers. However, this is a craft-based discipline without an adequate theoretical or empirical basis for justifying its activities and results. We show that both the automated tool and skill-based methods of pen testing are unsatisfactory, because we need to provide understandable evidence to clients about their weaknesses and offer actionable plans to fix the critical ones. We use attack patterns to help develop a pen-testing framework to help avoid the limitations of current approaches.

1 Introduction

The problems of system security are well known, but no satisfactory methods to resolve them have ever been discovered. It is often suggested that security should be 'baked into' systems from the outset, but this is unachievable considering their complexity and the pace of technological change. If we accept that security flaws are with us for the foreseeable future, we must find ways of finding and remediating flaws in operational systems. It is important to test systems even if the components are secure, as security is a system property that relates to organisational objectives, system configuration and usage scenarios.

One heuristic method is to pen test systems with the rationale of finding flaws before malicious threat actors. However, this is a craft-based discipline without an adequate theoretical or empirical basis for justifying its activities and results. The results should be explained in organisational terms so that management can show

C. Blackwell (✉)
Department of Computing and Communication Technologies, Oxford Brookes University,
Wheatley Campus, Wheatley, Oxford OX33 1HX, UK
e-mail: CBlackwell@brookes.ac.uk

C. Blackwell and H. Zhu (eds.), *Cyberpatterns*, DOI: 10.1007/978-3-319-04447-7_11,   135
© Springer International Publishing Switzerland 2014

there is a better return on investment for fixing major security issues compared to productive activities. We show that both the automated tool and skill-based methods of pen testing are unsatisfactory, because we need to provide comprehensible evidence to clients, and offer adequate remediation plans to fix the critical flaws.

We use attack patterns to suggest a pen-testing framework to help avoid the limitations of current approaches. Structured attack patterns help understand attacks better and formulate adequate test cases giving comprehensive coverage and consequently better-substantiated results, holding out the prospect of offering relevant and realisable advice about suitable remediation measures.

We introduce attack patterns followed by discussion of the current state of pen testing and testing techniques in general. We follow with our efforts to tackle the current issues by structuring and extending attack patterns to help develop realistic test suites that address organisational goals rather than simple implementation flaws.

2 Attack Patterns

In software engineering, a design pattern is a general reusable solution to a commonly occurring problem in software design, made famous in the software engineering community by the Design Patterns or 'Gang of Four' book [1]. It captures the context and structure of a general repeatable solution to a common problem archetype rather than its low-level implementation details. A design pattern represents desirable, intentional and expected system behaviour.

Attack patterns [2] are based on design patterns, and apparently emerged around 2001 in the security community, appeared first in the literature in Moore et al. [3], before greater elaboration in Hoglund and McGraw's book [4]. These are not patterns in the sense of design patterns, as most sections are missing from their templates.

Finally, Barnum and Sethi [2] standardised what is now understood as an attack pattern with a comprehensive template consistent with design patterns. They subsequently described the use of attack patterns [5] to help testers act like attackers attempting to break into systems, alluding to our concept of aiding pen testing of operational systems. Subsequently, attack patterns were classified in the Common Attack Pattern Enumeration and Classification (CAPEC) schema [6] of which there are currently around 400.

An attack pattern is analogous to a design pattern, as it describes how a particular type of attack is performed as a conceptual pattern, ignoring low-level implementation details. However, attack patterns are specified from the attacker's viewpoint, and therefore they represent undesirable, unintentional and unexpected behaviour. Here, the common problem targeted by the pattern represents the objective of the attacker, and the pattern's solution represents known methods of performing the attack.

We describe how our attack pattern template [7], adapted from the CAPEC schema [6], gives extensive information about attack types thereby helping pen testers to develop appropriate test cases for simulating attacks realistically.

3 Critique of Penetration Testing

A common way to check the protection of an operational system is to simulate attacks using a penetration test or vulnerability scan. A pen test actively exploits weaknesses, whereas a vulnerability scan merely passively discovers them, but we characterise them both as pen testing for simplicity in this paper. Pen testing can be characterised by two different methods at the ends of a spectrum of possibilities. We proceed to criticise the limitations of these extreme endpoints, at the risk of simplistic and crude stereotyping, in order to demonstrate clearly how attack patterns may help develop an effective pen-testing framework.

At one end of the spectrum, pen testing can be criticised as tool-driven, where various tools are executed to discover low-level system and application flaws automatically. The tool then provides an extensive report that gives the exploitability and significance of the discovered weaknesses. However, tools do not adequately emphasise and prioritise the crucial flaws that need remediation, because they do not consider the wider system context to distinguish serious threats that could have significant organisational effects from minor annoyances. For example, access to sensitive data is hard to detect using automated tools, because they do not understand its meaning, purpose or possible damage from disclosure.

Our pen-testing framework using attack patterns may offer a higher-level perspective to classify and characterise attacks within a wider context, including their intent and potential gains for the perpetrator and harm to the victim, rather than focussing on low-level bugs and weaknesses. An attack pattern can include the envisaged effects in the consequences or impact section of its template, incorporating possible unintentional side effects. For example, a data leak may also cause accidental loss of availability if the targeted data is removed or destroyed when it is copied.

At the other end of the scale, skilled pen testers have a theoretical and empirical rationale and framework for their activities based on their prior knowledge and experience, and check for significant weaknesses based on the system goals, environment, critical functions and likely weaknesses. A skilled pen tester may be able to find many issues that automated tools would not detect, by effectively formulating and testing pattern-matching hypotheses.

However, their conceptual models may lack valid foundation and empirical support. A skilled pen tester may attempt a particular attack in one or two ways that have worked in the past, but not try all variations for which an automated tool would be superior. We want to establish the extent and range of possible attacks, so that we can deal with all its manifestations rather than just fix isolated flaws. An attack pattern repository can provide an aide mémoire that might suggest relevant tests to ensure that everything significant is covered.

Secondly, a pen tester may discover an attack, such as the lack of adequate protection for sensitive data, but not fully comprehend the subsequent issues resulting from unauthorised disclosure. Attack patterns include detailed information about the context of the attack, such as the purpose of the targeted data, its meaning and the possible effects from exposure or destruction. Finally, attack patterns aid documentation and reporting by providing the wider context beyond the low-level technical details provided by tools.

We conclude that both the automated tool and skill-based methods are unsatisfactory, because the pen tester needs to provide convincing, comprehensible and complete evidence to clients about their weaknesses, and offer an adequate, timely and cost-effective remediation plan to fix the critical ones in support of organisational objectives.

4 Testing Fundamentals

4.1 Black Box Testing

The use of attack patterns for black box or white box testing of software [5] can also be used for pen testing of entire systems. Black box testing involves investigating the external behaviour of a system without any knowledge of its inner workings. White box testing involves deeper and more systematic analysis of the system based upon knowledge of its internal structure and detailed operations.

Black box testing [8] focuses on determining whether a program or system meets its functional specification. A black box test considers only the input and output of the software or system without regard to its internal operation. A system fails a test case if there is a departure from specification called a failure.

Black box testing most closely replicates attacks by an external attacker with no prior knowledge of the targeted systems. However, adversaries nowadays can often obtain good information about targeted organisations from the data they publish or expose about their systems (deliberately or accidentally), which can potentially be collected automatically using various reconnaissance tools. Although black box testing simulates general hacker activity and is good for finding specific known issues, it is not as effective at finding more specialised and obscure issues as white box testing. Fuzz testing or fuzzing [9] is one black box technique that provides invalid, unexpected or random data inputs to programs that is useful in pen testing.

4.2 White Box Testing

White box testing [10] considers the internal mechanisms of a system or component with full visibility of its logical operations and structure. A failed test usually indicates the problem or fault and so aids correction. White box tests aim to cover all possible paths and at least should exercise every operation. It helps to focus attention on specific issues and generally produces results sooner than black box testing.

In white box pen testing, the testers are given complete access to information about the systems they are attacking, including detailed system diagrams and application code. So-called 'security by obscurity' is known to offer weak security, so it is considered better to assume complete knowledge of the system by sophisticated and knowledgeable attackers. However, white box tests do not realistically model most attacks that do not exploit detailed code even in insider and advanced cyber threats. White box tests are more suitable for security testing of bespoke software in development.

4.3 50 Shades of Grey

The goal of grey box testing [11] is to find more obscure bugs and flaws not found in black box testing because of lack of detailed understanding of system structure. Grey box testing provides combinations of inputs and outputs as in black box testing, but also uses some information about system internals as in white box testing. A grey box tester has partial knowledge of internal system structure from the documentation, but does not use information about the detailed code. Grey box testing attempts to approach complete system coverage, whilst avoiding the exponential complexity of white box testing.

Pen testing is usually grey box testing [12], where the particular shade of grey is dependent on the degree to which it approaches the black or white end of the spectrum. Pen testers realise that black box pen testing has limitations just as with black box testing of software in terms of coverage. The general pen tester is not usually interested in the specific code as in white box testing, but is interested in the general structure and organisation of targeted systems including their networks, hosts and applications. This includes knowledge of internal communication paths, system configuration, and specific software vulnerabilities either disclosed on the Internet or incorporated into hacking tools. The scripted attacks using automated tools such as Nessus and Metasploit are grey box tests as they exploit weaknesses discovered through previous analysis or testing of gross program behaviour rather than detailed code.

Grey box testing simulates attackers who have knowledge of the system internals and is a reasonable assumption for privileged or sophisticated adversaries such as the insider threat and advanced cyber threats. We assume adversaries have some degree of initial system access and knowledge, but they do not have access to or exploit internal program structure. We note that the goal of the pen tester is different from the attacker who only has to find and exploit one weakness, whereas the tests requires high coverage to show there is limited attack potential. In addition, there may be movement towards the white end as the test progresses, because the gained information and greater access is subsequently used to probe for more internal weaknesses.

Attack patterns can highlight areas of system risk and thereby indicate the areas that the grey box analysis should focus upon and together with automation will make such analysis more tractable. Grey box testing is aided by extending some attack pattern sections with UML diagrams to help design and structure the test cases.

4.4 Security Testing

Ordinary testing exercises anticipated functionality, whereas security testing checks for unexpected behaviour. Security testing involves verifying security mechanisms to ensure that their functionality is properly implemented. Incorrect designed or implemented functionality is often straightforward to detect, as the erroneous behaviour often manifests itself under typical usage conditions.

Security is an emergent property of a system, not just about the correctness of security mechanisms and features, as all systems have greater functionality than known and required. Therefore, security testing also checks for unexpected functionality and requires new skills of 'thinking outside the box'.

Many of these flaws are not violations of system specification, as a process might behave correctly according to requirements, but perform additional unspecified tasks in addition to legitimate actions. For example, a SQL injection attack might legitimately read a table row, but then append an illicit command in the same line. An example is:

SELECT * FROM userinfo WHERE id=me; DROP TABLE users; where my record is correctly selected, but followed by an instruction to delete the users table.

We need to understand possible attacks better to facilitate simulation of the attacker's approach with suitable tests. We claim that a sensible way of investigating germane threats is to use attack patterns to specify attacks clearly and precisely including describing both the wider context and specific attack vectors. The CAPEC attack pattern schema encapsulates expert knowledge and thereby helps testers develop suitable tests that realistically simulate attacks.

5 Proposed Penetration Testing Framework

5.1 Introduction and Rationale

We propose a pen-testing framework based on attack patterns to help formulate comprehensive test plans covering possible attack scenarios. An attack pattern provides a space of possible attacks that scope or bound possible individual instances. The testing framework takes advantage of the long established and successful discipline of software testing described briefly above and applies it to the security of operational systems.

We can instantiate attack patterns by binding parameters to possible values, including systematic testing of different combinations of values and mutating known attack vectors. The framework may help to hypothesise novel attacks by instantiating attack patterns by allocating possible, but never previously observed values to parameters, or bringing unseen combinations of variables together into novel attack instances by techniques that give high test coverage such as Orthogonal Array Testing [13].

Another possibility is to use existing attack instances as exemplars, and then adapt or extend them by changing their parameters, a bit like fuzzing [14], except in a meaningful and relevant way to the attack being executed. In so-called smart fuzzing using a tool such as Sequitur [15], test cases can be generated from scratch or by mutating existing cases.

This could lead to a testing framework that provides comprehensive coverage to address some of the limitations in both the skill-based and automated approaches to pen testing described before. The proposed framework could offer comprehensive tests similar to the current automated tool-driven testing, but at a more meaningful scale of analysing complete attacks against the entire system rather than atomic exploits on particular targeted components. We may be able to show that certain attacks cannot occur, by testing all variations of the attack pattern. The resulting pen-testing plan would offer a comprehensible view of the tests linked to organisational objectives, thereby helping to make the results actionable by the client.

5.2 Existing Standards

We indicate the utility for pen testing of relevant sections of our attack pattern template [7] that were adapted and expanded from the CAPEC schema [6]. The pattern template sections give generic information about the type of attack, which can be particularised by incorporating known information about the system under test to aid grey box testing.

Firstly, we discuss relevant security frameworks used in pen testing. Most security testing templates have few sections and focus on the specific test data without considering the surrounding context.

The Information Systems Security Assessment Framework (ISSAF) [16] from the Open Information Systems Security Group (OISSG) is a very comprehensive framework that combines high-level organisational security concerns such as policy, standards, governance and compliance with detailed validation strategies such as pen testing. There is a detailed pen-testing template containing the fields: Description, Objective, Expected Results, Prerequisite, Process, Example/Results, Countermeasures, Further Reading and Contributors. This looks like an abbreviated version of an attack pattern, and in fact, our template includes all these sections, albeit called by different names.

The Open Source Security Testing Methodology Manual (OSSTMM) [17] produced by the Institute for Security and Open Methodologies (ISECOM) is a manual for security testing and analysis of operational systems that takes a more conceptual viewpoint rather than focusing on tools. Test results are reported with the Security Test Audit Report (STAR) [18] that provides a comprehensive form for the overall report with sections for the different types of possible test, but does not provide a detailed template for individual test cases.

The Penetration Testing Execution Standard [19] is designed to provide both businesses and security service providers with the baseline expectations from a pen test and detailed description and scope of the different types of test. They aim to create a formal standard using a common language for pen testing, but it is still a work in progress. At present, there are lists of testing concerns in Sect. 6 on Reporting, but they are undeveloped placeholders and need contributions from the community.

Finally, OWASP provides a comprehensive testing guide [20] for verifying the security of running applications with several different types of test, including Penetration Testing as well as Manual Inspections and Reviews, Threat Modelling and Source Code Review. It describes a general Testing Framework along with practical techniques for implementation, including a Web Application Penetration Testing methodology discussing a large set of scenarios taking up the greater part of the guide. Each threat scenario is described under the headings: Summary, Description of the Issue, Black Box Testing (and Example), Grey Box Testing (and Example) and References.

5.3 Threat Modelling

Threat modelling often analyses adversarial threats by modelling their behaviour with attack trees [21] or their effects using the STRIDE classification [22] (Spoofing identity, Tampering with data, Repudiation, Information disclosure, Denial of service, Elevation of privilege). Attack patterns are more comprehensive as they characterise the threats contextually by considering the wider organisational system and environment, along with the knowledge, skill and motivation of potential attackers.

UML [23] is used widely in all aspects of software development, and, inter alia, helps move from system specification to test cases that verify correct operation. We include UML diagrams in different attack pattern sections to go from textual descriptions of attack vectors to structured diagrammatic representations that help the creation of effective test cases. We show the attack pattern template together with its potential use in pen testing in Table 1.

Class and object diagrams visually show the involved participants and their relationships, including system agents that inadvertently aid the attack. Process diagrams visually show the attack performance and path within the execution section of the template. Sequence and activity diagrams are common and help to consider attacks from the wider perspective of interfering with system processes rather than exploiting low-level code.

The threat model informs test planning and provides traceability to system goals and plausible attacks. The threat model together with any provided (grey box) or inferred (black box) system models aids the design and prioritisation of tests, their application and anticipated results, much like any decent software test plan.

Table 1 Attack pattern template (abridged) [24] for penetration testing

Section	Description of contents	Use in pen testing
Name	Generic name for attack	Suggestive name is helpful
Description	Textual description summarising the type of attack	Supports knowledge acquisition in an easily digestible form
Perpetrator	Helps to flesh out their motivation, abilities and methods	Taking the adversary's perspective makes the attack appear more real
Motivation	Answers why the attacker would act in this way	Aids discovery of suitable tests
Resources	Includes resources initially available to the adversary or that need to be acquired before use	The greyness of the test determines the initial access to internal resources
Attacker skill	Including inherent abilities and tool skills	Attacker sophistication helps to scope likely attacks. Test suites can be designed to simulate different skill sets
Attacker knowledge	Including both general knowledge and specific system information	Grey box testing is needed for simulating the insider threat and advanced cyber threats, and so the tester needs extensive system documentation
Context or prerequisites	Description of the conditions needed for the attack to succeed	Includes level of access required and existence of suitable weaknesses
Activation zone	Location within the system where the offensive activities occur	Helps determine the scope of the pen test and restrict undesirable side effects on legitimate activities
Execution	Describes how the attack can be performed	Helps to establish attack scope and discover new instances by varying each independent aspect
Target	System must host a suitable target instance accessible to the attacker	Tests are included within the test suite only if the target is within scope
Security or immediate impact	Violations of access control, authentication, accountability, confidentiality, integrity and availability	Helps to understand side effects of attacks and poorly executed pen tests
System or ultimate impact	The wider service, financial and reputational effects	Test objective is to find serious organisational effects not security breaches that are only the means of attack
Instances	Description of known scenarios where the attack occurred	Helps to determine test applicability and design test cases

5.4 Benefits of Attack Patterns

There is a need for effective and efficient testing methods and tools to help us deal with system size and complexity, and attacker ingenuity and evolution. We must move away from dumping tool output in 1,000 page reports containing all the discovered vulnerabilities without highlighting the key ones needing rapid remediation. This requires abstraction away from tool implementations as implicit attack descriptors, to adequate test specifications describing testing goals such as high coverage and organisational objectives such as potential impact from exploited weaknesses.

The attacker often cunningly constructs malicious inputs to exploit obscure weaknesses, and so we need to generate test cases beyond simple techniques that aim for high coverage like fuzzing (black box) and simple path or statement coverage (white box). These techniques are unlikely to discover devious combinations of inputs, and so we need better ways of developing malicious test cases that model attacks and the system weaknesses they exploit.

Attack patterns help the creation of more adequate test suites that map better to system objectives. They help to decide which attacks are relevant to the system under test by scoping the relevant attack types comprehensively and clearly. Attack patterns help to develop test cases that simulate variations of known attacks using some of the testing techniques previously described by clearly scoping the possible inputs for each variable. This allows the determination of unusual and unexpected input combinations to simulate the construction of malicious attack vectors by allowing the systematic search for or random variation of known attacks within the attack space delineated by the pattern.

Tests are become increasingly complex to exercise the business logic where multiple applications (such as in the cloud) work together to provide a service, rather than focusing on single applications and exploits. The tests should exercise relevant combinations of inputs and system states, rather than the low-level canned tests typically implemented by common tools with limited understanding of system functionality.

It is therefore important to know (grey box) or infer (black box) what system states are critical and how they may be reached. Grey box testing is usually more suitable, as we need to investigate potential attackers and compromised components inside the system. The attack pattern template may help to provide a superstructure to help design a test plan to discover and test internal system state and behaviour.

The provision of standardised attack pattern templates aids objectivity by providing a rational basis for testing and helps to challenge incorrect security assumptions. We can apply regression testing [25] to pen testing using attack patterns. Regression testing [26] involves the replay of relevant test cases after making an upgrade or repair to discover if the changes have caused other issues.

It is particularly apposite to rerun pen tests after fixing security issues, as test repeatability helps to define a baseline for system security and model improvement (or decline) over time. In addition, we can supplement the basic regression tests by making slight variations in test cases with new values within the attack pattern space to check that reported flaws have been successfully mitigated in their entirety. We can update and extend tests as new attack variants are discovered by consulting the attack patterns for appropriate instances rather than simply making ad hoc additions to test suites.

This level of organisation is rare with pen tests, but is important, as many clients use pen testing for tick box compliance only and do not update their security adequately to counter test failures. Adequate structuring of test plans could potentially enable their development and distribution in the community. Attack patterns could come supplied with a range of devious inputs or test case generators, although this might of course also be beneficial to potential adversaries.

5.5 Organisational Considerations

Risk cannot be eliminated as not everything can be completely protected (the best is the enemy of the good). As with counting software bugs, the number of discovered vulnerabilities in systems is not a good guide to security. Security is always relative to the value of information and services being protected, the skills and resources of adversaries, the impact from exploitation and the costs of potential remedies. Attack patterns help to bridge the divide between technical and organisational concerns by providing guidance that depicts security issues in business terms.

We therefore need to correlate the discovered weaknesses with their possible impact accounting for the organisational risk profile to create a remediation plan justified by estimated return on investment. Post exploitation tests are crucial to determine ways to inflict maximum damage and loss whilst avoiding detection.

The outcome of a soundly executed pen test should be a set of recommendations closely aligned with organisational goals. The report should identify important vulnerabilities including architectural, design and conceptual weaknesses, as well as technical. It should prioritise the discovered vulnerabilities based on the ease/likelihood of exploit, difficulty/cost to mitigate and system criticality/impact if materialised, rather than a laundry list of weaknesses in a 1,000 page report.

The report could include suitable test templates structured according to the sections in the attack pattern, so that the empirical test evidence is presented intelligibly to clients. A suitable template indicating the causes, methods and effects of the simulated attacks helps link the tests to organisation goals.

Attack patterns can help develop suitable test cases especially if standard generic tests are developed that simply need adaptation for the specific environment. We can start with the CWE/SANS Top 25 Most Dangerous Software Errors [27] or OWASP Top Ten Web Application Security Risks [28] for the largest impact, possibly modelling some of the most serious and common attacks like buffer overflow, SQL injection and cross-site scripting.

6 Conclusions and Further Work

Pen testers need to raise their game by providing better service to the clients who pay their wages, and they need to establish a firmer foundation for the discipline. We showed that both the automated tool and skill-based methods of pen testing are unsatisfactory, because we need to provide comprehensible and complete evidence to clients about their weaknesses, allowing them to take effective remediation measures.

We suggested using attack patterns to help develop a pen-testing framework to address the current issues of validity and completeness in pen testing. The resulting pen-testing plan would offer a comprehensible view of the tests linked to organisational objectives, thereby helping to make the report results actionable by the client. In addition to the tangible practical benefits, the results will have improved validity over current practice and therefore could play a part in the increasingly important 'science of cybersecurity'.

Tools encapsulate expert knowledge, but they remain too low-level to characterise organisational concerns, especially as the business benefits come mainly from applications, not the infrastructure supporting them. We need to assess and describe the impact and severity of vulnerabilities in both technical and organisational terms and provide a link between the two with the results interpreted with respect to the system and security requirements.

We also see attack patterns as educational resources for pen testers learning from the experience of more experienced professionals in the community. The attack pattern schema CAPEC has established a knowledge base encapsulating current understanding of threats, which can help pen testers analyse attacks more conceptually and take the adversarial perspective. However, attack patterns need more structure and clarity beyond sections containing simple freeform text, which can be provided by including structured language and UML diagrams.

We might hope that our framework could lead to a systematic theory of pen testing and corresponding remediation. We may be able to show empirically that certain attacks cannot occur by testing all variations of the attack pattern. This may give some form of security assurance, but the evidence must satisfy clear and convincing criteria relevant to system objectives.

Eventually, we might hope this could lead to a formal theory of pen testing and corresponding defensive controls, by adapting and extending the formalisation of design patterns [29] to attack patterns. For example, if both the attack and defensive systems have a formal representation, we may be able to prove that certain attacks are impossible, assuming the system realises the formal model.

Composition of attack patterns is also relevant and can also bootstrap off existing work in design patterns [30]. Attack patterns could be composed to help create complex, structured and realistic tests similar to real attacks that need to compromise multiple weaknesses in several stages to achieve their goals, but we leave this avenue of investigation for later.

References

1. Gamma E, Helm R, Johnson R, Vlissides J. Design patterns: elements of reusable object-oriented software. Boston: Addison-Wesley; 1995.
2. Barnum S, Sethi A. Introduction to attack patterns. Cigital Inc. (2006). (Revised 14 May 2013). https://buildsecurityin.us-cert.gov/bsi/articles/knowledge/attack/585-BSI.html. Accessed 23 Sept 2013
3. Moore AP, Ellison RJ, Linger RC. Attack modeling for information security and survivability. No. CMU-SEI-2001-TN-001. Software Engineering Institute, Carnegie Mellon University, Pittsburgh; 2001.
4. Hoglund G, McGraw G. Exploiting software: how to break code. Boston: Addison-Wesley; 2004.
5. Barnum S, Sethi A. Attack patterns as a knowledge resource for building secure soft-ware. Cigital Inc. http://capec.mitre.org/documents/Attack_Patterns-Knowing_Your_Enemies_in_Order_to_Defeat_Them-Paper.pdf. (2007). Accessed 23 Sept 2013.
6. Mitre Corporation: Common attack pattern enumeration and classification (CAPEC). http://www.capec.mitre.org (2013). Accessed 23 Sept 2013.
7. Blackwell C. Formally modelling attack patterns for forensic analysis. In: 5th international conference on cybercrime forensics education and training. Canterbury; 2011.
8. Williams L. Testing overview and black box testing techniques. Open seminar in software engineering. North Carolina State University. http://agile.csc.ncsu.edu/SEMaterials/BlackBox.pdf. (2006). Accessed 26 September 2013.
9. Miller BP, Barton P, Fredriksen L, So B. An empirical study of the reliability of UNIX utilities. Commun ACM. 1990; 33(12):32–44.
10. Williams L. White black box testing. Open seminar in software engineering. North Carolina State University. http://agile.csc.ncsu.edu/SEMaterials/WhiteBox.pdf. (2006). Accessed 26 September 2013
11. Kicillof N, Grieskamp W, Tillmann N, Braberman V. Achieving both model and code coverage with automated gray-box testing. In: Proceedings of the 3rd international workshop on advances in model-based testing. ACM. 2007; pp. 1–11.
12. Geer D, Harthorne J. Penetration testing: a duet. In: Proceedings of the 18th annual computer security applications conference (IEEE); 2002.
13. Hedayat AS, Sloane NJA, Stufken J. Orthogonal arrays: theory and applications. New York: Springer; 1999.
14. Takanen A, DeMott JD, Miller C. Fuzzing for software security testing and quality assurance. Norwood: Artech House; 2008.
15. Kaminsky D. Black ops 2006: Pattern recognition. Usenix LISA '06. https://www.usenix.org/legacy/events/lisa06/tech/slides/kaminsky.pdf. (2006) Accessed 7 Oct 2013.
16. OISSG: The information systems security assessment framework (ISSAF) Draft 0.2.1. OISSG. http://www.oissg.org/files/issaf0.2.1.pdf. (2005). Accessed 5 Oct 2013.
17. Barceló M, Herzog P. Open Source security testing methodology manual (OSSTMM) ver 3. ISECOM. http://www.isecom.org/mirror/OSSTMM.3.pdf. (2010). Accessed 5 Oct 2013.
18. ISECOM: Security test audit report. ISECOM. http://www.isecom.org/mirror/STAR.3.pdf. (2010). Accessed 5 Oct 2013.
19. Penetration Testing Execution Standard Team: Penetration testing execution standard. www.pentest-standard.org (2013). Accessed 5 Oct 2013.
20. Meucci M, Keary E, Cuthbert D. OWASP testing guide ver 3.0. OWASP foundation. https://www.owasp.org/images/5/56/OWASP_Testing_Guide_v3.pdf. (2008). Accessed 5 Oct 2013.
21. Schneier B. Attack trees: modeling security threats. Dr. Dobb's J. 1999;24:21–29.
22. Swiderski F, Snyder W. Threat modeling. Redmond: Microsoft Press; 2004.
23. Fowler M. UML distilled: a brief guide to the standard object modeling language. 3rd ed. Reading: Addison-Wesley Professional; 2003.
24. Blackwell C. A strategy for formalising attack patterns. Cyberpatterns 2012. In: Cyberpatterns: unifying design patterns with security, attack and forensic patterns. Springer; 2014.

25. Myers G. The art of software testing. Chichester: Wiley; 2004.
26. Kolawa A, Huizinga D. Automated defect prevention: best practices in software management. New York: Wiley-IEEE Computer Society Press; 2007. p. 73.
27. Christey S, Brown M, Kirby D, Martin B, Paller A. CWE/SANS Top 25 most dangerous software errors. Mitre corporation. http://cwe.mitre.org/top25/archive/2011/2011_cwe_sans_top25.pdf. (2011). Accessed 9 Oct 2013.
28. Williams J, Wichers D. OWASP top 10–2013. OWASP foundation. https://www.owasp.org/index.php/Category:OWASP_Top_Ten_Project. (2013). Accessed 9 Oct 2013.
29. Bayley I, Zhu H. A formal language for the expression of pattern compositions. Int J Adv Softw IARIA. 2011; 4(3,4):354–366.
30. Taibi T. Formalising design patterns composition. IEE Proc. Softw. IET. 2006; 153(3):127–136.

Chapter 12
A Method for Resolving Security Vulnerabilities Through the Use of Design Patterns

Nick Walker, Natalie Coull, Ian Ferguson and Allan Milne

Abstract Most software development companies conduct in-house testing of their code prior to releasing their product, yet software vulnerabilities are still found every single day in the most prevalent of applications. Memory corruption vulnerabilities are amongst the most difficult to detect, but can be the most dangerous. This research presents both an effective taxonomy of these vulnerabilities, which can be used to identify software threats and a methodology to maximize the number of memory corruption vulnerabilities that are identified during software testing. A means of cataloguing such vulnerabilities was required: As design patterns were already familiar to software engineers the use of a pattern language seemed appropriate, particularly as the solution to the vulnerabilities lay in the software engineering domain.

1 Introduction

By far the most diverse and prevalent type of software bugs, with the greatest security implications are memory corruption vulnerabilities. A survey undertaken by Chen, Xu and Nakka [1] indicated that memory corruption vulnerabilities account for 67 % of all software flaws identified. These memory corruption vulnerabilities can manifest themselves in various forms and occur when the contents of a memory location

N. Walker · N. Coull (✉) · I. Ferguson · A. Milne
School of Science, Engineering, and Technology,
University of Abertay Dundee, Bell Street, Dundee DD1 1HG, UK
e-mail: 0801554@abertay.ac.uk

N. Coull
e-mail: n.coull@abertay.ac.uk

I. Ferguson
e-mail: i.ferguson@abertay.ac.uk

A. Milne
e-mail: a.milne@abertay.ac.uk

C. Blackwell and H. Zhu (eds.), *Cyberpatterns*, DOI: 10.1007/978-3-319-04447-7_12,   149
© Springer International Publishing Switzerland 2014

are modified unintentionally or maliciously and result in the corruption of data, through logic or programming errors. These vulnerabilities can exist at a number of different stages in program execution [2], making it extremely challenging to locate them during normal software testing procedures, especially if the tester has limited understanding of them and how to find them. A further difficulty is encountered when analyzing the effects of memory corruption in order to identify the source of a given vulnerability. The source of a memory corruption vulnerability and how it manifests in terms of the program crash may be far apart in terms of covered program code, with tedious links between source and manifestation. If true security is to be achieved, then programmatical issues must be identified and countermeasures applied proactively by fixing the erroneous code, rather than trying to reactively prevent exploitation of the system. To achieve this requires considerable understanding of the different types of memory corruption vulnerabilities and a well-planned systematic approach to identify the existence of these errors must be undertaken.

Design patterns, originally popularised by the "Gang of Four" book [3], have been widely adopted in the software engineering community as an effective means of documenting recurring software problems and possible solutions. As such, the use of patterns to catalogue idiom from the security field seemed like an appropriate way of presenting such ideas to practising software engineers. As the type of vulnerabilities under consideration (memory corruption) is largely created by ignorance during the software development process, anything that could be done to communicate an awareness of the both problem and of appropriate solutions would be beneficial.

2 Summary of Work

This work presents a taxonomy of memory corruption errors and a methodology for testing software to maximise the number of errors that are identified.

2.1 Taxonomy

This taxonomy was created through an evaluation of existing taxonomies and conducting a thorough vulnerability test of software to identify the full range of errors that can lead to memory corruption. The taxonomy consists of nine different types of memory corruption bugs, and details them according to the following criteria:

1. Origin of vulnerability
2. Behaviour of vulnerability
3. Criteria required to leverage vulnerability
4. Impact of vulnerability
5. Countermeasures required to solve the vulnerability.

Table 1 Taxonomy of memory corruption vulnerabilities

Name	Defining origin	Behavior	Exploitation reqs	Impact	Countermeasures
Strcpy() overflow	Originates where a call to strcpy() is made where the size of the string in the source buffer is larger than that of the destination buffer.	A write operation exceeds the target memory allocated for it, and overwrites core variables on the stack such as ret or the base pointer.	Requires that the attacker has some level of control over the *src string. It is also possible to cause a bounds checked overflow to corrupt memory if the attacker is able to affect the allocation size of the buffer prior to the call.	Arbitrary code execution. Corruption of stack variables.	Bounds check all strcpy() functions dynamically based on sizeof(*dest)+1.
Strncpy() termination failure	Originates where the source buffer is of equal size or greater than the space allocated to store it, especially where n is also greater than the allocated number of bytes.	Variable based on context. Either creates string in memory that is not null terminated (and therefore corrupted in the eyes of functions like strcpy() or overwrites EIP in a similar manner to strcpy() overflows.	Requires that either: - Attacker controls the size of buffer *dest - Attacker controls the integer N. - Attacker controls the size of the string in *src.	Arbitrary code execution and corruption of stack variables.	Throw an exception if strlen(*src)+1 > sizeof(*dest). Determine the number of bytes to copy dynamically using sizeof.
Memcpy() overflow	Originates where the number of bytes to be copied into *dest is greater than the sizeof(*dest).	A write operation exceeds the target memory allocated for it, and overwrites core variables on the stack such as ret or the base pointer.	Requires that either: - Attacker controls size of *dest, and contents of *src - Attacker controls content of src and an integer >sizeof (*dest) is used as an argument to memcpy().	Arbitrary code execution and corruption of stack variables	Ensure that the number of bytes to be copied is not greater than sizeof *dest prior to making the function call.

(continued)

Table 1 (continued)

Name	Defining origin	Behavior	Exploitation reqs	Impact	Countermeasures
Free of non-dynamic memory	Originates where a buffer which has not been dynamically allocated is passed to free().	The free() accepts the pointer as a valid argument and attempts to modify the linked list structures which keep track of the heap with invalid values.	Requires that the attacker be able to manipulate the pointer in such a way to affect the free() procedure to cause later function calls to execute unexpected code.	Possible arbitrary code execution and corruption of the process heap.	Only free() pointers returned from malloc(), realloc() or calloc(). It is recommended to keep a "shadow table" of all pointers returned from these functions for verification.
Free after malloc() failure	Originates where a free() call is made to a pointer which was previously passed to malloc() where the memory allocation failed.	A free() attempts to remove the invalid pointer from the heap structures, and corrupts the process heap.	Requires that the attacker be able to manipulate the pointer in such a way to affect the free() procedure to cause later function calls to execute unexpected code.	Possible arbitrary code execution and corruption of the process heap.	Always check the return values of malloc(). If a call fails for any reason, set the value of the pointer to NULL, protecting the heap from corruption in subsequent calls to free().
Double free()	Originates where a call to free() is made using a pointer which has already been free()'d and never reallocated in between the calls to free.	A free() attempts to remove the invalid pointer from the heap structures, and corrupts the process heap.	Requires that the attacker be able to manipulate the pointer in such a way to affect the free() procedure to cause later function calls to execute unexpected code.	Possible arbitrary code execution and corruption of the process heap.	After freeing a pointer ensure that it is immediately set to NULL, as a free on a NULL pointer will have no effect on the heap, and prevent corruption.

(continued)

Table 1 (continued)

Name	Defining origin	Behavior	Exploitation reqs	Impact	Countermeasures
Array out of bounds	Originates where a process attempts to read or write data outwith the bounds of a declared array.	The process reads data from other sections of memory. In an unbounded write, the write can overwrite data outside the array, causing memory corruption.	Requires that the attacker be able to control both the index of the array, and the contents of the write.	Arbitrary code execution and the corruption of the stack/heap (depending on where the array was declared).	Check that the array index is not outwith the bounds of the array before performing any read or write operations.
Pointer reassignment to double free	Originates where a two malloc()'ed pointers are reas-signed to point to one of the pair. Later, when calling free()', the programmer fails to take the reassignment into account, and performs a double free on the same address.	A free() attempts to remove the invalid pointer from the heap structures, and corrupts the process heap.	Requires that the attacker be able to manipulate the pointer in such a way to affect the free() procedure to cause later function calls to execute unexpected code.	Possible arbitrary code execution and corruption of the process heap.	After freeing a pointer ensure that it is immediately set to NULL, as a free on a NULL pointer will have no effect on the heap, and prevent corruption.
Pointer reassignment to double free	Originates where a process makes a call to a function which requires a format specifier such as printf() without passing the format specifier.	The formatting function interprets any format specifiers in the string passed to it in the variable, and performs the appropriate methods.	Requires that the attacker be able to control the contents of the variable passed to the formatting function, and that no format specifier be provided by the developer.	Arbitrary code execution and disclosure of memory.	Always pass a format specifier to a function that requires it.

These criteria became the "fields" of the ad-hoc pattern language.

The taxonomy is shown in Table 1.

The Taxonomy relies on simple behavioral facts about the target code, rather than relying on the highly variable contextual criteria in order to identify them. This behavior-based approach at categorizing software vulnerabilities proves very effective in determining the existence of software vulnerabilities, as the mechanisms that introduce issues into a code base are polymorphic in nature. This means that slight changes at a source code level can have cascading effects on the compiled instance of the code, making successful categorization based on either source code or decompilation techniques improbable. The focus on behavioral criteria gives the taxonomy its strength when used to determine the existence of a software issue. It should be noted that this taxonomy is unique in criteria 3 and 5, which could be very useful for a software tester to determine the impact of the vulnerability and how to solve it. The nine bugs were identified using a combination of techniques to determine their existence, which have been abstracted into the proposed methodology.

2.2 Methodology

An overview of the methodology can be seen in Fig. 1.

The proposed methodology combines a number of best practice techniques from static code analysis and reverse engineering.

1. The first step in the procedure requires a full source code audit. This should consist of:

   - A manual text based search through the codebase for the use of functions which may lead to memory corruption as identified in the taxonomy.
   - Identifying the variables used in the functions, and determine whether these variables could be used in an invalid way which may introduce memory corruption, by cross referencing the behavior seen within the program against the taxonomy.

2. The second step uses reverse engineering techniques in order to identify compiler level vulnerabilities. Like the source code audit, the test should comprise of:

   - A search through the codebase for use of functions which may lead to memory corruption
   - Identify the variables used in the functions, and attempt to determine whether it is possible that these variables are used in an invalid way which could introduce memory corruption, by cross referencing the behavior seen within the program against the taxonomy.

3. Incorporate countermeasures based on the mitigations described in the taxonomy for each identified vulnerability in the target.

Fig. 1 Overview of
methodology

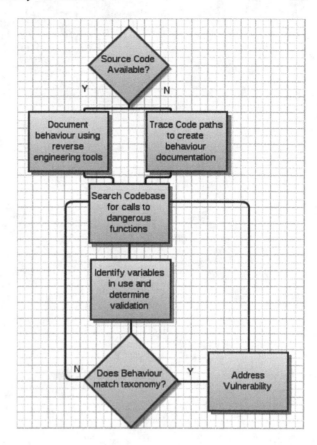

Only subjective evidence of the ease with which these particular security vulnerabilities could be recorded and disseminated using patterns currently exists. Future
work will seek to study the efficacy of patterns as a means of documenting security
concerns with a full-scale user study. The establishment of common (trial) pattern
languages in the area would go a long way to enabling comparative studies.

References

1. Chen S, Xu J, Nakka N, Kalbarczyk Z, Iyer RK. Defeating memory corruption attacks via pointer
   taintedness detection. In: IEEE international conference on dependable systems and networks
   (DSN). 2005;. doi:10.1109/DSN.2005.36.
2. Klein T. A bug hunter's diary: a guided tour through the wilds of software security. San Francisco,
   CA: No Starch Press; 2011.
3. Gamma E, Helm R Johnson. Design patterns: elements of reusable object-oriented software.
   Reading, Mass: Addison-Wesley; 1995.

Chapter 13
'Weird Machine' Patterns

Sergey Bratus, Julian Bangert, Alexandar Gabrovsky, Anna Shubina, Michael E. Locasto and Daniel Bilar

Abstract You do not understand how your program *really* works until it has been exploited. We believe that computer scientists and software engineers should regard the activity of modern exploitation as an applied discipline that studies both the actual computational properties and the practical computational limits of a target platform or system. Exploit developers study the computational properties of software that are not studied elsewhere, and they apply unique engineering techniques to the challenging engineering problem of dynamically patching and controlling a running system. These techniques leverage software and hardware composition mechanisms in unexpected ways to achieve such control. Although unexpected, such composition is not arbitrary, and it forms the basis of a coherent engineering workflow. This chapter contains a top-level overview of these approaches and their historical development.

1 Introduction

When academic researchers study exploitation, they mostly concentrate on two classes of attack-related artifacts: "malicious code" (malware, worms, shellcode) and, lately, "malicious computation" (exploits via crafted data payloads containing no native code, a popular exploiter technique. These techniques have been discussed

S. Bratus (✉) · J. Bangert · A. Gabrovsky · A. Shubina
Dartmouth College, Hanover, New Hampshire, USA
e-mail: sergey@cs.dartmouth.edu
http://www.cs.dartmouth.edu/ sergey/

M. E. Locasto
University of Calgary, Alberta, Canada
http://pages.cpsc.ucalgary.ca/locasto/

D. Bilar
Siege Technologies, Manchester, New Hampshire, USA
http://www.siegetechnologies.com/

C. Blackwell and H. Zhu (eds.), *Cyberpatterns*, DOI: 10.1007/978-3-319-04447-7_13,   157
© Springer International Publishing Switzerland 2014

in the hacker community since before early 2000s ([1] offers a brief history sketch). They were brought a decade later to the attention of academia by Shacham [2, 3] in 2007. These artifacts are tackled with a variety of approaches, from machine learning on either captured payloads or execution traces to automatic construction of exploit payloads for specific targets. The goals of such studies also vary, from straightforward detection of particular payloads in network traffic to finding and removing vulnerabilities or asserting that a vulnerability is not exploitable beyond a crash or denial-of-service. Considerable technical depth has been reached in all of these directions, yet we seem no closer to the ultimate goal of constructing trustworthy, non-exploitable software.

We argue that focusing on just these two classes of artifacts is a limiting factor in our understanding of exploitation (and therefore of how to prevent it). We believe that, as a means of making progress toward the goal of more fundamentally secure software, we must understand how exploitation relates to *composition*, which is fundamental to all modern software construction. Understanding the patterns of this relationship will expose new artifacts to study and indicate new technical directions.

We note that practical exploitation has long been about *composing* the attacker computation with the native computation of the target, allowing most of the target's functions to proceed normally, without undue interference. We posit that such composition is the source of the most powerful and productive concepts and methodologies that emerge from exploitation practice.

When researchers focus on attack artifacts alone, they frequently miss an important point of successful exploitation: the exploited system needs to remain available and reliably usable for the attacker.

In order to support this assertion and further discuss exploitation, we need to make an important terminological point. The word *hacking* is used to refer to all kinds of attacks on computer systems, including those that merely shut down systems or otherwise prevent access to them (essentially achieving nothing that could not be achieved by cutting a computer cable). Many activities labeled as "hacking" lack sophistication. In this chapter we focus on *exploitation* or, more precisely, *exploit programming*. We take *exploitation* and *exploit programming* to mean subverting the system to make it work for the attacker—that is, lend itself to being programmed by the attacker. Exploiters are less interested in causing BSODs, kernel panics, and plain network DOS attacks that merely result in a DoS on the target and cannot otherwise be leveraged and refined to take control over the system rather than disabling it.

Not surprisingly, preventing a disabling crash and subsequently "patching up" the target into a stable running state requires significantly more expertise and effort than, say, a memory-corrupting DoS. By achieving this state exploiters demonstrate a sophisticated understanding of the target platform,[1] often beyond the ken of its developers or even system programmers.

In this chapter we review a series of classic exploitation techniques from the perspective of composition. Many of these techniques have been extensively described

---

[1] It also serves as an excellent teaching aid in advanced OS courses; see, e.g., [4].

and reviewed from other perspectives; however, their compositional aspect is still treated as ad hoc, and has not, as far as we know, been the subject of systematic analysis. Specifically, we regard composition as the basic unit of activity in an engineering workflow, whether that workflow is a traditional software engineering workflow or a workflow focused on engineering an exploit. We compare these workflows in the Sect. 2.

Since our focus is on composition, we do not distinguish between techniques used by *rootkits* vs. *exploits*. Rootkits are traditionally separated from other exploit-related artifacts such as exploits proper, "shellcode", etc., since they are meant to be installed by the successful attacker who already attained the "root" level of privilege by other means. However, we note that such installation often involves means of composition that are only available to developers, not administrators however privileged; thus, composing parts of a rootkit with the system poses challenges due to lacking information and limited available context. The complexity of such challenges may vary, but they have the same nature as those faced by an exploit programmer, and indeed similar techniques are used to overcome them. In our discussion, we draw equally upon rootkit and exploit examples.

We posit that composition-centric analysis is required for designing defensible systems (see Sect. 4). The practical properties of composition in actual computer systems uncovered and distilled by hacker research have often surprised both designers and defenders. We believe that the relevant methods here must be cataloged and generalized to help approach the goal of *secure composition* in future designs.

2 A Tale of Two Engineering Workflows

"Language design is library design."

– B. Stroustrup

Hacking, vulnerability analysis, and exploit programming are generally perceived to be difficult and arcane activities. The development of exploits is still seen as something unrepeatable and enabled only by some unfortunate and unlikely combination of events or conditions. Almost by definition, something as imbued with arbitrary chance cannot or should not be an engineering discipline or workflow. Popular perception casts these activities as requiring specialized cross–layer knowledge of systems and a talent for "crafting" input.

This chapter asserts that what seems arcane is really only unfamiliar. In fact, although it may be difficult to conceive of exploit development as anything other than fortunate mysticism, we argue that its structure is exactly that of a software engineering workflow. The difference emerges in the specific constructs at each stage, but the overall activities remain the same. A software developer engineers in terms of sequences of function calls operating on abstract data types, whereas an exploit developer engineers in terms of sequences of machine–level memory reads and writes. The first one programs the system in terms of what its compile-time API promises; the other programs it in terms of what its runtime environment actually contains.

This section contains a brief comparison of these two engineering workflows. We do so to help give a conceptual frame of reference to the enumeration of exploit techniques and composition patterns detailed in Sect. 3.

The main difference between the two workflows is that the exploit engineer must first recover or understand the semantics of the runtime environment. In either case, programming is composition of functionality.

In the "normal" workflow of software engineering, the programmer composes familiar, widely-used libraries, primitive language statements (repetition and decision control structures), and function calls to kick input data along a processing path and eventually produce the result dictated by a set of functional requirements.

In the exploit workflow, the reverser or exploit engineer attempts to build this programming toolkit from scratch: the languages and libraries that the software engineer takes for granted are not of *direct* use to the exploit developer. Instead, these elements define a landscape from which the exploit developer must compose and create his own toolkit, language primitives, and component groups. The first job of the vulnerability analyst or reverse engineer is therefore to understand the latent functionality existing in runtime environments that the software engineer either neglects or does not understand.

2.1 The Software Engineer

Based on functional requirements, a software engineer's goal is to cause some expected functionality happen. In essence, this kind of programming is the task of choosing a sequence of library calls and composing them with language primitives like decision control structure and looping control structures. Data structures are created to capture the relevant properties of the system's input; this structure usually dictates how processing (i.e., control flow) occurs.

A software engineer follows roughly this workflow path:

1. design and specify data types
2. design data flow relationships (i.e., an API)
3. write down source code implementing the data types and API
4. ask compiler and assembler to translate code
5. ask OS to load binary, invoke the dynamic linker, and create memory regions
6. run program according to the control flow as conceived in the source level.

In this workflow, we can see the software engineer engaged in: memory layout, specifying control flow, program construction, program delivery (loading) and translation, and program execution. As we will see below, the exploit engineer engages in much the same set of tasks.

The software engineer's goal is to bring order to a composition of procedures via compilation and assembly of machine code. One does this through tool chains, design patterns, IDEs, and popular languages—the software engineer therefore does not need to relearn the (public) semantics of these operations every time he prepares to program.

These conventions are purely an effort–saving device aimed at increasing productivity by increasing the lines of code and features implemented in them. These patterns, tools, and aids reduce the level of thought required to emit a sequence of function calls that satisfy the functional requirements. They are an effort to deal with complexity. The goal of software engineers in dealing with complexity is to eliminate or hide it.

2.2 The Exploit Engineer

In contrast, exploit engineers also deal with complexity, but their goal is to manipulate it—expressiveness, side effects, and implicit functionality are a collective boon, not a bane. Any operations an exploit engineer can get "for free" increase his exploit toolkit, language, or architecture. A software engineer attempts to hide or ignore side effects and implicit state changes, but the very things encouraged by traditional engineering techniques like "information hiding" and encapsulation on the other side of an API become recoverable primitives for a reverser or exploit engineer.

The main difference in the workflows is the preliminary step: you have to learn on a case by case or scenario by scenario basis what "language" or computational model you should be speaking in order to actually begin programming toward a specific functional end. Based on some initial access, the first goal is to understand the system enough to recover structure of "programming" primitives. The workflow is thus:

1. identify system input points
2. recapture or expose trust relationships between components (functions, control flow points, modules, subroutines, etc.)
3. recover the sequencing composition of data transformations (enumerate layer crossings)
4. enumerate instruction sequences / primitives / gadgets
5. program the process address space (prepare the memory image and structure)
6. deliver the exploit.

In this workflow, we can see the exploit engineer engaged in: recovering memory layout, specifying control flow, program construction, program delivery (loading) and translation, and program execution. We note that these steps may not (and need not be) sperabale: Unlike the software engineering workflow, the delivery of an exploit (i.e., loading a program) can be mixed up and interposed with translation of the program and preparation of the target memory space. Even though these activities might be more tightly coupled for an exploit developer, much of the same discipline remains.

Recent academic advances have the potential of automating (at least partially) the preparatory steps (1–4) the exploiter's workflow. Holler's *LangFuzz* tool automates black-box fuzz testing of context-free grammar engines. It generates test cases from a given context-free grammar to exposes via fault generation inter-components' trust relations [5]. Caballero proposed and implemented the *Dispatcher* tool for automatic protocol reverse-engineering given an undocumented protocol or le format. Thus includes the structure of all messages that comprise the protocol in addition to the protocol state machine, which captures the sequences of messages that represent valid sessions of the protocol. As a proof of concept, his group managed to extract the grammar of Mega-D (a spam botnet), which sported an undocumented, encrypted Command & Control protocol [6]. The output of these tools can be repurposed for defenses. Samuels proposed a simple but clever approach against certain type confusion attacks through a generalizable annotated parse-tree-grammar scheme. Such annotated grammars can be converted to push-down automata from which input stress test can be derived [7]. The urgent need for such defenses is demonstrated by Shmatikov and Wang analysis of and attacks against AV parsers and undefined behavior in C language compilers, respectively [8, 9].

One major challenge exists for the exploit engineer: recovering the unknown unknowns. Although they can observe side effects of mainline execution or even slightly fuzzed execution, can they discover the side effects of "normally" dormant or latent "normal" functionality (e.g., an internationalization module that is never invoked during normal operation, or configuration code that has only been invoked in the "ancient past" of this running system)? This challenge is in some sense like the challenge a software engineer faces when exploring a very large language library (e.g., the Java class library API).

2.3 A Simple Example of Exploit Programming

Before we turn our attention to reviewing the composition patterns of hacking, we give a brief example of constructing an exploit as a programming task, to show the kind of workflow involved. The reader already familiar with such concept may skip directly to Sect. 3.

Assume a Program P that reads the contents of a file F into a buffer located on the stack and displays this content to standard output.

Note that our point here is not to say that stack-based buffer overflows are of independent or modern interest; rather, we use this scenario as the simplest illustration of exploitation as programming, where most readers likely already have a conception of some of the issues in play, from both the software developer side (why this vulnerability exists: failure to check lengths) and the exploit engineer side (where to inject and how to structure shellcode)—it is popularly "understood" enough.

The simplest possible core task in the exploit engineer's workflow in this scenario is to map input data to memory space. Concretely: where will the bytes that overwrite the return address and saved ebp land? And what should the content of my new return address be (i.e., the address of the file's content on the stack)?

In this scenario, file F is simultaneously:

- bytes in persistent storage
- bytes traversing kernel space via the read (2) implementation (and callchain)
- data for the program (i.e., contents of a buffer)
- an overlay of some part of the process address space
- bytecode for an automaton implicitly embedded in the target program (the so-called "weird machine", see Sect. 3) that will carry out malicious computation
- shellcode for the CPU.

Understanding the layout of this memory is vital to actually constructing an input file (i.e., bytecode) to program the exploit machine. In addition to understanding the memory layout as a living artifact generated by both the compiler and the runtime system (i.e., how the OS sets up the process address space and memory regions), an exploit engineer must also understand other implicit operators, transformers, and parsers co-existing in the *real* computational machine. He must understand where they interpose on the processing path, how they are invoked, and what *actual* set of transformations they have on the data (i.e., bytecode) as it journeys through the system toward various resting places. He must ask: is my data filtered? Does it have a simple transformation or encoding applied to it (e.g., Base64 encoding, `toupper()`)? Do certain special bytes (i.e., NULL) truncate the data? Is the data copied to new locations? Is the data reshuffled or reorganized internally?

When considering more complex examples, an exploit engineer must map and understand other memory regions, including the heap and its management data structures, dynamic data embedded within various memory regions, and threading (concurrency). Such things now present additional computational primitives to place in context and understand. In some sense, the sum total composition of all these mechanisms is a compiler, translator, or interpreter for your bytecode—and you must first understand how that compiler works. When you do, you can undertake the process of writing and constructing bytecode appropriate to accomplishing your goal, whether that is to drop shell, open a port, install a rootkit, exfiltrate a file, etc.

3 Patterns

3.1 Exploitation as Programming "Weird Machines"

Bratus et al. [1] summarized a long-standing hacker intuition of exploits as *programs, expressed as crafted inputs, for execution environments implicitly present in the target as a result of bugs or unforeseen combination of features* ("weird machines"), which are reliably driven by the crafted inputs to perform unexpected computations. More formally, the crafted inputs that constitute the exploit drive an input-accepting automaton already implicitly present in the target's input-handling implementation, its sets of states and transitions owing to the target's features, bugs or combinations thereof.

The implicit automaton is immersed into or is part of the target's execution environment; its processing of crafted input is part of the "malicious computation" — typically, the part that creates the initial compromise, after which the exploiter can program the target with more conventional means. The crafted input is both a program for that automaton and a constructive proof of its existence. Further discussion from the practical exploit programming standpoint can be found in Dullien [10], from a theory standpoint in Sassaman [11].

This perspective on exploit programming considers the exploit target as harboring a virtual computing architecture, to which the input data serve as *bytecode*, similar to, say, how compiled Java bytecode drives the Java virtual machine. In other words, the target's input is viewed as an actual program, similar to how the contents of a Turing machine's tape can be considered a program. Thus what is liable to be seen by developers as "inert data" such as inputs or metadata is in fact conceptually promoted to a vehicle of programming the target; in a sense, the exploiter treats the data as running and acting on the target program, not the other way around. Further discussion of this can be found in Shapiro [12].

In the following items, we focus on one critical aspect of the implicit exploit execution environments and the computations effected in them by exploit-programs: they must reliably co-exist with the native, intended computations both for their duration and in their effects, while their composition is done in contexts more limited and lacking critical information as compared to the system's intended scenarios. This is far from trivial on systems where state that is "borrowed" by the exploit computation's thread of control is simultaneously used by others. It involves dissecting and "slimming down" interfaces to their actual implementation primitives and finding out unintended yet stable properties of these primitives.

3.2 Recovering Context, Symbols, and Structure

To compose its computation with a target, an exploit must refer to the objects it requires in its virtual address space (or in other namespaces). In essence, except in the most trivial cases, a "name service" of a kind (ranging from ad-hoc to the system's own) is involved to reconstruct the missing information.

Early exploits and rootkit install scripts relied on hard-coded fixed addresses of objects they targeted, since back then memory virtual space layouts were identical for large classes of targets.[2] As targets' diversity increased, naturally or artificially (e.g., OpenWall, PaX, other ASLR), exploits progressed to elaborate address space layout reconstruction schemes and co-opting the system's own dynamic linking and/or trapping debugging.

---

[2] This fact was not well understood by most engineers or academics, who regarded below-compiler OS levels as unpredictable; Stephanie Forrest deserves credit for putting this and other misconceptions into broader scientific perspective.

Cesare [13] describes the basic mechanism behind ELF linking—based on little more that careful reading of the ELF standard. However, it broke the opacity and resulted in an effective exploit technique, developed by others, e.g., [14]. In [15] mayhem builds on the same idea by looking into the significance and priority of ELF's .dynamic symbols. Nergal [16] co-opted Linux's own dynamic linker into an ROP[3] crafted stack frame-chaining scheme, to have necessary symbols resolved and libraries loaded. Oakley [17] showed how to co-opt the DWARF-based exception handling mechanism.

Skape [18] takes the understanding of ELF in a different direction by showing how its relocation mechanism works and how that could be used for unpacking obfuscated Windows binaries. Recent work by Shapiro [12] demonstrated that the relocation metadata in ELF binaries is actually enough to drive Turing-complete computations on the Linux dynamic linker-loader. The ABI metadata in these examples serves as "weird machine" bytecode for the Turing machine implicitly embedded in the RTLD code.

In all of the above detailed understanding of a mechanism comes before the insight of how an exploit could be built; in fact, once the mechanism is clear at the "weird machine" level, its exploitation use is almost an afterthought.

3.3 Preparing Vulnerable System State

Earlier classes of exploits leveraged conditions and configurations (such as memory allocation of relevant objects) present in the target's state through all or most runs. Subsequent advancements such as Sotirov's [19] demonstrated that *otherwise non-exploitable targets can have their state carefully prepared by way of a calculated sequence of requests and inputs for an exploitable configuration to be instantiated.*

This pattern of pre-compositional state-construction of targets is becoming essential, as protective entropy-injecting techniques prevent setting up an effective "name service". Recent examples [20, 21] show its applications to modern heaps (the former for the Windows low fragmentation heap), in presence of ASLR and DEP. Moreover, this method can target the injected entropy *directly*, by bleeding it from the target's state (e.g., [22]).

3.4 Piercing Abstraction

Developers make use of abstractions to decrease implementation effort and increase code maintainability. However, abstractions hide the details of their implementation and as they become part of a programmers daily vocabulary, the implementation

---

[3] Which it pre-dates, together with other hacker descriptions of the technique, by five to seven years.

details are mostly forgotten. For example, few programmers worry about how a function call is implemented at the machine level or how the linking and loading mechanisms assign addresses to imported symbols.

Exploit engineers, however, distill abstractions into their implementation primitives and synthesize new composition patterns from them. Good examples of this are found in [16], who modifies the return addresses on the stack to compose existing code elements into an exploit, and the LOCREATE [18] packer which obfuscates binary code by using the primitives for dynamic linking.

3.5 Balancing Context Constraints

> Wherever there is modularity there is the potential for misunderstanding: Hiding information implies a need to check communication.
>
> A. Perlis

When a software architect considers how much context to pass through an interface, he has to balance competing constraints (see Sect. 4.2 in [23] for discussion of etiology and formalization sketch). Either a lot of context is passed, reducing the flexibility of the code, or too little context is preserved and the remaining data can no longer be efficiently validated by code operating on it, so more assumptions about the input have to be trusted. Exploiters explore this gap in assumptions, and distill the unintended side-effects to obtain *primitives*, from which weird machines are constructed [10, 24, 25]. We posit that understanding this gap is the way to more secure API design.

3.6 Bit Path Tracing of Cross-Layer Flows

When an exploiter studies a system, he starts with bit-level description of its contents and communications. Academic textbooks and user handbooks, however, typically do not descend to bit level and provide only a high-level description of how the system works. A crucial part of such bit-level description is the flow of bits between the conceptual design layers of the system: i.e. a binary representation of the data and control flow between layers.

Constructing these descriptions may be called the cornerstone of the hacker methodology. It precedes the search for actual vulnerabilities and may be thought of as the modeling step for constructing the exploit computation. The model may ignore large parts of the target platform but is likely to punctiliously describe the minutiae of composition mechanisms that actually tie the implementations of the layers together.

For example, the AlephOne Phrack article [26] famous for its description of stack buffer overflows also contained a bit-level description of UNIX system calls, which for many readers was in fact their first introduction to syscall mechanisms. Similarly, other shellcode tutorials detailed the data flow mechanisms of the target's ABIs (such as various calling conventions and the structure of libraries). In networking, particular attention was given to wrapping and unwrapping of packet payloads at each level of the OSI stack model, and libraries such as libnet and libdnet were provided for emulating the respective functionality throughout the stack layers.

What unites the above examples is that in all of them exploiters start analyzing the system by tracing the flow of bits within the target and enumerating the code units that implement or interact with that flow. The immediate benefits of this analysis are at least two-fold: locating of less known private or hidden APIs and collecting potential exploitation primitives or "cogs" of "weird machines", i.e. code fragments on which crafted data bits act in predictable way.

Regardless of its immediate benefits, though, bit-level cross-layer flow descriptions also provide useful structural descriptions of the system's architecture, or, more precisely, of the mechanisms that underly the structure, such as the library and loadable kernel functionality, DDKs, and network stack composition.

For instance, the following sequence of Phrack articles on Linux rootkits is a great example of deep yet concise coverage of the layers in the Linux kernel architecture: *Sub proc_root Quando Sumus (Advances in Kernel Hacking)* [27] (VFS structures and their linking and hijacking), *5 Short Stories about execve (Advances in Kernel Hacking II)* [28] (driver/DDK interfaces, different binary format support), and *Execution path analysis: finding kernel based rootkits* [29] (instrumentation for path tracing). Notably, these articles at the cusp where three major UNIX innovations meet: VFS, kernel state reporting through pseudo-filesystems (e.g., /proc), and support for different execution domains/ABI. These articles described the control and data flows through a UNIX kernel's component layers and their interfaces in great detail well before tools like DTrace and KProbes/SystemTap brought tracing of such flows within common reach.

It is worth noting that the ELF structure of the kernel binary image, the corresponding structure of the kernel runtime, and their uses for reliably injecting code into a running kernel (via writing /dev/kmem or via some kernel memory corruption primitive). In 1998, the influential *Runtime kernel kmem patching* [30] made the point that even though a kernel may be compiled without loadable kernel module support, it still is a structured runtime derived from an ELF image file, in which symbols can be easily recovered, and the linking functionality can be provided without difficulty by a minimal userland "linker" as long as it has access to kernel memory. Subsequently, mature kernel function hooking frameworks were developed (e.g., *IA32 Advanced function hooking* [31]).

Dynamic linking and loading of libraries (shared binary objects) provide another example. This is a prime example of composition, implicitly relied upon by every modern OS programmer and user, with several supporting engineering mechanisms and abstractions (ABI, dynamic symbols, calling conventions). Yet, few resources exist that describe this key mechanism of interposing computation; in fact, for a long time hacker publications have been the best resource for understanding the underlying binary data structures (e.g., *Backdooring binary objects* [32]), the control flow of dynamic linking (e.g., *Cheating the ELF* [33] and *Understanding Linux ELF*

RTLD internals [34]), and the use of these structures for either binary infection (e.g., the original *Unix ELF parasites and virus*) or protection (e.g., *Armouring the ELF: Binary encryption on the UNIX platform* [35]).

A similar corpus of articles describing the bit paths and layer interfaces exists for the network stacks. For the Linux kernel stack, the *Netfilter* architecture represents a culmination of this analysis. By exposing and focusing on specific hooks (tables, chains), Netfilter presents a clear and concise model of a packet's path through the kernel; due to this clarity it became both the basis of the Linux's firewall and a long series of security tools.

Not surprisingly, exploitative modifications of network stacks follow the same pattern as other systems rootkits. *Passive Covert Channels Implementation in Linux Kernel* [36] is a perfect example: it starts with describing the interfaces traversed on a packet's path through the kernel (following the Netfilter architecture), and then points out the places where a custom protocol handler can be inserted into that control flow, using the stack's native protocol handler interfaces.

3.7 Trap-Based Programming and Composition

In application programming, traps and exceptions are typically not treated as "first-class" programming primitives. Despite using powerful exception-handling subsystems (such as GCC's *DWARF*-based one, which employs Turing-complete bytecode), applications are not expected to perform much of their computation in traps or exceptions and secondary to the main program flow. Although traps are obviously crucial to systems programming, even there the system is expected to exit their handlers quickly, performing as little and as simple computation as possible, for both performance and context management reasons.

In exploit programming and reverse engineering (RE), traps are the *first-class programming primitives*, and trap handler overloading is a frequently used technique. The target platform's trap interfaces, data structures, and contexts are carefully studied, described, and modeled, then used for reliably composing an exploit or a comprehension computation (i.e., a specialized tracer of debugger) with the target.

The tracing and debugging subsystems in OS kernels have long been the focus of hacker attention (e.g., *Runtime Process Infection* [37] for an in-depth intro to the `ptrace()` subsystem). Not surprisingly, hackers are the leading purveyors of specializes debuggers, such as *dumBug*, *Rasta Debugger*, and the *Immunity debugger* to name a few.

For Linux, a good example is *Handling Interrupt Descriptor Table for fun and profit* [38], which serves as both a concise introduction to the x86 interrupt system and its use on several composition-critical kernel paths, as well as its role in implementing various OS and debugging abstractions (including system calls and their place in the IDT). This approach was followed by a systematic study of particular interrupt handlers, such as the *Hijacking Linux Page Fault Handler* [39].

Overloading the page fault handler in particular has become a popular mechanism for enforcing policy in kernel hardening patches (e.g., *PaX*[4] and *OpenWall*[5]). However, other handlers have been overloaded as well, providing, e.g., support for enhanced debugging not relying on the kernel's standard facilities—and thus not conflicting with them and not registering with them, to counteract anti-debugging tricks. Since both rootkits (e.g., the proof-of-concept *DR Rootkit* that uses the x86 debug registers exclusively as its control flow mechanism) and anti-RE armored applications (e.g., Skype, cf. *Vanilla Skype* [40]; also, some commercial DRM products). In particular, the *Rasta Debugger* demonstrates such "unorthodox debugging" trap overloading-based techniques.

Notably, similar trap overloading techniques are used to expand the semantics of classic debugger breakpoint-able events. For instance, *OllyBone*[6] manipulated page translation to catch an instruction fetch from a page just written to, a typical behavior of a malware unpacker handing execution to the unpacked code. Note the temporal semantics of this composed trap, which was at the time beyond the capabilities of any debugger. A similar use of the ×86 facilities, and in particular the split instruction and data TLBs was used by the *Shadow Walker* [41] rootkit to cause code segments loaded by an antivirus analyzer to be fetched from a different physical page than the actual code, so that the analyzer could receive innocent data—a clever demonstration of the actual vs assumed nature of ×86 memory translation mechanism. For an in-depth exploration of just how powerful that mechanism can be, as well as for background on previous work, see Bangert [42].

4 Conclusion

Exploit engineers will show you the unintended limits of your system's functionality. If software engineers want to reduce this kind of latent functionality, they will have to begin understanding it as an artifact that supports the exploit engineer's workflow.

Software engineers should view their input data as "acting on code", not the other way around; indeed, in exploits inputs serves as a de-facto bytecode for execution environments that can be composed from the elements of their assumed runtime environment. Writing an exploit—creating such bytecode—is as structured a discipline as engineering "normal" software systems. As a process, it is no more arcane or unapproachable than the ways we currently use to write large software systems.

Yet, a significant challenge remains. If, as hinted above, we want to have a practical impact on the challenge of secure composition, can we actually train software engineers to see their input parameters and data formats *as bytecode* even as they specify it? Even as they bring it into existence, where it is by definition partially

---

[4] http://pax.grsecurity.net/

[5] http://www.openwall.com/Owl/

[6] http://www.joestewart.org/ollybone/

formulated, can they anticipate how it might be misused? We posit that this constant and frequent self-check is worth the effort: Software engineers should familiarize themselves with anti-security patterns lest preventable 'weird machines' arise in critical applications.

References

1. Bratus S, Locasto ME, Patterson ML, Sassaman L, Shubina A. Exploit programming: from buffer overflows to "weird machines" and theory of computation. login: Dec 2011.
2. Shacham H. The geometry of innocent flesh on the bone: return-into-libc without function calls (on the ×86). In: Proceedings of the 14th ACM conference on computer and communications security, CCS '07. New York: ACM; p. 552–561.
3. Roemer R, Buchanan E, Shacham H, Savage S. Return-oriented programming: systems, languages, and applications. ACM Trans Inf Syst Secur. 2012;15(1):2:1–2:34.
4. Dan R. Anatomy of a remote kernel exploit. http://www.cs.dartmouth.edu/-sergey/cs108/2012/Dan-Rosenberg-lecture.pdf (2011).
5. Holler C, Herzig K, Zeller A. Fuzzing with code fragments. In: Proceedings of the 21st USENIX conference on security symposium, Security'12. Berkeley: USENIX Association; 2012. p. 38–38.
6. Caballero Juan, Song Dawn. Automatic protocol reverse-engineering: message format extraction and field semantics inference. Comput Netw. 2013;57(2):451–74.
7. Samuel M, Erlingsson Ú. Let's parse to prevent pwnage invited position paper. In: Proceedings of the 5th USENIX conference on Large-scale exploits and emergent threats, LEET'12. Berkeley, USA: USENIX Association; 2012. p. 3–3.
8. Jana s, Shmatikov V. Abusing file processing in malware detectors for fun and profit. In: IEEE symposium on security and privacy'12; 2012. p. 80–94.
9. Xi W, Haogang C, Alvin C, Zhihao J, Nickolai Z, Kaashoek MF. Undefined behavior: what happened to my code? In: Proceedings of the Asia-Pacific workshop on systems, APSYS'12. New York, USA: ACM; 2012. p. 9:1–9:7.
10. Dullien T. Exploitation and state machines: programming the "weird machine", revisited. In: Infiltrate conference, Apr 2011.
11. Sassaman L, Patterson ML, Bratus S, Locasto ME, Shubina A. Security applications of formal language theory. Dartmouth College: Technical report; 2011.
12. Shapiro R, Bratus S, Smith SW. "Weird machines" in ELF: a Spotlight on the underappreciated metadata. In: 7th USENIX workshop of offensive technologies. https://www.usenix.org/system/files/conference/woot13/woot13-shapiro.pdf. 2013
13. Cesare. S. Shared library call redirection via ELF PLT, Infection. Dec 2000.
14. Sd, Devik. Linux On-the-fly Kernel patching without LKM, Dec 2001.
15. Mayhem. Understanding Linux ELF RTLD internals. http://s.eresi-project.org/inc/articles/elf-rtld.txt (2002).
16. Nergal. The advanced return-into-lib(c) Exploits: PaX Case Study. Phrack Mag. 2001;58(4).
17. Oakley J, Sergey B. Exploiting the hard-working dwarf: Trojan and exploit techniques with no native executable code. In WOOT. 2011. p. 91–102.
18. Skape. Locreate: an anagram for relocate. Uninformed. 2007;6.
19. Sotirov A. Heap feng shui in javascript. In: Blackhat; 2007.
20. Redpantz. The art of exploitation: MS IIS 7.5 remote heap overflow. Phrack Mag. 68(12), Apr 2012.
21. Huku, Argp. The art of exploitation: exploiting VLC, a jemalloc case study. Phrack Maga. 2012;68(13).
22. Ferguson J. Advances in win32 aslr evasion, May 2011.

23. Bilar D. On callgraphs and generative mechanisms. J Comput Virol. 2007;3(4).
24. Richarte D. About exploits writing. Core security technologies presentation 2002.
25. Gera, Riq. Advances in format string exploitation. Phrack Mag. 2002;59(7).
26. One A. Smashing the stack for fun and profit. Phrack 1996;49:14. http://phrack.org/issues. html?issue=49&id=14.
27. Palmers. Sub proc_root auando sumus (Advances in Kernel hacking). Phrack 2001;58:6. http:// phrack.org/issues.html?issue=58&id=6.
28. Palmers. 5 Short stories about execve (advances in Kernel hacking II). Phrack 2002;59:5. http:// phrack.org/issues.html?issue=59&id=5.
29. Rutkowski JK. Execution path analysis: finding Kernel based rootkits. Phrack 2002;59:10. http://phrack.org/issues.html?issue=59&id=10.
30. Cesare S. Runtime Kernel kmem patching. 1998. http://althing.cs.dartmouth.edu/local/vsc07. html.
31. Mayhem. IA32 advanced function hooking. Phrack 2001;58:8. http://phrack.org/issues.html? issue=58&id=8.
32. Klog. Backdooring binary objects. Phrack 2000;56:9. http://phrack.org/issues.html?issue=56& id=9.
33. The Grugq. Cheating the ELF: subversive dynamic linking to libraries, 2000.
34. Mayhem. Understanding Linux ELF RTLD Internals, 2002. http://s.eresi-project.org/inc/ articles/elf-rtld.txt.
35. Grugq, Scut. Armouring the ELF: binary encryption on the UNIX platform. Phrack ; 2001;58:5. http://phrack.org/issues.html?issue=58&id=5.
36. Rutkowska J. Passive covert channels implementation in Linux Kernel. 21st chaos communi- cations congress, 2004. http://events.ccc.de/congress/2004/fahrplan/files/319-passive-covert- channels-slides.pdf.
37. (Anonymous author). Runtime process infection. Phrack 20025;9:8. http://phrack.org/issues. html?issue=59&id=8.
38. Kad. Handling interrupt descriptor table for fun and profit. Phrack 2002;59:4. http://phrack. org/issues.html?issue=59&id=4.
39. Buffer. Hijacking Linux page fault handler exception table. Phrack 2003;61:7. http://phrack. org/issues.html?issue=61&id=7.
40. Desclaux F, Kortchinsky K. Skype V. REcon. http://www.recon.cx/en/f/vskype-part1.pdf (2006).
41. Sparks S, Butler J. "Shadow Walker": Raising the bar for rootkit detection. BlackHat; 2005. http://www.blackhat.com/presentations/bh-jp-05/bh-jp-05-sparks-butler.pdf.
42. Bangert J, Bratus S, Rebecca S, Sean WS. The page-fault weird machine: lessons in instruction- less computation. In: 7th USENIX workshop of offensive technologies. Aug 2013. https://www. usenix.org/system/files/conference/woot13/woot13-bangert.pdf.

Part V

Socio-technical Aspects of Patterns

Clive Blackwell

There have been several collections of patterns modelling people participating in general organisational activities [1] and for security in particular [2]. In addition, much attention has been given to usability and interaction design patterns [3,4]. The first chapter in this part describes an application of patterns to help understand cybercrime, whereas the other two emphasise the social aspects in pattern creation and use.

Chapter 14, *Towards a Simulation of Information Security Behaviour in Organisations* by Ruskov, Ekblom and Sasse, addresses the important concern of the human factor in information security, calling for security models that capture the complexity of the broader socio-technical systems. They adapt a framework based on prior theoretical and empirical research into general crime prevention [5] to the cybercrime domain. The proposed framework unifies traditional offender-oriented approaches and situational crime prevention, with the proximate causes of crime captured within 11 generic headings called the Conjunction of Criminal Opportunity. These reflect the necessary conditions that must coalesce for crimes to occur, ranging in a continuum from offender factors such as criminal disposition all the way to situational factors such as the crime target and its surroundings. The authors also use Crime Scripts [6] that are sequences of events characteristic of recurring or similar crimes, including both the preparatory and following activities, thus providing a wider context for how crime commonly occurs. They can model the interaction between various agents occupying diverse roles using scripts as well. They mention the idea of script clashes as promising future work, where counter-scripts used by security staff and other employees can interact with and possibly defeat Crime Scripts.

Chapter 15, *Security Design Patterns in the MASTER Workbench* by Kearney, Sinclair and Wagner, describes the pattern-related aspects of the Protection and Assessment Workbench that aims to provide a methodology and infrastructure to facilitate the monitoring, enforcement and auditing of regulatory and security compliance and business best practice. A Protection and Regulatory Model (PRM) is essentially a control-process design pattern that incorporates proven strategies in a reusable form. The Workbench is intended to incorporate a library of PRMs allowing users to browse this library looking for relevant PRMs for the specific application context, similar to searching a conventional pattern catalogue. An analyst initially builds models from templates with placeholders filled in by entities present in the investigated system. Successful strategies are recast in abstract form as PRMs and deposited in the library for potential reuse, allowing the Workbench to be used as an 'organisational memory' for design practices that accumulate and improve over time. This increases productivity as models are constructed partly from pre-fabricated components, and improves quality from adopting proven solutions.

Chapter 16, *Evaluating the Implications of Attack and Security Patterns with Premortems* by Faily, Parkin and Lyle, presents a framework for evaluating the implications of security and attack patterns by applying the concept of premortems [7]. Security and attack patterns are useful ways of describing, packaging and applying existing knowledge about security issues to help develop possible defensive solutions. Instead, the authors use patterns to understand the security problem space by creating suitable premortems. These are hypothetical scenarios describing failed systems, inviting discussion about the potential causes from domain experts or stakeholders. The authors evaluated the implications of applying security and attack patterns by combining them together, and then estimated the risk impact in the resulting premortem scenario. Using KAOS goal and obstacle modelling techniques [8], the underlying causes for possible failures in the premortem scenario are elicited as implicit requirements. The elicited obstacles and goals are then used to refine the selected attack and security patterns. This approach uses the open-source CAIRIS requirements management tool specifically developed for security and usability concerns [9].

References

1. Graham I. Business rules management and service oriented architecture: a pattern language. John Wiley and Sons; 2007.
2. Schumacher M, Fernandez-Buglioni E, Hybertson D, Buschmann F, Sommerlad P. Security patterns: integrating security and systems engineering. Wiley; 2005.
3. Borchers JO. A pattern approach to interaction design. John Wiley and Sons; 2001.
4. Graham I. A pattern language for web usability. Addison-Wesley Longman; 2002.
5. Ekblom P. Gearing up against crime: a dynamic framework to help designers keep up with the adaptive criminal in a changing world. Int Risk Secur Crime Pre. 1997;2/4:249–265.
6. Cornish D. The procedural analysis of offending and its relevance for situational prevention. Crime prevention studies. Lynne Rienner Publishers. 1994; Vol 3: pp. 151–196. www.popcenter.org/library/CrimePrevention/Volume_03/06_cornish.pdf. Accessed 14 Nov 2013.

7. Klein G. Performing a project premortem. Harvard Business Review. 2007; Vol 85: No 9: pp. 18–19.
8. van Lamsweerde A. Requirements engineering: from system goals to UML models to software specifications. John Wiley and Sons; 2009.
9. Faily S. CAIRIS web site. GitHub. http://github.com/failys/CAIRIS. Accessed 14 Nov 2013.

Chapter 14
Towards a Simulation of Information Security Behaviour in Organisations

Martin Ruskov, Paul Ekblom and M. Angela Sasse

Abstract In this chapter we propose the fundaments of a design of an exploratory simulation of security management in a corporate environment. The model brings together theory and research findings on causes of information security risks in order to analyse diverse roles interacting through scripts. The framework is an adaptation of theoretical and empirical research in general crime prevention for the purposes of cybercrime. Its aim is to provide insights into the prerequisites for a more functional model (Information security; Conjunction of criminal opportunity; Crime scripts; Simulation).

1 Introduction

Recent research, e.g. [1, 2] demonstrates the importance of addressing the human factor in information security: attackers often obtain information, access to systems or money by tricking customers or employees. This calls for security models that capture the complexity of the wider socio-technical system. Examples of such models are the Mechanics of Trust [3] and the Compliance Budget [4]. Of interest is the unification of these models in the search for a more general theory of how we can design systems that prevent such attacks.

M. Ruskov (✉) · M. A. Sasse
Information Security Resarch Group, University College London, London, UK
e-mail: m.ruskov@cs.ucl.ac.uk

M. A. Sasse
e-mail: a.sasse@cs.ucl.ac.uk

P. Ekblom
Design Against Crime Research Centre, Central Saint Martins College of Art and Design,
London, UK
e-mail: p.ekblom@csm.arts.ac.uk

C. Blackwell and H. Zhu (eds.), *Cyberpatterns*, DOI: 10.1007/978-3-319-04447-7_14,   177
© Springer International Publishing Switzerland 2014

In 2004 in a report for the UK Government Foresight Programme, Collins and Mansell [5] suggest the adoption of a framework from conventional crime science—the Conjunction of Criminal Opportunity (CCO) framework [6, 7]—as a basis for developing and designing resilient systems and effective defences against cyber threats. The CCO framework presents a systematic and conceptually rigorous categorization of immediate contributing causes to criminal events. Such a focus on precursors makes it possible to trace chains of causes back to distal events. Compared with prior frameworks it captures a much wider range of causes for attacks. The CCO framework unifies traditional offender-oriented approaches with situational crime prevention and is explained further in this chapter along with its potential application in cybercrime. It has already been suggested [6] that CCO can combine well with the Crime Scripts approach [8] in which the interaction between various agents is modelled. The objective is to represent how attackers (or offenders in CCO terminology) exploit or harm the technical settings, often combining factors from the physical environment and cyberspace.

This makes CCO generally applicable, yet simple enough to serve as a framework in which other theories of causation of criminal events could be unified in an exploratory simulation. Such a reusable framework that incorporates domain knowledge could be seen to be very similar to the formal patterns used in architecture [9] and software engineering [10]. A potential resulting simulation can deliver a learning experience exploring an actual research framework. Moreover, challenges encountered during simulation design provide feedback that tests the consistency of the theoretical research, as has been done with simulations in conventional crime science by Birks, Townsley and Stewart [11].

Quantitative simulation models already exist. For example, the Naval Postgraduate School developed a game to spread awareness about cyber security called CyberCIEGE [12]. It is a customizable platform that allows designers to develop scenarios for their organisations. A typical scenario in CyberCIEGE is about preventing users from letting malware into the corporate intranet, preventing social engineering and safeguarding data. Unlike CyberCIEGE however, the simulation model proposed here seeks theoretical (and eventually empirical) validity.

2 Background

In his research on insider attacks Schultz [13] considers the CMO model consisting of capability to commit attack, motive to do so and opportunity to do it. In his work Schultz also reviews a model of insider attackers by Tuglular and Spafford [14] allegedly featuring factors such as personal characteristics, motivation, knowledge, abilities, rights and obligations, authority and responsibility within the organisation, and factors related to group support. Parker [15] develops the SCRAM model. The abbreviation reflects the factors considered: skills, knowledge, resources, authority and motives.

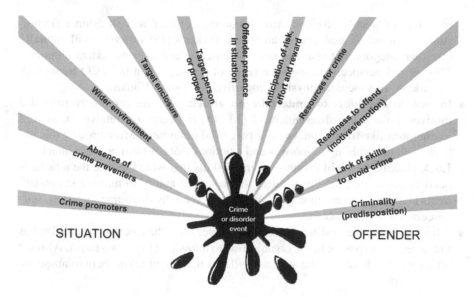

Fig. 1 The diagram visualizing the 11 generic causes in the Conjunction of Criminal Opportunity framework, a simplified version of the diagram found in ([7], p. 141). In CCO the term offender is being used to represent the attacker

The CCO framework considers eleven overarching classes of complementary causes which come together to provide a criminal opportunity. The number of these classes may seem high, but that is to model all potential contributory causes of crime in the real world. To model the contributory causes of cyber crime, the classes of causes can be considered to fit in three wider groups—personal, technical and social factors. These all are represented in Fig. 1.

The personal (attacker) factors are:

- **Criminality** and wider personal traits influencing attacker's tolerance towards immoral or criminal deeds. This is where *personal characteristics* [14] being addressed. Examples for such treats could be severe childhood or family problems, criminal background, abuse with drugs and/or alcohol, or indebtedness beyond control.
- **Anticipation of risk, effort and reward**—the rational decision and utility behind the attack. This combines attacker's rational appraisal of the situation, notably how much effort is required to conduct the attack, what is the expected reward and what are the possible risks, related to the endeavour. Financial assessment is only one possible way to analyse these. A simpler review of most probable outcomes is another common way to make this judgement.
- Abundance of **resources to commit crime** includes cognitive resources and capabilities, and social factors such as trust, but also technical hacking tools—the attacker needs to be both aware of their existence and be able to operate them. Schultz's [13] *capability* and *opportunity* can be viewed as part of the cognitive

resources of hostile insiders, thus combining personal and situational circumstances that act as enablers for an attack. Parker's [15] *resources* fall naturally into this category, but also his *skills*, *knowledge* and to some extent *authority*. This second perspective shows the range of resources that the CCO framework considers—this includes physical, cognitive and social affordances.

- Immediate **readiness to undertake an attack**, e.g. the commonly modelled motives to do it like disgruntlement [13, 15] or search for retaliation, as well as emotions like frustration, envy or perceived unfairness. More broadly this has to do with the build-up of motives and emotions that lead to a possible attack.
- **Lack of skills to avoid crime**—potential skills that would reduce the attacker's need to commit crime. For insiders this could be ability to manage stress, soft skills to improve common understanding of potentially discouraging issues, self-perceived independence etc.
- **Attacker presence in situation**—circumstances like the fact that the attacker has the necessary exposure to the organisation to allow picking it as a target. Also the attacker could have specific access privileges that might allow them to abuse the organization.

Situational factors contributing to the criminal opportunity capture the predisposition of the environment to allow for criminal behaviour. In the context of cybercrime as such can be seen aspects like *scamming* and *social engineering*[2]. These could be both social and technical and are represented by the following:

- **Presence of crime promoters**—people (or roles, or organisations) that deliberately, recklessly or unintentionally make the crime more likely. Deliberate promoters could be potential buyer of stolen data, hacker technology providers. Non-deliberate promoters might not pay due attention to suspicious events happening around them or carelessly not log out from the system after having used it. Regardless if such activities by possible promoters are a result of wrong judgement or inability to understand of the problem these are behaviours that make it easier to carry out an attack.
- **Absence of crime preventers**, i.e. people that intentionally or not would discourage or deter attackers. Similar to the case with promoters this could be deliberate or not. Examples for the former could be security officers, technology providers or management and staff ready to help disgruntled colleagues resolve their grudges. The latter could be represented by colleagues providing a friendly environment, or random passers-by that could potentially become witnesses in case of an attack.
- The **target** of the attack. In the context of cyber crime commonly information or finances become targeted. Still, indirectly the target could also be the person or organisation which might suffer from a security breach. The character of the target could determine what attacks are possible and probable. For example when information is unencrypted or self-contained, this might turn it into much more desirable target.
- In the context of cyber security the **enclosure around the target** becomes a much broader notion. It still includes means of controlling the physical access like locked

hardware storing valuable information or more advanced access control management. However, a digital dimension is also present in the form of e.g. firewalls and system access monitoring.

- The **wider environment** which could contribute towards attacks and discourage or restrict potential preventers. This could include something as tangible as the specific affordances of the environment like visibility of transactions, to something abstract like the organisational culture. *Authority* can be thought of as a feature of the organisational environment that allows misuse, e.g. lifting doubt from people with authority that demand information which they don't possess.

The issue of *authority* as considered by previous models comes to illustrate the interactions of these different factors. On one hand *authority* is a *resource* that a potential offender possesses and enables them to commit the attack. On the other one's *authority* also is a function of the *wider environment*—it is the organisational culture that allows authority to be exercised without protective questioning from others.

3 Crime Scripts

One technique used in conventional crime prevention is that of crime scripts [8]. These are sequences of events characteristic of recurring, or similar, attacks. Typically a script would also capture the preparatory and consummatory sequences of actions that attackers engage in before and after the actual attack, thus providing a wider picture and context to how attacks commonly happen.

Research in design against crime has revealed that not only are the scripts of attackers insightful tools, but also the scripts typical of ordinary users who may or may not be acting in the role of crime preventers [6]. Being a normal business routine, this category of non-criminal scripts can typically be extracted from the established business processes in an organisation. These processes could either be designed or ad-hoc; with the former it could be that the actual routine is different from the one designed, e.g. in cases when users find it difficult to comply with designed procedures [4].

Examples of scripts of attackers and regular users are illustrated below:

Users' generic script:

1. User is asked to create an account.
2. User generates a password, according to own cognitive scheme.
3. User stores password (either mentally or physically).
4. If stored physically password needs to be secured.
5. User devises restoration procedures, e.g. reminder question or location to where file is stored.
6. Generation of procedure to restore passwords.
7. Using password (or subset of its letters) for authentication.
8. Make sure password is not retrievable after end of use.

Script instance illustrating misuse:

1. Change password (due to a system request to change regularly).
2. Store new password on a piece of paper, convenient for frequent referencing.
3. Because it is already stored externally and thus easier to reuse, use new password for several systems in company.
4. Skip anti-virus checks so that they do not slow down work.
5. Reschedule anti-virus checks for non-working hours.
6. Log out when done working for the day.

Hostile insider script:

1. Decide to cause harm to company and identify target and what to do with it (e.g. upload internal financial data onto internet).
2. Choose mode of access and tactics to reach target (e.g. plan on time when target company's office will be unlocked and empty).
3. Acquire target's externally stored password (e.g. on piece of paper).
4. Access target system, retrieve asset and copy it (e.g. physically access office computer of Accounts department, deploy trojan).
5. Distribute valuable asset to market analysis.

External attacker script:

1. Try target technical system for potential backdoors or exploits.
2. Research social networks of potential human targets that have access to system.
3. Infect a computer of trusted peer of user.
4. Have trusted computer send trojan to user.
5. Infect computer with access to secured network.
6. Copy data out of the secured network.

4 Script Clashes

Scripts on their own depict the procedural nature of everyday and criminal situations. However, they represent the routine of an individual and not the dynamics resulting from the inevitable interaction of these routines upon an encounter between their corresponding performers. For example, if a potential attack is being suspected, security officers could decide to reduce the number of people that have access to valuable data. This would be a counter-move trying to prevent data theft. It is natural that when seeing the new obstacle the attacker would decide to change their tactics of access. As a result devising a counter-counter-move which could be trying to get access through an unsuspecting colleague, trusted enough to still have the wished access.

Such steps of interruption lead to branching from routine scripts that demonstrates the complexity of dynamic modelling of crime, and cybercrime in particular. Over time, the scripts and counter-scripts become steadily more elaborate. But potentially there may be only a limited number of archetypical script clashes to address (such as 'conceal move versus detect move') [6]. Such a hypothesis makes the exploration and modelling of scripts a potentially promising endeavour.

5 Conclusion and Future Work

In the process towards a simulation of cyber crime this position paper contributes in two ways. First, it proposes an adaptation of the CCO framework to information security. And second, it suggests modelling of script clashes and discussion of potential reactive adaptations of scripts. These two patterns of representation both contribute to the fundaments of a design for a simulation of information security behaviour in a potential crime situation.

Designing and implementing a simulation of information security behaviour is a challenging task. A computer simulation typically requires a finite (and thus mathematically closed) representation. On the other hand there is an arms race between attackers and security officers which requires continuous adaptation and innovation [16]—a potentially infinite space of ideas or steps. A way out of this contradiction could be to address only the recurring attacks, but not the innovative ones. This way the hope is to get coverage of the "20 % of scripts occurring 80 % of the time".

The domain of simulation can be built utilizing the currently developed CCO browser game prototype [17]. This prototype features neither any simulation elements, nor crime scripts yet. Instead it guides users through a facilitated process of brainstorming crime interventions. Still, the game prototype could be used to analyse attacker scripts thus collecting user generated counter-moves. Data will be collected with the game prototype until certain level of saturation of ideas is achieved. The collected data could then be used to describe (hopefully enumerate) the space of counter-moves within certain abstraction and simplification.

References

1. Adams A, Sasse MA. Users are not the enemy: why users compromise security mechanisms and how to take remedial measures. Commun ACM. 1999;42:40–6. doi:10.1145/322796.322806.
2. Stajano F, Wilson P. Understanding scam victims: seven principles for systems security. Commun ACM. 2011;54:70–5. doi:10.1145/1897852.1897872.
3. Riegelsberger J, Sasse M, McCarthy J. The mechanics of trust: a framework for research and design. Int J Hum-Comput Stud. 2005;62:381–422. doi:10.1016/j.ijhcs.2005.01.001.
4. Beautement A, Sasse MA, Wonham M. The compliance budget: managing security behaviour in organisations. In: Proceedings of the 2008 workshop on New security paradigms. ACM, Lake Tahoe, California, USA, p. 47–58, doi:10.1145/1595676.1595684.
5. Collins BS, Mansell R. Cyber trust and crime prevention: A synthesis of the state-of-the-art science reviews. 2004. London, UK. http://eprints.lse.ac.uk/4252/. Accessed 16 Sept 2013.

6. Ekblom P. Happy returns: ideas brought back from situational crime prevention's exploration of design against crime. In: Farrell G, Tilley N, editors. The Reasoning Criminologist: Essays in Honour of Ronald V. Clarke. Routledge, p 163–204; 2011.

7. Ekblom P. Crime prevention, security and community safety using the 5Is framework (Crime Prevention and Security Management). Palgrave Macmillan; 2010.

8. Cornish D. Crimes as scripts. In: Zahm D, Cromwell P, editors. Proceedings of the International Seminar on Environmental Criminology and Crime Analysis. Tallahassee: Florida Criminal Justice Executive Institute; 1994. p. 30–45.

9. Alexander C, Ishikawa S, Silverstein M. A pattern language: towns, buildings, construction. Later printing. Oxford: Oxford University Press; 1977.

10. Gamma E, Helm R, Johnson R, Vlissides J. Design patterns: elements of reusable object-oriented software, 1st ed. Addison-Wesley Professional; 1994.

11. Birks D, Townsley M, Stewart A. Generative explanations of crime: using simulation to test criminological theory. Criminology. 2012;50:221–54. doi:10.1111/j.1745-9125.2011.00258.x.

12. Cone B, Irvine CE, Thompson MF, Nguyen T. A video game for cyber security training and awareness. Comput Secur. 2007;26:63–72. doi:10.1016/j.cose.2006.10.005.

13. Schultz. A framework for understanding and predicting insider attacks. Comput Secur. 2002; 21:526–531, doi:10.1016/s0167-4048(02)01009-x.

14. Tuglular T, Spafford EH. A framework for characterisation of insider computer misuse; 1997.

15. Parker DB. Fighting computer crime: a new framework for protecting information. Wiley; 1998.

16. Ekblom P. Gearing up against crime: a dynamic framework to help designers keep up with the adaptive criminal in a changing world. Int J Risk Secur Crime Prev. 1997;2:249–65.

17. Ruskov M, Celdran JM, Ekblom P, Sasse MA. Unlocking the next level of crime prevention: development of a game prototype to teach the conjunction of criminal opportunity. Information Technologies and Control 8; 2013.

Chapter 15
Security Design Patterns in the MASTER Workbench

Paul J. Kearney, David A. Sinclair and Sebastian Wagner

Abstract We describe the pattern-related aspects of the prototype Protection and Assessment (P&A) Workbench that was developed as part of the MASTER EU 7th Framework collaborative research project. The Workbench supports a model-driven design process within the overall MASTER methodology. It includes a Protection and Regulatory Model (PRM) tool that is a step towards turning the Workbench into an 'organisational memory' for design practices that accumulates and improves over time. PRMs are essentially control process design patterns that incorporate proven strategies in a re-usable form, saving time and improving quality and consistency.

1 Introduction

We will describe the pattern-related aspects of the prototype Protection and Assessment Workbench developed as part of the MASTER EU 7th Framework[1] collaborative research project. MASTER ran from 2008–2011 with the aim of providing a methodology and infrastructure that facilitates the monitoring, enforcement, and

---

[1] This work was supported by EU FP7 project MASTER (Grant Agreement No. 216917).

P. J. Kearney (✉)
BT Technology, Service and Operations, pp3/7/Rm21 Orion Building, BT Adastral Park, Martlesham Heath, Ipswich, Suffolk IP5 3RE, UK
e-mail: paul.3.kearney@bt.com

D. A. Sinclair
School of Computing, Irish Software Engineering Research Centre, Dublin City University, Glasnevin, Dublin 9, Ireland
e-mail: david.sinclair@computing.dcu.ie

S. Wagner
Institute of Architecture of Application Systems, University of Stuttgart, Universitaetsstrasse 38, 70569 Stuttgart, Germany
e-mail: Sebastian.wagner@iaas.uni-stuttgart.de

C. Blackwell and H. Zhu (eds.), *Cyberpatterns*, DOI: 10.1007/978-3-319-04447-7_15,

auditing of regulatory and security compliance, as well as business best practice, especially where highly dynamic service oriented architectures are used to support business process enactment in single, multi-domain, and iterated contexts.

The Protection and Assessment (P&A) Workbench is a prototype graphical software tool that supports a model-driven design process within the overall MASTER methodology. The term 'Protection and Assessment' reflects the focus of MASTER on the design and execution of processes that enforce regulatory and security policies and measures their effectiveness. The P&A Workbench is intended for use by an analyst/designer working in conjunction with a variety of business stakeholders to develop a Design Model. Typically, a Design Model is constructed, evaluated and elaborated iteratively until stakeholders agree that it describes an effective and affordable P&A solution that complies with control objectives that define the regulatory and business obligations of the intended solution. It is then refined further until the description is sufficiently concrete to provide the basis for implementation of a P&A system based on the MASTER infrastructure. The MASTER run-time infrastructure provides monitoring, enforcement and assessment run-time components. These components are configured by policy files generated by the P&A Workbench. The monitoring component watches for specific events and generates aggregated events from the base events. The enforcement component implements the Control Activities. The assessment component gathers data to calculate the key indicators and monitor the overall system.

The Verification and Simulation (V&S) tools are used to help confirm that the implemented system will indeed be fully compliant with the control objectives. The main output derived from the Design Model is a Policy Document that specifies rules that are interpreted by the run-time P&A system and determine its behaviour.

The Workbench comprises an extensible set of graphical modelling and transformation tools within a loosely coupled architectural framework, and a Repository in which interim and final models and other documents are stored. Collections of documents related to the same project are checked out of the Repository into a local workspace while being worked on using the Workbench tools. Documents in the Repository, notably Policy Documents, may be made available for deployment to, or consultation by, the MASTER infrastructure components at run-time. Not strictly part of the Workbench, but closely related to it, are the MASTER Verification and Simulation tools. These are invoked from the workbench in order to test certain properties of the Design Model.

2 Usage Scenario

A typical usage scenario for the workbench is as follows. A company already has a service-oriented infrastructure that it uses to partially automate the enactment of certain key business processes. It has identified that some high level security policies are relevant for the enactment of these business processes and the resources used. We are not concerned at this point whether the policies are due to regulatory requirements, industry codes of practice, or are of company-internal origin. The company now wishes to deploy IT controls to ensure as far as is practical that the policies are complied with and that the extent of any non-compliance is measured.

The company has decided to use the MASTER infrastructure to implement the controls. Company IT and security staff are now faced with a range of design decisions regarding how to use the 'vanilla' MASTER software to create an appropriate set of controls and indicators that interacts correctly with the existing infrastructure. The main means of customising the MASTER run-time infrastructure to implement the controls is to deploy a set of Signalling, Monitoring, Enforcement and Assessment policies to it.

Major requirements on the workbench are:

- To support the application of MASTER Methodology steps that guide the analyst and business stakeholders through description of the business context, selection and refinement of Control Objectives (COs) and Control Activities (CAs), specification of Key Assurance and Key Security Indicators (KAIs and KSIs), and definition of Control Processes (CPs) that implement the CAs.
- To use the Verification and Simulation (V&S) tools to help confirm the correctness of the CPs, i.e. that composing the CPs with the relevant target business process will result in compliance with the COs.
- To facilitate implementation of these design decisions by automating the creation of MASTER Signaling, Monitoring, Enforcement and Assessment policies.

Furthermore, the company wants compliance to be auditable to provide its management, shareholders, customers, partners, and legal and regulatory authorities with confidence that the policies are indeed being followed. This means it must be easy to check that appropriate controls are deployed and that they have been implemented correctly. Here, 'appropriate' means that the controls are suitable to achieve the intention of the policies taking into account the anticipated threat environment and the risk appetite and budget of the organisation. The workbench therefore needs, in addition, to enable an independent auditor to review and verify design and deployment decisions to ensure that appropriate choices have been made to implement the high level policies

The company will need to update the controls as requirements and business, technology and threat environments change. Furthermore, it is unlikely that the company will implement controls for a single process in isolation (except as a pilot), but rather would roll MASTER out for all relevant business processes as part of a major compliance or Business Process Re-engineering initiative. The Workbench therefore needs to support the maintenance of controls over time and ideally, re-use of successful controls and accumulation of experience.

3 Security Patterns

Schumacher et al. [1] inspired by the approach to pattern-oriented software architecture taken in [2] give the following definition: "A security pattern describes a particular recurring security problem that arises in specific contexts, and presents a well-proven generic solution for it. The solution consists of a set of interacting roles that can be arranged into multiple concrete design structures, as well as a process to create one particular structure". Security problems typically deal with constraining the behaviour of systems to uphold confidentiality and integrity properties while continuing to provide a service to legitimate users, in the face of malicious or misguided agents. A security pattern establishes an approach to solving a class of security problems by generalising over related successful cases.

Schumacher at al. regard humans as being the *only* audience for patterns. They further say that it is not practical to make patterns machine-readable and automatable, as it is all but impossible to formalise them. They contrast patterns with "other design or modelling techniques such as the Unified Modelling Language" that result in artefacts that are intended to be readable by machines and humans. This view is not universal, however. For example, Sowa [3] identifies three kinds of pattern (syntax, semantics and pragmatics) and three kinds of notation (natural language, linear notations for logic and computation, and graphical diagrams and movies) in his work applying conceptual graphs to knowledge design patterns.

The approach taken in MASTER attempts to bridge the two worlds of patterns and modelling languages. A MASTER pattern (termed a Protection and Regulatory Model, PRM) includes fields for free form textual entries that are aimed purely at a human audience and are broadly similar to those found in 'classical' patterns. However, it also contains corresponding design fragments expressed in the MASTER modelling language.

The intention is that the Workbench will incorporate a library of PRMs. In the course of developing a design model, the analyst and stakeholders will browse this library looking for PRMs that are relevant to the application context and the aspect of the model being worked on. For example, the analyst may be working on a control objective aimed at minimising opportunities for insider fraud and find a pattern describing how to do this using the principle of separation of duties. This stage is similar to searching a conventional pattern system.

The analyst then turns to the model fragments described in the PRM. These are templates with placeholders that must eventually be unified with entities in the model. The template is instantiated and added to the model, and the analyst stitches it into place by associating existing entities with placeholders. Often, the existing model will need to be re-worked to enable a good fit, for example, a role in a business process might have to be divided into two simpler roles to allow separation of duties. Sometimes, the changes required to achieve a fit may be judged excessive, and the pattern will be discarded and a new one sought. Not all the placeholders need to match existing model elements; indeed some may give rise to further searches of the pattern library.

Use of patterns in this way results in improved quality (as a result of adopting proven solutions and best-practice) and also in increased productivity as models are constructed partly from pre-fabricated components rather than always working at the level of the primitives of the modelling language.

Once a project is completed, the model is reviewed with the aim of identifying successful strategies with potential for re-use. These are recast in more abstract form, documented as PRMs and deposited in the library. PRMs that have been used should also be critiqued as part of this review and comments added to the record in the library. If appropriate, a PRM may be modified or elaborated in the light of experience, or even deleted if it has proved unsuccessful on several occasions. In this way, the Workbench will become an 'organisational memory' for design practices that accumulates and improves over time.

PRMs are now covered in more detail, before moving on to describe an early prototype PRM tool that was implemented as part of Workbench during the MASTER project.

4 Protection and Regulatory Models

Each PRM describes a design pattern that captures "best practice" in designing control processes for a specific control objective in a specific context. The essence of a PRM is a set of parameterised fragments of control processes, and each PRM is linked to a generalised control objective. The control process fragments in each PRM are composed and sequenced in a specific manner. Each control process fragment is defined by a set of allowed event traces. An event trace is a sequence of observable events. These event traces may consume events from or add events to its enclosing environment that consists of the business process and other control processes. Some of the events in the traces may be bound to terms in the PRM's control objective or the events that are consumed or added to its enclosing environment. These events are defined as *exposed PRM events* and are included in the parameters of the PRM. Non-exposed events, *internal PRM events*, are not visible to the actors who interact with the PRM. Internal PRM events can be renamed without any impact on actors and processes that interact with the PRM. Exposed PRM events are typically the input and output events of the PRM, but may also include intermediate events.

Each PRM contains the following elements.

(1) A textual description that describes the purposes of the PRM, its associated control objective(s) and the type of environments in which the PRM is envisaged to be deployed. This description should be brief enough to allow a user to browse this description within a collection of PRMs, yet it should contain sufficient information to allow a user to make a preliminary decision on whether a PRM is appropriate for a particular design.
(2) A description of the parameters of the PRM.
(3) A description of the context in which the problem that is being solved arises. In addition to describing the attacks that the PRM is addressing, the section also describes the organisational context in which the PRM can be used. More specifically the PRM describes the requirements and restrictions on the organisational structure in which the PRM can be used in terms of:

   (a) The *entities* participating in the solution: Actor roles, Goals, Activities, and Resources.

(b) The *structural dependencies* among entities. These structural dependencies can arise due to the context of the problem the PRM is addressing or due to the structure of an organisation. An organisation can impose dependencies on entities and actors. For example, the organisation may require certain entities to collaborate together. It may define which actors are subordinate to other actors, and which actors have incompatible roles and hence require a separation of their duties.

(4) A description of any infrastructural services required by the PRM. For example, an authentication PRM may require a service that associates a set of roles with each actor.

(5) A description of the control objective implemented by the PRM. This is given by a textual description and a formal statement of the control objective using the MASTER Property Specification Language.

(6) A formal description of the control process fragments that implement the PRM. This description is specified in the M-calculus, which has both a graphical and textual representation. The M-calculus is a process calculus that extends Milner's π-calculus [4] to include timed events and probabilistic events. The motivation for describing the control process fragments formally is that this enables the PRM designer to prove that the PRM implements its control objective in the specified contexts.

(7) A description of the possible impact of the PRM on the overall system. This section should address, but not be limited to, issues such as availability, confidentiality, integrity, performance and usability.

When composing multiple PRMs, care needs to be taken that the names of the exposed PRM events do not conflict. Internal PRM events can be renamed to avoid any conflict with events in the target processes, control processes or other PRMs. Since the exposed PRM events are all parameters of the PRM, each PRM is instantiated with events from the target and control processes. If two PRMs reference the same event from the target and/or control processes, this event is called a *conflicted event*. Conflicted events may require special handling, such as duplication to ensure that each PRM can consume the event, or amalgamation to ensure that conflicted events produced by both PRMs do not invalidate the system's control objectives when consumed by the environment.

Since PRMs represent "best practice" they have an added significance in an environment with multiple trust domains. While organisation X may be reluctant to disclose the details of the control processes it is providing to organisation Y, if organisation X agrees to provide a specific authentication PRM then organisation Y can be sure of that the corresponding control objective is achieved (subject to the PRM's assumptions on its environment) without organisation Y revealing, or allowing access, to the control infrastructure within organisation Y.

The use of PRMs can be illustrated by looking at how one could be used to represent a control taken from ISO 17779-2005 [5]. The ISO standard describes Control 11.1.1 "Access Control Policy" as "*An access control policy should be*

*established, documented and reviewed based on the business and security require-
ment for access"*. The text does not describe how to implement Control 11.1.1, but
it does describe some properties that any implementation of the control 11.1.1 must
have. The corresponding PRM would capture a "best practice" implementation of this
control in specific contexts and outline how the properties specified for this control
can be proved in these contexts. The main objective of PRM is to capture precisely
and formalise the knowledge required to implement a control process aiming to be
compliant with control objective derived from a business objective or regulation. The
control objectives describe "patterns" that compliant control processes must match
and PRMs formalise these patterns.

5 PRM Tool

The prototype PRM tool is an Eclipse plugin that is a step towards turning the
Workbench into an 'organisational memory' for design practices that accumulates
and improves over time. As mentioned in the previous section, PRMs are essentially
control process design patterns that incorporate proven strategies in a re-usable form,
saving time and improving quality and consistency. They map security compliance
objectives to control processes and architectures that achieve them in defined business
and technical contexts. The tool allows new PRMs to be created and stored in the
Repository, and retrieved and instantiated as part of a new model when required.

During its initial creation the PRM elements and properties (name, description,
problem context, parameters etc.) can be defined with the PRM tool. A PRM includes
its control objectives and implementation artefacts, i.e. control processes and the corresponding infrastructure services, and can be directly linked to elements modelled
within the design workbench. Hence, if they are modified with their corresponding
workbench tools (e.g. a process model editor) these modifications are immediately
visible within the PRM. Moreover, this has the advantage that these elements can be
also used in other PRMs.

Separation of Duty (SoD) ensures that critical operations within a business process
are played by two separate agents. As SoD is a pattern with high re-use potential in
different business scenarios it is decided to model it as a PRM by using the PRM
Tool (Fig. 1).

The PRM has two parameters *targetProcessRole* and *controlProcessRole* that
have to be specified during the instantiation of the PRM (see below). The first parameter represents the definition of the business process where the PRM instance is
applied on during runtime. The second parameter represents the control process that
enforces the control objective of the PRM. The control process must comply with the
M-Calculus control process fragments specified in the *SoDPRMWrapperTemplate*.
The PRM requires the infrastructural service *AUTHZ* that acts as authorization manager for user actions. This service monitors the user actions and can be also used by
the control process to prohibit users from performing certain actions.

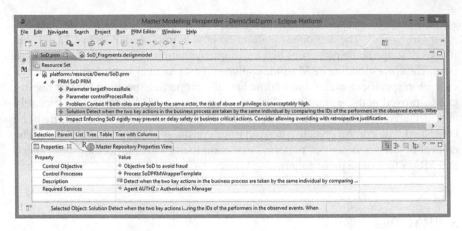

Fig. 1 PRM tool with SoD PRM

Parameters, control objectives, control process fragments, and services must be defined in one or several Design Models before they can be referenced from a PRM model. For each parameter its type has to be specified. During the instantiation of the PRM the type of the element that is specified as parameter value must correspond to this parameter type. For instance, the parameters *targetProcessRole* and *control-ProcessRole* in Fig. 1, specify that their values must be of type *Process*. The PRM tool provides a wizard that guides the user through the instantiation of a PRM. As shown in Fig. 2 the wizard lists all parameters of a PRM and the user can provide concrete values for the listed parameters. This means that the user can supply concrete design model elements from arbitrary design models from the workbench or the repository, respectively. In order to do that, for each parameter the path to the design model that contains the element that has to serve as parameter value is provided. Then the design model element can be selected from the combo box.

In the following example, our SoD PRM will be applied to a Drug Dispensation process to avoid fraudulent dispensation of drugs, i.e. it ensures that the person dispensing the drug and the one who wrote the prescription are not the same (see Sect. 6). Hence, as shown in Fig. 2 the *targetProcessRole* parameter is instantiated with a *Drug Dispensation Process*. The parameter value combo boxes list only those elements of a design model that match the type of the parameter defined in the PRM model. Therefore, to instantiate the parameter *controlProcessRole* only those elements of the selected design model *ControlProcessLibrary* are listed in the combo box that have the type *Process*. In the example in Fig. 2 these are three control processes of type *Process*. The control processes *SoD Control Process V1.1* and *SoD Control Process V2.0* enforce the SoD requirement on the *Dispensation Process* by monitoring the persons that perform the prescription and dispensation of the drugs and by prohibiting the dispensation if both persons are the same.

After the user has provided the values for each parameter she finishes the wizard and the PRM is instantiated by creating a new design model out of it that is stored

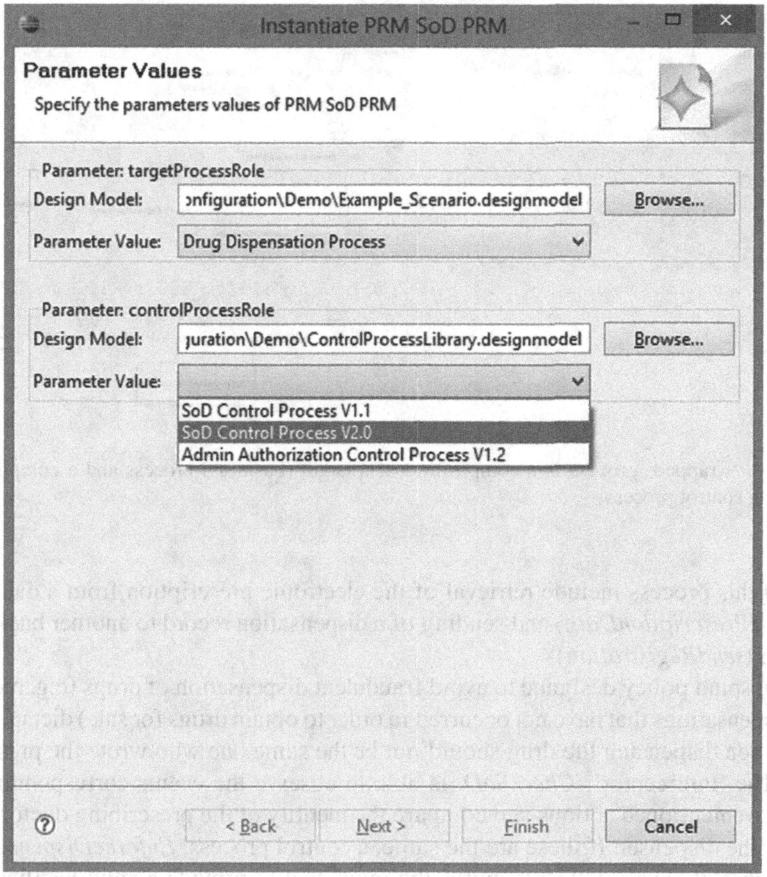

Fig. 2 PRM instantiation wizard

in the workbench. In our example a design model is created that contains *Drug Dispensation Process* and the SoD control process *SoD Control Process V2.0*.

6   An Example

We will now give a simple example of creation and application of a PRM based on the main application case study from the MASTER project. The case study is to design a system to automate a hospital business process concerning dispensation of prescriptions to outpatients that must comply with local regulations and hospital policy. Figure 3 shows a detail from the design model. The business process fragment *RegisterDrugs* involves the person dispensing a prescription to recording the drugs that have actually been provide to the outpatient. Actions performed as

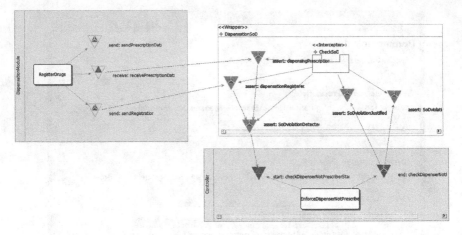

Fig. 3 A 'wrapped' process is a composition of a target (business) process and a compliance-enforcing control process

part of this process include retrieval of the electronic prescription from a database (*receivePrescriptionData*) and sending of a dispensation record to another back-end system (*sendRegistration*).

A hospital policy designed to avoid fraudulent dispensation of drugs (e.g. recording dispensations that have not occurred in order to obtain drugs for sale) dictates that the person dispensing the drug should not be the same one who wrote the prescription. The 'Interceptor', *CheckSoD*, is able to observe the events corresponding to the abovementioned actions and compare the identity of the prescribing doctor with that of the dispenser. If these are the same, a control process, *EnforceDispenserNot Prescriber*, is invoked. This requires the individual to provide a valid justification, and if this is not done, a separation of duties (SoD) violation is raised. Note that use of Interceptors to wrap target business processes with control processes aids modularity and encourages reusability.

During a retrospective design review, it is recognised that separation of duties is a pattern with high re-use potential, and it is decided to encode it as a PRM. A new PRM object is created and stored in the Respository (Fig. 4). It has two parameters, being placeholders for the target process and the control process. The solution element references a Control Objective (*SoD to avoid fraud*), and *SoDPRMWrapperTemplate*, which is a generic form of the wrapper that we saw earlier (Fig. 5).

To apply the pattern, the *Instantiate PRM* command is used. The user is asked to select objects in the design model to replace the parameters in the template. Selecting the original target and control process results in Fig. 6. At present, the user still has to connect the actions in the instantiated template manually with those in the processes replacing the parameters. The user may also choose to replace the generic names of the objects created from the template with ones that are more meaningful in the context of the application.

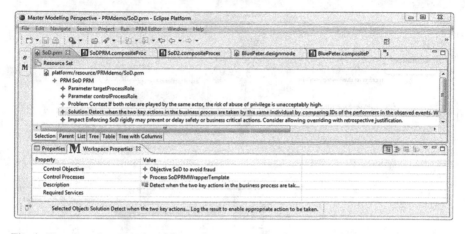

Fig. 4 The separation of duties PRM

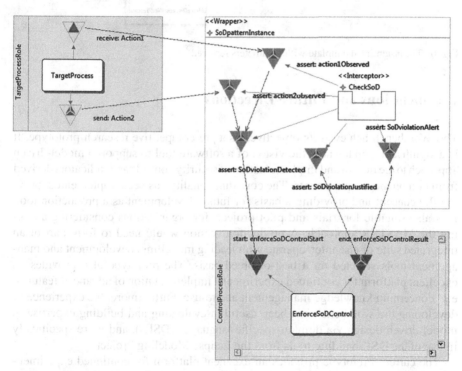

Fig. 5 The SoD template and parameterized roles

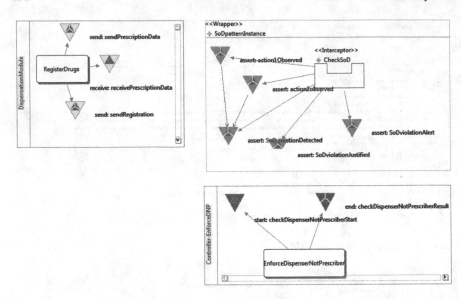

Fig. 6 The instantiated template with parameters replaced

7 Conclusions and Future Directions

The Workbench achieved its objectives as a pre-competitive research prototype. It is a significant step towards the vision of a software tool to support a model-driven approach to the design and implementation of security controls and indicators derived from compliance requirements. The core functionality has been implemented, proving the concept and providing a basis for future development as a production tool. It is also suitable for trials and pilot projects for organisations considering adopting the MASTER approach. A production version would need to form part of an integrated suite or else inter-operate with leading modelling, development and management tools selected on a best-of-breed basis. The prototype also provides an excellent platform for continued experimental implementation of advanced features, e.g. concerning knowledge management and re-use. Furthermore, the experience of developing the workbench has been useful in evaluating and building expertise in model-driven design via domain-specific languages (DSLs), and more specifically in use of the DSL-building tools from the Eclipse Modeling Project.

The current prototype provides an excellent platform for continued experimental implementation of aspects of the Workbench vision that we did not have time to investigate or implement fully during the MASTER project. Re-use of parameterised models in design patterns is already present in the workbench in the form of the PRM tool. While this is effective in proving and demonstrating a viable approach there are many details to be fleshed out. Once a framework for re-use has been established, PRM libraries need to be developed providing abstract solutions to compliance requirement commonly appearing in regulations and corporate policies.

PRMs are only one form of knowledge management that would be useful in a Workbench. The design process makes extensive use of knowledge derived from experience. Traditionally, this has been held in the heads of experts, and in text books, codes of practice and standards. A future research project could incorporate an expert system into the Workbench to provide advice on design decisions. The knowledge base of the expert system could be seeded with generic guidance, and expanded over time with enterprise-specific and sector-specific knowledge to become a living means of continuous improvement. An important aspect of the project would be investigation of means of capturing new knowledge and otherwise maintaining the knowledge base.

References

1. Schumacher M, Fernandez-Buglioni E, Hybertson D, Buschmann F, Sommerlad P. Security patterns: integrating security and systems engineering. 1st ed. Chichester: Wiley; 2005.
2. Buschmann F, Meunier R, Rohnert H, Sommerlad P, Stal M. Pattern-oriented software architecture, vol. 1. 1st ed., A system of patterns. Chichester: Wiley; 1995.
3. Sowa JF. Knowledge design patterns—combining logic, ontology and computation. 2012. http://www.jfsowa.com/talks/kdptut.pdf. Accessed 8 Sept 2013.
4. Milner R. Communicating and mobile systems: the Pi-calculus. 1st ed. Cambridge: Cambridge University Press; 1999.
5. ISO/IEC. International Standard ISO/IEC 17799:2005. Information technology—security techniques—code of practice for information security management. Geneva: ISO Copyright Office; 2005.

Chapter 16
Evaluating the Implications of Attack and Security Patterns with Premortems

Shamal Faily, Simon Parkin and John Lyle

Abstract Security patterns are a useful way of describing, packaging and applying security knowledge which might otherwise be unavailable. However, because patterns represent partial knowledge of a problem and solution space, there is little certainty that addressing the consequences of one problem won't introduce or exacerbate another. Rather than using patterns exclusively to explore possible solutions to security problems, we can use them to better understand the security problem space. To this end, we present a framework for evaluating the implications of security and attack patterns using *premortems*: scenarios describing a failed system that invites reasons for its failure. We illustrate our approach using an example from the EU FP 7 *webinos* project.

1 Contextualising Patterns for Security Design

Because security knowledge isn't readily available in design situations, there is considerable value in codifying and packaging it. Given both the adversarial nature of security, and the dangers of over or underestimation of security issues when this nature is misunderstood, it also seems useful to package knowledge about attacks as patterns. From a practitioner perspective, it seems surprising that, despite an abundance of examples of how security knowledge can be codified as patterns, e.g. [1], and the claim that building attack patterns is evidence of organisational security

S. Faily (✉)
Bournemouth University, Poole BH12 5BB, UK
e-mail: sfaily@bournemouth.ac.uk

S. Parkin
University College London, London WC1E 6BT, UK
e-mail: s.parkin@ucl.ac.uk

J. Lyle
University of Oxford, Oxford OX3 0NH, UK
e-mail: john.lyle@cs.ox.ac.uk

C. Blackwell and H. Zhu (eds.), *Cyberpatterns*, DOI: 10.1007/978-3-319-04447-7_16,   199
© Springer International Publishing Switzerland 2014

maturity [2], there is a dearth of work describing the application of attack patterns in security design.

Characterising attack and misuse patterns, e.g. [3], has been helpful in illustrating how patterns can tackle specific problems, but patterns need to be contextualised to be useful. One way of contextualising attack patterns involves better understanding the motives and capabilities of an attacker. Steps towards this goal are being made via profiling techniques [4], and the reuse of open-source intelligence for building attacker personas [5]. However, even when contextualised, such representations remain only partial representation of an attacker's knowledge. Although these provide inspiration for undirected ideation activities, more relevant qualitative data is needed to augment profiles or patterns to understand what specific attacks they might carry out in specific contexts. If such data was available then attacks would be self-evident, thereby eliminating the need for attack patterns.

2 Patterns as an Exploratory Tool

We may never have the assurances that we would like about a pattern's efficacy; while a pattern may be one possible solution to a problem, we can never be completely sure that this solution itself doesn't introduce further complications we have yet to identify. This is a symptom of the lack of clarity about what it means to secure a system. This, in turn, makes it difficult to devise tests for proving a system is secure, and a grasp of all possible solutions for satisfying a specified security problem [6]. Patterns have the potential to provide this clarity because not only do they help solve security problems, they can also help understand the problem space security is concerned with as well. When we apply patterns, we also make value judgements about how attacker patterns might exploit systems, or how different security patterns might be a satisficing security design solution. These value judgements help us understand and delimit the solution space. Therefore, not only are patterns effective at structuring knowledge, they also explore the consequences of their application. If we can better understand these consequences, we can also better understand what is important to us when thinking about system security.

Interestingly, the value associated with applying patterns to delimit the problem space is obtained whether or not they successfully address the problem we had in mind. While it seems paradoxical that we would apply a security pattern knowing that it will ultimately fail, such an approach is analogous to a *premortem*. In business scenario planning, these operate on the assumption that a solution has failed and, rather than reflecting on what might have gone wrong, designers instead generate plausible reasons for explaining the solution's failure [7]. Although the known structure, motivation, and consequences of security patterns provide some insight into the causes of such a failure, when combined with attack patterns, they allow us to reflect on the motivations of a perceived attacker, and how his capabilities and motivations ultimately led to an exploit. More interestingly, if the mapping between patterns is not clear, the lack of data also provides clues about what additional evidence is needed before the "cause of death" can be established.

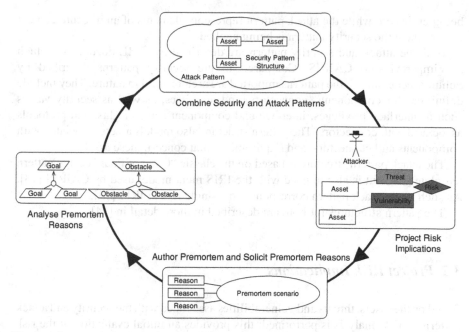

Fig. 1 A framework for evaluating patterns with premortems

3 Approach

To make the most of the exploratory power of both patterns and premortems, we have devised an approach to evaluate the implications of applying security and attack patterns. This entails combining security and attack patterns, and statically evaluating the risk posed as a result. The risk impact is described using a premortem scenario, and reasons for the failure described are solicited from domain experts or stakeholders. Using KAOS goal and obstacle modelling techniques [8], the underlying causes for these reasons are elicited as implicit requirements that hold when the security pattern is applied. The obstacles and goals elicited are then used to refine the select attack and security patterns respectively.

This approach, which we illustrate in Fig. 1, relies on the open-source CAIRIS security requirements management tool [9, 10]. It also relies on goal and risk modelling techniques developed as part of the IRIS framework [11].

This approach is described in more detail in the following sub-sections.

3.1 Combine Security and Attack Patterns

The first step involves selecting a security and attack pattern to form the basis of evaluation. The security pattern represents some aspect of a system architecture being evaluated, while the attack pattern represents elements of an insecure context of use where the security pattern is being applied.

Both the attack and security pattern are described by XML documents, which are imported into CAIRIS. Compared to the security patterns described by Schumacher et al. [1], the patterns imported are architectural in nature. They include definitions for components, connectors, and interfaces, as well as security values such as interface privileges, interface and component access rights, and protocols associated with connectors. The pattern structure also models assets associated with components and connectors, and requirements that concern these assets.

The attack pattern structure is based on the classic "Gang of Four" design pattern template [12], but is also aligned with the IRIS meta-model used by CAIRIS [13]. As such, each attack pattern corresponds to a single risk in IRIS [13].

The pattern structures for both are described in more detail in [14].

3.2 Project Risk Implications

Based on the assets, threats and vulnerabilities associated with the security and attack patterns, a risk analysis is performed; this provides an initial evaluation of the risk implications of the pattern combination.

This analysis is automatically carried out by CAIRIS based on the imported security and attack patterns. The results are visualised using CAIRIS' risk modelling notation; this is described in more detail by Faily and Fléchais [15].

3.3 Author Premortem and Solict Premortem Responses

Using inspiration from both the patterns and the risk analysis, a premortem scenario is written to characterise a system failure resulting from this application of both patterns. Reasons for these failures can be elicited from a variety of different people. These range from direct stakeholders, such as customers or project team members, to indirect stakeholders, such as domain experts or members of the public.

Because premortems are not conceptually supported by CAIRIS, this scenario is modelled as a misuse case [16] and associated with the risk resulting from the pattern combination.

3.4 Analyse Premortem Reasons

Using KAOS obstacle models, each premortem reason is modelled as a set of obstacles. Obstacles are abstracted to identify problems giving rise to these reasons; they are also refined to identify conditions that need to be present for the reasons to hold.

Where security pattern requirements mitigate these obstacles, obstacle resolution links are added to the obstacle model.

To capture the insights resulting from this evaluation, the obstacle model is incorporated into the structure of the CAIRIS attack pattern. To facilitate this, the Data Type Definition for attack pattern XML documents includes an implementation element. This element allows an attack to be described textually and visually using an obstacle model.

The implicit requirements that mitigate these obstacles are also incorporated into the security pattern. These requirements are represented as goals trees, which are associated with individual components in the pattern.

4 Example

We illustrate our approach by describing how it was used to evaluate aspects of the security architecture of *webinos*. *webinos* is a software infrastructure for running web applications across smartphones, PCs, home media centres, and in-car devices [17]. *webinos'* software architecture includes policy management components for facilitating cross-device access control [18].

The process used to carry out an architectural risk analysis process was described in [14]. Our approach complements that process by providing a framework for moving from the identification of general flaws and knowledge about known attacks, to the discovery of risks resulting from ambiguity and inconsistency in a system design.

4.1 Combine Security and Attack Patterns

We wanted to consider how resistant the policy management architecture might be to attempts to *footprint*, i.e. attempts to gather potentially exploitable information about the system.

The security pattern is characterised using the *Context Policy Management* architectural pattern [19]. This pattern realises the policy management requirements specified by Lyle et al. [18].

The initial attack pattern illustrated in Fig. 2 was constructed by searching for keywords associated with footprinting activities using open-source intelligence. In this example, attacks and exploits were found by searching the Common Attack Pattern Enumeration and Classification (CAPEC) and Common Weakness Enumeration (CWE) repositories [20, 21].

4.2 Project Risk Implications

When the patterns were imported into CAIRIS, a risk model was automatically generated and a "Test footprinting" risk added to characterise the attack pattern.

Name	Test footprinting
Likelihood	Occasional
Severity	Critical
Intent	Glean an understanding of what resources are available on a device by eavesdropping on requests.
Motivational Goal	Accountability (High)
Motivation	Ethan looks for test code which provides unauthorised resource access.
Applicable Environment	Complete
	Structure
Attack	Locate and Exploit Test APIs
Exploit	Allocation of Resources without Limits or Throttling
Participant	Ethan
Motives	Data theft
Responsibilities	Technology (Medium), Software (Medium), Knowledge/Methods (Medium)
	Collaboration
Target	Application Data
Exploit	Access Request

Fig. 2 Initial attack pattern structure

When this risk model, which is illustrated in Fig. 3, was automatically generated, the risk score seemed surprisingly low based on the colour of the risk diamond. In the risk model, the shade of red is used to indicate its seriousness; the darker the shade, the more serious the risk is. Based on the initial lightness of the shade, the risk was not considered significant. On further investigation, we discovered that this was because no security properties were associated with the exploited Application Data asset, despite an attack that compromised its accountability. This minimised the impact of the threat, thereby lowering the overall risk rating. However, initially contextualising the attack pattern with the *Ethan* attacker persona [22] indicated that both integrity and accountability of this data needed to be maintained. Adding these security properties to the Application Data asset subsequently lead to the criticality of risk being increased.

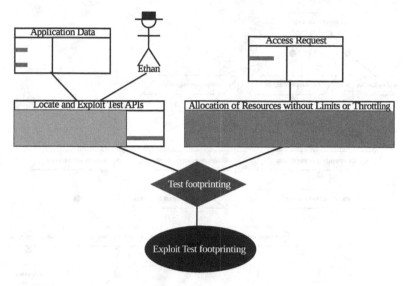

Fig. 3 CAIRIS risk analysis model of security and attack pattern elements

4.3 Author Premortem and Solict Premortem Responses

Inspired by the risk model, we developed the premortem scenario below to characterise the implications of an access control failure.

The Register picked up a story based on blog reports by irate mobile users complaining about increased email spam since they started using webinos applications; this spam is sufficiently targeted that it evades spam filters. This has led to lots of irate twitter posts appearing on the twitter feed on the webinos home page, especially from angry developers who users blame for this traffic. As the bad press grew and open-source advocates began to criticise the project, major partners began to leave the project, and EC funding was cut; this lead to the project being halted due to lack of money.

This premortem scenario was emailed to all members of the *webinos* project team, who were asked to reply to the email with their reasons for the described failure. Although the most active members of the project team were web app developers, the team also included participants with backgrounds in handset and car manufacturing, and mobile market analysis.

4.4 Analyse Premortem Reasons

Several possible reasons for this failure were proposed. These ranged from the re-selling of private application data, through to attackers actively footprinting the network infrastructure hosting the cloud-based hubs for *webinos* personal zones.

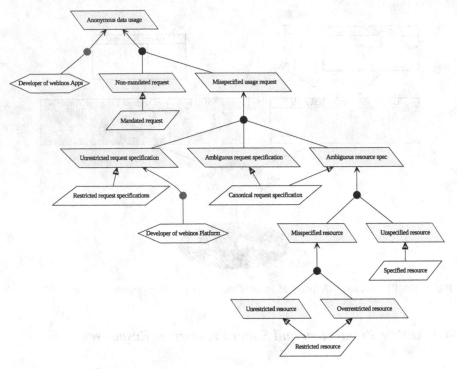

Fig. 4 Obstacle model associated with premortem reason

For reasons of brevity, we will consider only one of these: one team member suggested that *webinos*' access control policies might be open to ambiguity, and that this could lead to information being shared against the wishes of end users.

Using the ambiguity analysis techniques described in [14], it was possible to derive the obstacle model illustrated in Fig. 4. The Test Footprinting attack pattern was revised to incorporate this obstacle model as rationale for the attack [23]. Additionally, insights about these reasons lead to revisions to the access right, protocol, and privilege values associated with the Context Policy Management architectural pattern.

5 Implications

Devising and applying this premortems-based approach to pattern evaluation has broader implications on the design and evaluation of security. We describe some of these in the following sub-sections.

5.1 Analysing Incomplete Risk Models

The Test Footprinting attack pattern sketched in Fig. 2 made assumptions about both vulnerable assets, and assets used as part of a broader exploit. Because the IRIS meta-model assumes these assets are known when specifying risks, these assumptions needed to be made early. However, while indications about vulnerable assets may be known at an early stage, it's unlikely that details about exploited assets will be known. If inappropriate assets, or asset security properties are elicited at this early stage, the visual risk models can help identify this. However, inappropriate assets or asset values may also inspire inappropriate premortems; these are less easy to identify, and may lead to the exploration of inappropriate parts of the problem space. While there is no easy remedy to this problem, it does suggest that risk models may benefit from being less specific at an early stage; this has implications on how risks might be appropriately analysed and visualised using incomplete information.

5.2 Measuring Quality Concerns

As well as evaluating the implications of attack and security patterns, this approach also helps us measure quality concerns. Responses given by project team members may be complicated, simple, pessimistic, or optimistic. In each case, however, they say something about how confident team members are about either the system or the context it is situated in. This suggests that premortem responses are a useful tool for managers to keep in touch with the security reality of a project.

We can also use this approach to understand why security systems may not satisfy quality requirements we expect to hold. For example, we may expect a combination of security patterns to fail fast and predictably for different attack patterns. If we write a premortem describing a system that fails slowly and unpredictably then responses might help us to identify what we need to do to fix these problems.

5.3 Engagement with Hard to Reach Groups

Premortems allow organisational stakeholders with security interests, but a non-IT background, to engage in security design. While time-constrained stakeholders, such as senior managers, may find it difficult to take time out to engage in design activities, they might it easier to provide short, thought-provoking feedback to scenarios that capture their imagination. When these responses are recorded, they can formally acknowledge their contribution to the design process. However, because premortems are successful because contributors don't feel any responsibility for their contribution, acknowledging these responses may lead to less than honest responses.

5.4 Promoting Open Innovation

Although our approach relied on a predefined list of stakeholders for premortem responses, we could also use *Open Innovation* to collect responses from a broader base of external respondents. Open Innovation is a paradigm where both ideas and paths to market are generated from both within and outside an organisation [24]. This can be made possible by using premortems to describe contextual information; this is collected while combining patterns and projecting risks, particularly when risks are rated at a lower than expected value. Using premortems, this contextual information could be shared without disclosing sensitive information about the nature of the assets being exploited, potential attacks and attackers.

6 Conclusion

In this chapter we described an approach where premortems were used to better understand the problem and solution space associated with attack and security patterns. We illustrated this approach using an example where this exploration lead to more refined pattern descriptions.

We are currently exploring ways that CAIRIS can be updated to better address the lessons learned applying this approach. For example, we are currently investigating different ways of making the IRIS risk meta-model more permissive given the issues raised in Sect. 5.1. We are also considering more effective ways of supporting the premortem technique within CAIRIS and the broader IRIS framework. These include devising more effective ways of supporting the elicitation of premortem scenarios, and soliciting reason responses from appropriate stakeholders.

In future work, we will explore how this technique might be used by security testers, in particular ethical hackers, to support a deep-dive analysis of a system. In particular, we will consider how this approach provides a framework for taking fresh thinking that ethical hackers can provide, and aligning this thinking with both exploiting and mitigating system models.

Acknowledgments The work described in this chapter was funded by the EU FP7 *webinos* project (FP7-ICT-2009-05 Objective 1.2).

References

1. Schumacher M, Fernandez E, Hybertson D, Buschmann F. Security patterns: integrating security and systems engineering. Chichester: Wiley; 2005.
2. McGraw G, Migues S, West J. Building Security In Maturity model: BSIMMV. October 2013. http://bsimm.com. Accessed March 2014

3. Fernandez EB, Yoshioka N, Washizaki H, Jürjens J, VanHilst M, Pernul G. Using security patterns to develop secure systems. In: Mouratidis H, editor. Software engineering for secure systems: industrial and research perspectives. , New York: IGI Global; 2011. p. 16–31.
4. Chiesa R, Ducci S, Ciappi S. Profiling hackers: the science of criminal profiling as applied to the world of hacking. 1st ed. Boston: Auerbach Publications; 2008.
5. Atzeni A, Cameroni C, Faily S, Lyle J, Flechais I. Here's johnny: a methodology for developing attacker personas. In: Proceedings of the 2011 sixth international conference on availability, reliability and security. ARES '11. Washington: IEEE Computer Society; 2011. p. 722–7. http://dx.doi.org/10.1109/ARES.2011.115.
6. Faily S, Flechais I. To boldly go where invention isn't secure: applying security entrepreneurship to secure systems design. In: Proceedings of the 2010 workshop on new security paradigms. NSPW '10. New York: ACM; 2010. p. 73–84. http://doi.acm.org/10.1145/1900546.1900557.
7. Klein G. Performing a project premortem. Harvard Bus Rev. 2007;85(9):18–9.
8. van Lamsweerde A. Requirements engineering: from system goals to UML models to software specifications. West Sussex: Wiley; 2009.
9. Faily S, Fléchais I. Towards tool-support for usable secure requirements engineering with CAIRIS. Int J Secure Software Eng. 2010;1(3):56–70.
10. Faily S. CAIRIS web site; 2013. http://github.com/failys/CAIRIS.
11. Faily S, Fléchais I. Eliciting policy requirements for critical national infrastructure using the iris framework. Int J Secure Software Eng. 2011;2(4):114–9.
12. Gamma E, Helm R, Johnson R, Vlissides J. Design patterns: elements of reusable object-oriented software. Boston: Addison-Wesley Longman; 1995.
13. Faily S, Fléchais I. A meta-model for usable secure requirements engineering. In: Proceedings of the 2010 ICSE workshop on software engineering for secure systems. SESS '10. New York: ACM; 2010. p. 29–35. http://doi.acm.org/10.1145/1809100.1809105.
14. Faily S, Lyle J, Namiluko C, Atzeni A, Cameroni C. Model-driven architectural risk analysis using architectural and contextualised attack patterns. In: Proceedings of the workshop on model-driven security. MDsec '12. New York: ACM; 2012. p. 3:1–3:6. http://doi.acm.org/10.1145/2422498.2422501.
15. Faily S, Fléchais I. Analysing and visualising security and usability in iris. 2012 seventh international conference on availability, reliability and security 2010; p. 543–8.
16. Sindre G, Opdahl AL. Eliciting security requirements with misuse cases. Requir Eng. 2005;10(1):34–44. http://dx.doi.org/10.1007/s00766-004-0194-4.
17. Fuhrhop C, Lyle J, Faily S. The webinos project. In: Proceedings of the 21st international conference companion on World Wide Web. WWW '12 Companion. New York: ACM; 2012. p. 259–62. Available from: http://doi.acm.org/10.1145/2187980.2188024.
18. Lyle J, Monteleone S, Faily S, Patti D, Ricciato F. Cross-platform access control for mobile web applications. In: 2012 IEEE international symposium on policies for distributed systems and networks (POLICY);2012. p. 37–44.
19. webinos Consortium. Context Policy Management Architectural Pattern; July. https://github.com/webinos/webinos-design-data/blob/master/architecture/architecturalpatterns/ContextPolicyManagement.xml.
20. The MITRE Corporation. Common Attack Pattern Enumeration and Classification (CAPEC) web site; 2012. http://capec.mitre.org.
21. The MITRE Corporation. Common Weakness Enumeration (CWE) web site; 2012. http://cwe.mitre.org.
22. webinos Consortium. Ethan Attacker Persona; 2011. https://github.com/webinos/webinos-design-data/blob/master/personas/ethan.xml.
23. webinos Consortium. Test Footprinting Attack Pattern; July. https://github.com/webinos/webinos-design-data/blob/master/architecture/attackpatterns/TestFootprinting.xml.
24. Chesbrough HW. Open innovation: the new imperative for creating and profiting from technology. Boston: Harvard Business School Press; 2003.

Part VI
Pattern Recognition

Clive Blackwell

The focus of pattern recognition in this section is on the use of AI techniques to recognise and respond to anomalous patterns in large and diverse collections of data for cyber security and digital forensics. There are numerous issues in extracting and classifying relevant data, as its key attributes may be difficult to define, it may be distributed in multiple systems in different formats, methods of system compromise change rapidly and unpredictably, and the small proportion of anomalies makes it difficult to discover them reliably without causing large numbers of false positives. Russell and Norvig [1] is a relevant and comprehensive introduction to Artificial Intelligence for the uninitiated.

Chapter 17, *An Overview of Artificial Intelligence Based Pattern Matching in a Security and Digital Forensic Context* by Mitchell, discusses several cyber security and digital forensics challenges involving the analysis of large quantities of data, such as network traffic and hard disc contents. The concentration is on basic common AI techniques that could be adapted to the cyber security and digital forensics arena, giving a brief insight into their strengths and weaknesses and indicating their possible uses. She first indicates the foundational issue of knowledge representation, where we do not have good ontologies to represent basic concepts. She then discusses pattern recognition techniques describing different types of machine learning and knowledge discovery techniques. Pattern recognition becomes outdated through changes in system use and attacker behaviour, so the techniques must adapt to recognise new anomalous scenarios whilst ensuring existing issues are still recognised. She finally suggests Exploratory Data Analysis (EDA) [2] that is the combination of a pattern recognition system and data visualisation, allowing a human to explore and understand the data under investigation. This is in line with existing security technologies that provide numerous visualisation tools to spot anomalies in large quantities of data, and it is a relatively easy way to add AI to current systems, as the computer can be given computational tasks whereas the more complex reasoning can be performed by the human analyst.

Chapter 18, Partitional Clustering of Malware using K-Means by de Amorim and Komisarczuk, describes a novel method of clustering behavioural data containing malware collected from client interactions with websites. The data are captured and analysed with Capture-HPC which is a high-interaction client honeypot with a fully functional Web browser, which makes requests to multiple websites and then analyses the collected data to determine whether any attacks have taken place on the client. The data are very high-dimensional in both the number of websites and interesting features, leading to sparse data that is difficult to cluster, so they use the cosine distance or similarity with the distance d between x and y $d(x,y) = \Sigma x_i \cdot y_i / \Sigma x_i^2 \cdot \Sigma y_i^2$ rather than the more popular squared Euclidean distance $d'(x,y) = (\Sigma(y_i - x_i)^2)^{1/2}$. k-means clustering partitions the observations into k clusters in which each observation is placed in the cluster with the nearest mean value. As the problem is NP-hard, they use the intelligent K-Means [3] variant of K-Means that normally performs better. This starts with a heuristic initialisation for the K-Means algorithm using anomalous clusters (clusters of entities far from the centre of gravity of the entire dataset), where the algorithm iteratively finds each of these clusters and uses their means and the number of clusters as the parameters for K-Means. They were able to cluster the data collected from 17,000 websites with Capture-HPC in less than 2 min using intelligent K-Means.

Chapter 19, *Dynamic Monitoring of Composed Services* by Asim, Zhou, Llewellyn-Jones, Shi and Merabti, discusses monitoring issues in Service-Oriented Architecture (SOA). The composed services are highly dynamic and liable to change significantly at runtime, justifying the shift to monitoring throughout the lifetime of their execution, as traditional validation and verification techniques cannot predict many changes. The authors' develop security policies using BPMN (Business Process Modelling Notation) [4], and check that executing services comply with the policies and any violations are dealt with appropriately. Monitoring information can be combined from multiple services in order to automate complete business processes. Users can develop their own security policies based on business requirements, such as for loan processing or travel bookings, giving traceability of service execution to business workflow processes. The future work will focus on the process of transforming policies into monitoring patterns, as currently the patterns are translated manually into the policy language.

Chapter 20, *Where has this Hard Disk been?: Extracting Geospatial Intelligence from Digital Storage Systems* by Lallie and Griffiths, examines the diverse sources of geospatial data in computational devices, and discusses suitable methods for data extraction, analysis and visualisation to provide useful intelligence insights. The data take a number of forms in applications and operating system files, each of which requires particular types of processing to extract the geospatial data and resolve it into geographical coordinates. A feature-matching algorithm is applied to the input data such as an address, postcode, GPS coordinates or IP addresses, and the resulting outputs are correlated with coordinates in a geospatial reference dataset allowing the locations to be plotted on maps. Problems are caused by the large quantities of data and the diverse nature of data captured from numerous sources, causing difficulties in extracting the geospatial coordinates, resolving ambiguities such as names of locations and lack of data precision. The authors illustrate the use of geospatial data as an important source of intelligence in police investigations for discovering criminal organisation, communication, incidence and trends.

References

1. Russell S, Peter Norvig. Artificial intelligence: a modern approach. 3rd ed. Englewood Cliffs: Prentice Hall; 2009.
2. Tukey JW. Exploratory data analysis. Pearson. 1st ed. Boston: Addison-Wesley; 1977.
3. Mirkin B. Clustering: a data recovery approach. 2nd ed. Boca Raton: Chapman and Hall/CRC Press; 2012.
4. Object Management Group. Business Process Model and Notation. Object Management Group. http://www.bpmn.org. Accessed 14 Nov 2013.

Chapter 17
An Overview of Artificial Intelligence Based Pattern Matching in a Security and Digital Forensic Context

Faye Rona Mitchell

Abstract Many real world security and digital forensics tasks involve the analysis of large amounts of data and the need to be able to classify parts of that data into sets that are not well or even easily defined. Rule based systems can work well and efficiently for simple scenarios where the security or forensics incident can be well specified. However, such systems do not cope as well where there is uncertainty, where the IT system under consideration is complex or where there is significant and rapid change in the methods of attack or compromise. Artificial Intelligence (AI) is an area of computer science that has concentrated on pattern recognition and in this extended abstract we highlighted some of the main themes in AI and their appropriateness for use in a security and digital forensics context.

1 Introduction

In [1] we outline, from an academic and practitioner perspective, three of the main challenges in digital forensics

1. the exponential growth in storage capacity, in single drives (hard drives, USB sticks, optical media, ...)
2. the growth in distributed systems and the sophisticated forms of attack that can now be launched
3. the degree of technical sophistication employed by opponents and the apparent inability of existing tools and methodologies to keep pace [2].

F. R. Mitchell (✉)
Department of Computing and Communication Technologies, Oxford Brookes University, Wheatley Campus, Wheatley, Oxford OX33 1HX, UK
e-mail: frmitchell@brookes.ac.uk

C. Blackwell and H. Zhu (eds.), *Cyberpatterns*, DOI: 10.1007/978-3-319-04447-7_17,
© Springer International Publishing Switzerland 2014

In [3] we add a fourth challenge

4. the ubiquity of electronic storage and the range and prevalence of disparate storage systems.

Although these challenges were originally specified with respect to digital forensics, they are also important challenges to be dealt with in the cyber security arena.

From a practical point of view however, these challenges all involve the requirement to deal with large amounts of rapidly changing information in a timely fashion. For cyber security, timely will normally mean in close to real time response as is possible. In digital forensics, there is not this requirement for real time (although the time taken must be bounded), but the amount of potential data to be investigated is significantly larger.

2 Artificial Intelligence

For the sake of this paper, we will use a pragmatic definition of AI as "*a computer process or set of processes that acts in a manner that an ordinary person would deem intelligent*". Furthermore, we will limit our discussion to the areas of AI that have direct relevance to cyber security and digital forensics and in particular, we will focus on techniques that perform some aspect of pattern matching. We will not consider techniques such as robotics (as they have limited application to cyber security and digital forensics) nor we will consider techniques such as expert systems (which although technically classifiers are limited in their pattern matching scope).

2.1 Knowledge Representation

Knowledge representation is a key part of any AI system and is the means by which we represent both the knowledge and the reasoning about that knowledge. It also forms a key part in attack patterns, as there needs to be a representation language for the concepts used in the patterns. From a cyber security perspective an ideal knowledge representation language has the properties of being inferential (you can reason using it), flexible & comprehensive (sometimes known as a language's representational adequacy), extensible, usable (normally this relates to how easy it is for humans to interpret) and community support.

The inferential property is simply a matter of making sure that the language is consistent and supports some sort of inference engine, and as such is not difficult to achieve. Similarly, the usability property is normally a function of how close the language is to a conventional spoken language (yet still avoiding ambiguity), and is also not unique to the cyber security domain and is achievable. Flexibility, comprehensiveness and extensibility are normally addressed by using a lower level knowledge representation language which has those properties (e.g. XML or Ontolingua [4]).

Perhaps the hardest property to address is the most pragmatic of all, a languages support by the community that it is designed for. It is a well-known catch 22 situation that until a representation language receives buy in from the community it is aimed at it will not have sufficient support in the associated community and the tools they use for it to achieve its desired functionality.

There does exist some specific knowledge representations for cyber security [5] and digital forensics [6] and there are standard knowledge representations for specific technologies (e.g. Cisco ACLs, IP chains rulesets). However, these do not at present satisfy the requirements for an ideal knowledge representation language. [5] perhaps comes the closest in that it satisfies the inferential, flexible, comprehensive and extensible properties however it is debatable whether or not it satisfies the usability concept because of its complexity and that it shows no evidence of being supported widely by the community. Paradoxically the representations that do have community support tend to be niche languages like IP chains that cannot be said to satisfy many of the other ideal properties.

Fenz and Ekelhart [5] however does have the feature that it can be transformed into generic OWL [7] ontology[1] and this could help in starting to provide the foundations of a domain ontology.

A domain ontology would provide standard definitions of common concepts in an extensible format, which could then be used to generate a knowledge representation language that meets our ideal language requirements. In particular, if it was widely supported by the community and the tools used in the community it would greatly facilitate the sharing of knowledge between tools and resources. It would also facilitate the creation of a well described collection of test cases with known behaviours which could be used to test cyber security tools and techniques in a similar manner to what the UCI ML Repository [8] does for Machine Learning.

In digital forensics, there is recognition that such work to provide a domain ontology is required, but little has been undertaken so far. In cyber security, this is not yet seen by many as a problem. However, without addressing it, many of the modelling or reasoning techniques that cyber security would benefit from can only be at best partially successful.

2.2 Pattern Recognition Techniques

Pattern recognition techniques are classifiers that allow the efficient description and recognition of sets of data that are of interest to the user, based on a description or statement of a certain pattern. Key features of most pattern-recognition techniques are the notions of *generalisation* and *specificity*. Suitable patterns must be specific

---

[1] OWL is a web markup language for creating *ontologies*. The term *ontology* is used to mean a shared vocabulary and taxonomy that can be used to describe the concepts and relationships in a given domain. The main difference between an ontology and a knowledge representation is that an ontology is designed to be shared, whereas a knowledge representation language is not.

enough to match all known cases of the set, and nothing that is not in the set, but also general enough to recognise previously unseen examples of the set.

2.2.1 Machine Learning

The problem with naive pattern matching techniques is in the creation of the description of the patterns—often we can say X is an example of Y, but not be able to produce a suitable description that meets our generalisation and specificity requirements. (A good example is can be found in whiskey distillation where a master distiller can blend the different casks together to produce a fine whiskey but not be able to tell you why a particular set of casks should be combined.) Machine Learning (ML) is one of the branches of AI that tries to *learn* the classifications of interesting sets. ML techniques are generally thought of with respect to two dimensions—their representation format (symbolic or subsymbolic) and the amount of pre-classification needed (supervised or unsupervised learners).

Supervised Learners Supervised Learning is the name given to the ML techniques (such as decision tree generators or Artificial Neural Nets) where the information is pre-classified into the relevant sets before learning occurs. This is useful when we have examples of the sets, but are unsure of how to describe the sets. This is perhaps the most appropriate form of ML for cyber security and digital forensics as it can provide accurate descriptions of the attacks that we seen on our systems, and even with subsymbolic learners (see next page) can give reasonable explainability. However, it is not as good at adapting to previously unknown situations.

Unsupervised Learners Unsupervised learners (such as conceptual clusterers) are used when we do not know, or are unwilling to classify the available data into sets. This is particularly relevant when we are dealing with the large amount of data that is available when we are monitoring or investigating large systems. In general, the results given by unsupervised learners are not as accurate as those given by supervised learners for known issues, but they can perform much better on previously unseen issues.

Symbolic Learner Symbolic learners (such as Learning Apprentice Systems or decision tree generators) are ML techniques where the classifications gained by the learner are in a form that is relatively understandable by a human being and where distinct classification attributions can be critiqued and modified easily. Symbolic learners are therefore most useful when the results of a classification and/or action have to be explained to a human being. This is particularly of relevance in digital forensic investigations.

Symbolic learners are also much easier to tie into existing systems, both in terms of the knowledge-based systems but also more conventional security systems such as firewalls. For this reason, symbolic learners, particularly supervised symbolic learners can provide a useful first step in adding intelligence into cyber security systems and could provide a mechanism for automatically generating cyber attack/defence patterns.

Subsymbolic Learner Subsymbolic learners (such as Artificial Neural Networks or Hopfield Nets) are ML techniques where the classifications gained are in form of a weighted graph or other such notation that is not easily comprehended by a human. These learners lack the explainability of their symbolic counterparts, but are often faster in use (although not to learn) and provide better generalisation characteristics.

Subsymbolic learners are also very good at learning in unsupervised situations where the initial classification of the training examples is unknown, approximate or difficult to produce. However, this coupled with the lack of explainability can lead to the subsymbolic learner learning a different concept from the one the user thought the system was learning.[2]

This means that although they are suitable for use in defending against unknown attacks they are less likely to be used to play a significant part of a system's defence simply because humans do not normally trust systems where the reasoning cannot be explained. It is possible to combine both symbolic and subsymbolic systems (such as is found in First Order Neural Networks) to help alleviate this problem [9], but the generalisability of the system suffers as a result.

Despite a reluctance to use subsymbolic learners in many situations because of their unpredictability, their ability to handle unseen situations can make them worth consideration in the cyber security domain. Because they can be used to effectively recognise a normal baseline state and to detect previously unseen abnormal behaviour they can act as an alert system to flag possible attacks, even if they do not respond to them directly themselves. This flag, along with a subsymbolic learner generated summarisation of the abnormal behaviour can be passed directly on to a human being for action or as input to a more predictable symbolic learner that can act on the information.

Another interesting feature of subsymbolic learners that is of interest in a cyber security context is that they can often be used as an autoassociative and a bidirectional associative memory.[3] An autoassociative memory is particularly useful in detecting distributed attacks as it allows the possibility of recognising the nature of the attack from just a small component. A bidirectional associative memory enhances a subsymbolic learner's ability to detect the same attack in a completely different context. Together these can provide the ability to detect a wide range of attacks; however, both of these approaches suffer from the fact that they have no guarantees of recalling an existing memory that would be useful in cyber defence.

---

[2] This is best illustrated in a (possibly apocryphal) story about the US military who tried to train an ANN to recognise tanks hiding in trees. To this end they took pictures of forests with no tanks, pictures of forests with tanks and showed them to the ANN. Unfortunately the pictures without tanks were taken on a cloudy day and the pictures with tanks were taken on a sunny day so the ANN learnt how to tell if it was sunny or not. Because an ANN has no explainability power this fact was not found out until much later in the testing process.

[3] An *autoassociative memory* is a memory system that can retrieve an entire data set based on just a small part of that data. A *bidirectional associative memory* is a memory system that can retrieve a related but different dataset.

2.2.2 Knowledge Discovery

Knowledge Discovery (KD) is the use of ML, probabilistic and statistical analysis techniques to discover classifications and relationships in extremely large (normally sparse) data sets. It can be viewed as a form of pattern recognition and the ML techniques discussed in Sect. 2.2.1 form part of KD but the emphasis is on techniques that are not knowledge intensive and are efficient enough to perform, as these are tractable on large data sets (normally GB to PB in size).

Unfortunately, in any large collection of data there are going to be an extremely large collection of patterns and relationships, the vast majority of which are going to be of no use to the user. Therefore, a feature of KD is the use of an interestingness metric, normally referred to as a J measure. This is a mechanism by which we can control the amount and type of classifications that we generate and limit them to ones that are potentially useful to us. The advantage of this is that we can greatly speed up both the learning of classifications and the detection by limiting ourselves to only that which is relevant. The problem is one of specifying a correct J measure and this is normally done on a per domain instance although there are standard methodologies to help generate it.

KD systems are normally highly interactive and time consuming to run. This obviously rules out their use in many cyber security situations; however, they are good at examining historical data in detail and using that to find rules, relationships and classifications that can be used in a real time cyber security system. They can also be used to find attacks that might otherwise be below the noise threshold for more conventional ML techniques, in one instance detecting patterns that had previously been considered too small to be worth detecting [10].

2.3 Exploratory Data Analysis

Exploratory Data Analysis (EDA) is the combination of a suitable knowledge representation or ontology, a pattern recognition system and Data Visualisation (DV) so that a human can explore and understand the data under investigation. EDA is often seen as the poor man's alternative to ML or KD as it requires human input. However, in cyber security it is often perceived to be desirable to leave the final decision on the action taken to the human and to present the relevant information in such a way as facilitates that decision. This can also be thought of as a relatively easy way to add AI into a system as the computer can be given more mathematical and logical tasks and the bulk of the more complex reasoning can be offloaded to the human. (This also has the advantage that the human is more likely to accept the final results, as they trust their own judgement.)

A better use of EDA is to use the EDA to guide the discovery or learning process in KD and ML. This requires the ability to display high dimensionality data in a form the user can understand and process. Fortunately as [11] illustrates, the human perceptual system is able to process data with high dimensionality, in some case, if the data is presented properly, up to 25 simultaneous dimensions. When coupled with the human's pre-attentive focusing ability,[4] this allows EDA systems to rapidly and accurately process large amounts of data.

2.4 Knowledge Refinement

Unfortunately, the patterns in any pattern recognition system can and will become outdated. In particular, changes in the behaviour of a system's users can quickly result in pattern recognition systems generating many false negatives. One approach is to simply do the learning again and replace the existing patterns with the new learnt patterns. While this may be feasible for small cyber security scenarios, the effort involved in most cases renders it infeasible.

A better approach is to "patch" our knowledgebase of patterns. Unfortunately, manually patching such a complex knowledgebase is very error prone and automatically patching can be unpredictable and result in refining a knowledgebase to allow through previously blocked attacks.

One solution to this is to use a technique developed in the early days of Knowledge Refinement, that of a chestnut case [12], which is essential a test case which must succeed after the refinements have been made. This allows us to ensure that even after refining the knowledgebase, the main cyber security issues will still be detected.

3 Conclusion

AI techniques are very good at helping us find patterns in our data and as such have great potential for helping to solve cyber security and digital forensics issues. The difficulty is in selecting the appropriate tool for this domain and in this paper we have highlighted the main relevant approaches and commented on their appropriateness for the different aspects of cyber security and digital forensics.

This is by no means an exhaustive summary and there are many other possible AI techniques that might be applied to the domains of cyber security and digital forensics that we have insufficient space to discuss here (for instance, Support Vector Machines might be used to reduce the dimensionality of the problem, agent based systems could be used to better utilize distributed resources and to help defend against distributed attacks in large complex systems, conceptual clustering could be used to help identify important areas in the evidence under investigation and so on). Instead, we have tried to concentrate on the more basic and common AI techniques that could possibly, in

---

[4] Pre-attentive focusing is the name given to a human's ability to see patterns in apparently random data. The disadvantage of this is that humans can spot patterns when no pattern really exists.

one form or another, be used in the near future in the cyber security and digital forensics arena, and to give a brief insight into the strengths and weaknesses of such techniques and to indicate where they might be used.

References

1. Duce D, Mitchell F, Turner P. Digital forensics: challenges and opportunities. In: 2nd conference on advances in computer security and forensics (ACSF)', LJMU, Liverpool; 2007.
2. NIST: Computer forensics tool testing project. Available: http://www.cftt.nist.gov/ (2010). Accessed 10 Sept 2013.
3. Mitchell F. The use of artificial intelligence in digital forensics: an introduction. Digit. Evid. Electron. Sign. Law Rev. 2010;7:35–41.
4. Stanford University: Ontolingua. Available: http://www.ksl.stanford.edu/software/ontolingua/ (2008). Accessed 10 Sept 2013.
5. Fenz S, Ekelhart A. Formalizing information security knowledge. In: ACM symposium on information, computer and communication security (ASIACCS 2009). Sydney: Australia; 2009.
6. Turner P. Unification of digital evidence from disparate sources (digital evidence bags). Digit. Inv. 2005;2:223–8.
7. W3C: OWL web ontology language—overview. Available: http://www.w3.org/TR/owl-features/ (2012). Accessed 10 Sept 2013.
8. Frank A, Asuncion A. UCI machine learning repository. Available: http://archive.ics.uci.edu/ml (2010/2012). Accessed 10 Sept 2013.
9. d'Avila Garcez AS, Broda K, Gabbay DM. Symbolic knowledge extraction from trained neural networks: a sound approach. Artif. Intell. 2001;125:155–207.
10. Linari A. Abuse detection programme at nominet. In: 17th CENTR technical workshop, Amsterdam, The Netherlands, 2007.
11. Friedman R. Data visualization: modern approaches. Available: http://www.smashingmagazine.com/2007/08/02/data-visualization-modern-approaches/ (2007/2012). Accessed 10 Sept 2013.
12. Craw SM, Sleeman D. Automating the refinement of knowledge-based systems. In: Proceedings of the ninth european conference on artificial intelligence, 1990.

Chapter 18
Partitional Clustering of Malware Using K-Means

Renato Cordeiro de Amorim and Peter Komisarczuk

Abstract This paper describes a novel method aiming to cluster datasets containing malware behavioural data. Our method transform the data into an standardised data matrix that can be used in any clustering algorithm, finds the number of clusters in the data set and includes an optional visualization step for high-dimensional data using principal component analysis. Our clustering method deals well with categorical data, and it is able to cluster the behavioural data of 17,000 websites, acquired with Capture-HPC, in less than 2 min.

1 Introduction

Malware is a term, popular even among non-IT professionals, used to describe software designed to perform undesirable actions. There are a number of such actions, including: to gain unauthorised access to computing devices (PCs, laptops, mobiles, etc.), exfiltrate sensitive data, or simply disrupt the normal operation of computing devices.

Large amounts of malware are discovered daily, this number was already approaching 10,000 in 2010 [1]. Most importantly, there seems to be no reason to believe this number will decrease, particularly now with so much functionality, and private data, in new mobile devices. Such quantity of malware coupled with the possibility of financial gain have created a rather wide variety of attack/deployment strategies, giving birth to names such as viruses, worms, spyware, adware, etc.

R. C. de Amorim (✉)
Department of Computing, Glyndŵr University, Mold Road, Wrexham LL11 2AW, UK
e-mail: r.amorim@glyndwr.ac.uk

P. Komisarczuk
School of Computing Technology, University of West London, St Mary's Road, London W5 5RF, UK
e-mail: peter.komisarczuk@uwl.ac.uk

C. Blackwell and H. Zhu (eds.), *Cyberpatterns*, DOI: 10.1007/978-3-319-04447-7_18,   223
© Springer International Publishing Switzerland 2014

Malware has created a whole new industry focused in software tools for its development, deployment, detection and removal. Capture-HPC [2] is a high-interaction honeypot client that pays particular attention to the detection of malware. Honeypot clients work by monitoring the state of an unprotected network client normally using kernel call-back mechanisms. They look for changes in the file system, registry, network activity and so on, filtering out common state changes through an exclusion list. When a state change is detected, suggesting a possible malware activity, Capture-HPC updates a log file containing comprehensive information regarding the state change. This log file includes a list of files and registry keys changed, as well as launched processes and attempted tcp connections that may have happened.

The nature of Capture-HPC makes sure there are no false negatives, except when Capture-HPC itself is corrupted. In order to increase the detection rate of Capture-HPC for our experiments, we have given it the additional capability of emulating the presence of ActiveX components. This way any given malware will always detect as installed any ActiveX component it is trying to exploit.

We believe that organising malware into homogeneous clusters may be helpful to generate a faster response to new threats, and better understanding of malware activities. However, the large amount of malware released daily limits the algorithms that can be used in the real-world for this purpose. Algorithms with exponential time complexity are unlikely to be feasible. Clearly, one can generate different malware clusters by taking different points of view, such as the malware binaries or its behaviour. We have opted for the latter and Capture-HPC has proved to be an excellent tool to gather behavioural data of malware [3–5], being able to detect a high amount of different malware related activities.

The idea of homogeneity in a cluster is directly linked to similarity, and by consequence to a distance measure. The squared Euclidean metric is the most popular distance used in clustering algorithms, However, it does have its limitations. For instance, this distance is not the most appropriate when an entity is defined over a high number of features. In our scenario, the entities are the websites are defined over a rather large amount of possible activities a malware may initiate on an unprotected client. Such scenarios define a high-dimensional space and these can be difficult to organise due to the so called curse of dimensionality [6].

In this paper we present a fast method for malware clustering. Our method generates a data matrix from the behavioural data of malware gathered with Capture-HPC, standardise this data matrix and find the number of clusters in a dataset by using intelligent K-Means [7]. We show that the number of clusters obtained by our method is correct by ratify this number by analysing the Hartigan index [8], and perform visual analysis of the clusters by using the two first principal components of the data matrix.

Any method applied to a dataset based on the presence or absence of a particular malware activity presents difficulties. Such dataset would contain solely categorical data which can be difficult to analyse. Nevertheless, our method transforms these categorical features in numerical and clusters clusters 17,000 websites in less than 2 min.

2 Background and Related Work

Cova et al. [3] empirically showed that most cases Capture-HPC could not detect
a malware, it was because the malware was targeting a plugin not present in the
system. Without the presence of the targeted plugin the malware simply does not
make any state change in the unprotected client being monitored. Taking this into
account we have updated Capture-HPC to emulate the presence of any requested
ActiveX component by using AxMock.[1]

The organisation of malware could follow a supervised, semisupervised or unsupervised learning approach. Algorithms under the supervised learning framework
normally require a considerable amount of labelled samples for the algorithm to
learn from. It is not uncommon in the evaluation of such algorithms to use 10-fold
cross-validation, which means that 90 % of the data is used in the learning process.
Algorithms under the semi-supervised learning framework require a considerably
smaller amount of labelled samples, at times as low as 5 % of the data. Algorithms
under the unsupervised learning framework do not require any labelled sample stat-
ing that a particular behaviour should belong to a particular group. Such algorithms
are data-driven and attempt to learn the patterns in a dataset using solely the data
itself and a distance measure.

Although supervised and arguably semisupervised algorithms tend to have better
accuracy than unsupervised, their requirement of labelled data can be difficult to
meet in certain scenarios. Labelling a statistically significant, and diverse, amount
of data would require an impractical effort because of the high quantity of malware
being released everyday. Another issue is that this labelled data would have to be
highly accurate, otherwise the algorithm could learn incorrect patterns and classify
malware under the wrong groups. These facts made us opt for unsupervised learning.

In general, clustering algorithms can be divided into hierarchical and partitional.
The former, in its more popular agglomerative form, begins by setting each entity
in a dataset as a cluster, also called a singleton. It then merges such clusters, two at
a time, generating a tree-like structure that can be visualised through a dendogram.
A given entity then may belong to different clusters at different levels of the tree.
The time complexity of hierarchical algorithms is normally of $\mathcal{O}(n^3)$, but may reach
$\mathcal{O}(n^2)$ in some particular cases, for a dataset with n entities. Partitional algorithms
generate a single set of labels for the entities. The time complexity of K-Means [9,
10], the most popular partitional algorithm, is of $\mathcal{O}(nKt)$, where K is the number
of clusters and t the number of iterations the algorithm takes to converge. Although
t is unknown at the beginning of the clustering, we have shown that this tends to be
small [11]. In both cases the granularity of the clustering is defined by the number
of clusters in the dataset.

The use of clustering algorithms in datasets related to malware was introduced,
to the authors knowledge, by Bailey et al. [12] using, as most of the literature,

---

[1] Our new version of Capture-HPC will be available soon at https://projects.honeynet.org/capture-
hpc. AxMock can be downloaded at http://code.google.com/p/axmock/

hierarchical clustering. Because of the large amount of data and the so called zero-day attacks, we consider the time complexity of the clustering algorithm used to be crucial and have chosen to use partitional clustering in this research.

K-Means is arguably the most popular clustering algorithm there is. Assuming a dataset Y of n entities $y_i \in Y$ over features $V = \{v_1, v_2, \ldots, v_{|V|}\}$, in which the value of a particular feature, representing a malware behaviour at a particular website is given by y_{iv}, K-Means assigns each entity $y_i \in Y$, into K clusters around centroids $C = \{c_1, c_2, \ldots, c_K\}$ producing the clustering $S = \{S_1, S_2, \ldots, S_K\}$.

1. Assign values to K centroids $c_1, c_2, \ldots, c_K$, normally K random entities; $S \leftarrow \{\}$.
2. Assign each entity y_i in the dataset to its closest centroid c_k, generating the clustering $S' = \{S'_1, S'_2, \ldots, S'_K\}$.
3. Update all centroids to the centre of their respective clusters.
4. If $S \neq S'$ then $S \leftarrow S'$ and go to step 2.
5. Output the clustering $S = \{S_1, S_2, \ldots, S_K\}$ and centroids $C = \{c_1, c_2, \ldots, c_K\}$.

The above algorithm iteratively minimises the sum of the squared error over K clusters, we show the K-Means criterion in Eq. (1).

$$W(S, C) = \sum_{k=1}^{K} \sum_{i \in S_k} d(y_i, c_k), \tag{1}$$

where $d(y_i, c_k)$ is a function calculating the distance between the entity $y_i \in S_k$ and the centroid c_k. K-Means is a rather successful algorithm, its popularity is mainly due to its easy implementation, simplicity, efficiency, and empirical success [13]. One can easily find implementation of K-Means in popular data analysis software packages such as R, MATLAB and SPSS.

Due to its constant use, K-Means weaknesses are well known, among them: (i) it is a greedy algorithm. There is no guarantee its criterion will reach a global minima, meaning that the final clustering may not be optimal. Although there have been attempts to deal with this issue, most notably the classical solution of swapping entities between clusters given by Hartigan and Wong [14]. To reach global minima in (1) is a very difficult problem, particularly because the minimisation of (1) is a NP-Hard problem, we will leave this for future research; (ii) it requires the number of clusters to be known beforehand; (iii) the final clustering depends highly on the initial centroids given to the algorithm, these are normally found at random.

In a number of scenarios, including ours, the exact number of clusters K may not be known. The literature of malware clustering tends to use hierarchical clustering algorithms [12, 15, 16] seemingly because it is possible to run such algorithm without knowing K. However it can be difficult to interpret results when no granularity is set via K, possibly generating clusters with no significance, or a taxonomy where the number of taxons is still not known. Another issue is that hierarchical algorithms are known not to scale well. For instance, it may take 3 h to cluster 75,000 [15] while our method clusters 17,000 in less than 2 min (see Sect. 4). This time discrepancy is easily explained by comparing the time complexities of hierarchical algorithms with that of K-Means. We find that there is a considerable amount of research effort in attempting to find K that could be used in malware datasets [7, 8, 17–19].

Regarding the weakness (iii), K-Means is a non-deterministic algorithm. It may provide different clusterings if run more than once, this characteristic raises the question of which clustering to use. A common solution is to run K-Means a number of times, generating a number of clusterings, and pick the clustering S^* which is the closest to the K-Means data model. S^* will be the clustering with the smallest $W(S, C)$ given by the K-Means criterion, Eq. (1). This approach does seem to work in a number of scenarios, but it can be very lengthy when dealing with high amounts of data.

In order to deal with weaknesses (ii) and (iii) at once, we have decided to use Intelligent K-Means (iK-Means) [7] due to its considerable success in different scenarios [11, 17, 20–22]. The iK-Means algorithm provides an heuristic initialization for K-Means based on the concept of anomalous clusters. An anomalous cluster is a cluster of entities that are far from the centre of gravity of the dataset. The iK-Means algorithm iteratively finds each of these anomalous clusters and uses their centroids and number of clusters as the parameters for K-Means. This is a deterministic algorithm, which means there is no need to run it more than once. The algorithm is formalised below.

1. Assign a value to the parameter θ; set c_c as the centre of gravity of the dataset Y; $C_t \leftarrow \{\}$.
2. Set a tentative centroid c_t as the entity farthest away from c_c.
3. Apply K-Means using two centroids, c_t and c_c generating the clustering $S = \{S_t, S_c\}$, without allowing c_c to move.
4. If the cardinality of $S_t \geq \theta$ then $C_t \leftarrow c_t$, otherwise discard c_t. In any case, remove S_t from the dataset.
5. If there are still entities to be clustered go to step 2.
6. Run K-Means with the centroids in C_t and $K = |C_t|$.

To demonstrate the method works with malware data we have chosen to ratify the number of clusters it finds with visual inspection and the Hartigan index [8] mainly because of its easy of use and popularity. This index is based on the error W, the output of Eq. (1).

$$H(K) = (N - K - 1)(\frac{W_K - W_{K+1}}{W_{K+1}}) \qquad (2)$$

This index requires K-Means to be run with different values for K and may take time. We find intuitive that the centroids found by iK-Means can be used here making K-Means a deterministic algorithm. Visibly W is inversely proportional to K, the more clusters the less variance within them, the index is based on abnormal variances in $H(K)$.

Unfortunately, any real-world dataset containing malware behavioural data is very likely to be large in terms of both websites, given by n, and features, given by $|V|$, being clearly high-dimensional. The curse of dimensionality, a term coined by Bellman [6] states that as the number of dimensions increases so does the sparseness of data making entities to appear dissimilar, a very problematic fact for distance-based algorithms such as K-Means, as well as hierarchical clustering algorithms. This is further supported by research suggesting that the concept of nearest neighbours calculated using Euclidean distance becomes meaningless as the dimensionality of the data increases [23–25].

In order to cluster malware we need a method that supports high-dimensional spaces. There are different solutions with different degrees of success that can address this problem. For instance, one could perform feature selection removing then the dimensions of Y that are less informative. Of course this raises other problems, how to measure the degree of information in each feature? how to deal with features that are highly informative only when taken in a group? how to define a threshold used to define what features are less informative? A different, and perhaps easier solution for this particular problem would be to select an appropriate distance measure for K-Means. Although the literature tends to use the Euclidean distance this is not the most appropriate in high-dimensional spaces. Empirical experiments [26, 27] show that distances such as the cosine are more appropriated than the Euclidean distance. The cosine distance for the V-dimensional x and y is defined as:

$$d(x, y) = 1 - \frac{\sum_{v \in V} x_v . y_v}{\sum_{v \in V} (x_v)^2 . \sum_{v \in V} (y_v)^2} \tag{3}$$

A somewhat easier way to apply the cosine distance, is to perform an extra step in the pre-processing of data by dividing each row vector $y_i \in Y$ representing a website by the vector's norm $\sqrt{\sum_{v=1}^{V} y_{iv}^2}$ [23, 28, 29]. We find this particularly helpful to calculate the centroid of each cluster.

As final consideration for this section, a clustering algorithm regardless of being partitional or hierarchical, will not yield that a given cluster is composed of malware. Clustering algorithms simply find that two or more clusters are dissimilar according to a given distance measure and cannot state what they are actually composed of. In order to define what malware family a cluster contains one would need the analysis of a field expert. Clearly this expert would not need to analyse the whole cluster but solely the malware that is the closest to the cluster centroid.

3 Method

In order to apply any clustering method we need to create and standardise a data matrix representing the whole dataset Y. In this data matrix each instance of $Y = \{y_1, y_2, \ldots, y_n\}$ represents a website and each column $v = \{1, 2, \ldots, M\}$ a feature. In our method y_{iv} represents the presence or absence of a particular maware behaviour v, a features, in the website y_i. If the behaviour is present $y_{iv} = 1$, or $y_{iv} = 0$ otherwise.

The first step of our method is to apply Capture-HPC on each website, recording its activities in a log file. The amount of time used for recording stays as a parameter, but we suggest it should not be less than a minute as some websites may take time to load. The full list of activities these websites performed on an unsecured network client becomes our initial list of features.

The second step is to filter the list of features. Although Capture-HPC uses a exclusion list to filter out expected state changes, it records data such as time and process ID generating groups of features that represent in fact the same malware activity. We disregard any part of the log file that is not directly linked to the activities, but to management, such as timestamps, process IDs, paths to files and IP numbers in tcp-connections. This filtering ensures each feature is unique in terms of what states the malware is changing, effectively reducing the number of features.

The third step is to create the data matrix, by assigning a value to each y_{iv}, and standardise it. When creating the entry y_i in the data matrix we read the log file for this particular website and search for of the M features we have listed. If a feature v is found to be in the log file then y_{iv} is set to 1, otherwise 0. Each value in our data matrix is categorical, making its standardization less obvious. We have opted to use a method presented by Mirkin [7]. In this each feature is transformed into two new features (since we have only two possible categories given by the presence and absence of v in y_i). Only one of the new features is assigned 1, the new feature corresponding to the category in the original feature, the other is assigned 0. We then standardise the data numerically by subtracting each of the values y_{iv} by the new feature average $\bar{y}_v$ over each entity in Y, linking the final value of y_{iv} to the frequency of v in Y.

In the forth step we apply the intelligent K-Means algorithm with $\theta = 1$. We then sort the clusters in descending order by the number of websites found in each of them, in the anomalous cluster part of iK-Means. We choose the number of clusters by analysing when the cardinality of clusters stabilizes in a relatively small value.

Optionally, one can also ratify the number of clusters by using for instance the Hartigan index and the less reliable visual inspection. The former analyses the differences of the K-Means criterion shown in Eq.(1) under different values for K. Regarding visual inspection, we have chosen to plot the whole dataset over its two first principal components. Because the data is categorical in nature the clusters structure can be rather difficult to see. One may wish to add a small mount of uniformly random noise to help the visualization of cluster cardinalities.

4 Experiments

We acquired a list with 17,000 possibly infected IP addresses.[2] In the first step of our method we applied Capture-HPC for 2.5 min to each of these websites, generating a total of 133,327 features. By using our second step we were able to reduce the number of features to 231, making each feature truly representative.

---

[2] 3,273 from http://www.malwaredomainlist.com/update.php plus 13,763 from http://www.malware.com.br/lists.shtml

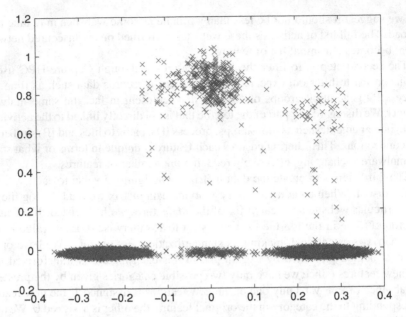

Fig. 1 A Dataset containing the behavioural data of 17,000 possibly infected websites over its two first principal components

We then created the data matrix of initially 17,000 websites over 231 by checking the logs of each website against the features we found. We finalised the data matrix by standardising it using Mirkin's method, effectively doubling the number of features.

In the next step we applied intelligent K-Means with $\theta = 1$, finding a total of 15 cluster with more than 1 entity each. We then sorted the clusters by the number of entities found in the anomalous part of the algorithm and found the cardinalities $8,439, 7,851, 381, 129, 121$ and very small numbers after these, suggesting the dataset had five clusters.

The popular Hartigan index helped us to ratify five as the number of clusters. After the 5th cluster the error given by Eq. (1) ceased to be significant. Although less reliable, we also found five clusters in this dataset by analysing visually the two first components of the dataset, extracted by using principal component analysis (PCA). The image can be seen in Fig. 1, to which we had to add random noise between 0 and 0.25 to increase clarity. It seems to us that Fig. 1 presents two clusters at the top, the one at the right being a bit more elongated, and three at the bottom, totally five clusters.

5 Conclusion

By using our method we were able to cluster a dataset of 17,000 malwares in less than 2 min. This was a particularly interesting dataset to work for three reasons: (i) the features were solely categorical; (ii) the cardinality of the clusters was uneven and (iii) it was a high-dimensional data matrix. Because of these three reasons the ordinary K-Means algorithm would constantly fail to cluster the dataset, generating empty clusters.

We solved the above issues by standardizing the data by transforming each feature into two new features allowing us to standardise them numerically through their frequencies in the dataset. We have also used the intelligent K-Means method to find the number of clusters in the dataset as well as the initial centroids for each of them. Finally, the issue of high-dimensionality was dealt by using the cosine distance rather than the more popular squared Euclidean distance.

This research assumes that the features obtained with Capture-HPC are all relevant. This sounds realistic since Capture-HPC uses an exclusion list for expected state changes, not leaving any reason why a client should suffer a change in state while not being used. Of course relevant features may have different degrees of importance for clustering particularly at different clusters. We intend to further developed a previous method used to find features weights called intelligent Minkowski K-means [20] so we can apply it to the clustering of malware.

Acknowledgments The authors would like to thanks Tiffany Youzhi Bao for her instrumental work developing AxMock ultimately allowing us to upgrade Capture-HPC to mock ActiveX components.

References

1. Lau B, Svajcer V. Measuring virtual machine detection in malware using DSD tracer. J Comput Virol. 2010;6(3):181–95. doi:10.1007/s11416-008-0096-y.
2. Capture-hpc. https://projects.honeynet.org/capture-hpc. Accessed Aug 2011
3. Cova M, Kruegel C, Vigna G. Detection and analysis of drive-by-download attacks and malicious javascript code. In: Proceedings of the 19th international conference on world wide web. Raleigh: ACM; 2010. p. 281–90. doi:10.1145/1772690.1772720.
4. Seifert C, Delwadia V, Komisarczuk P, Stirling D, Welch I. Measurement study on malicious web servers in the. nz domain. In: Boyd C, Nieto JC, editors. Information security and privacy. New York: Lecture Notes in Computer Science; 2009. p. 8–25. doi:10.1007/978-3-642-02620-1_2.
5. Seifert C, Komisarczuk P, Welch I. True positive cost curve: a cost-based evaluation method for high-interaction client honeypots. In: Third international conference on emerging security information, systems and technologies (SECURWARE'09). Athens: IEEE; 2009. p. 63–9. doi:10.1109/SECURWARE.2009.17.
6. Bellman R. Dynamic programming and lagrange multipliers. Proc Nat Acad Sci USA. 1956;42(10):767–9. doi:10.1090/S0025-5718-1959-0107376-8.
7. Mirkin BG. Clustering for data mining: a data recovery approach, vol. 3. Boca Raton: Chapman and Hall/CRC; 2005.
8. Hartigan JA. Willey series in probability and mathematical statistics. New York: Wiley; 1975.
9. Ball GH, Hall DJ. A clustering technique for summarizing multivariate data. Behav Sci. 1967;12(2):153–5. doi:10.1002/bs.3830120210.
10. MacQueen, J. Some methods for classification and analysis of multivariate observations. In: Proceedings of the fifth Berkeley symposium on mathematical statistics and probability, vol. 1. Bekerley. University of California Press; 1967. p. 281–97.
11. de Amorim RC. An empirical evaluation of different initializations on the number of K-means iterations. In: Batyrshin I, Mendoza MG, editors. Advances in artificial intelligence, vol. 7629.

New York: Springer, Lecture Notes in Computer Science; 2013. p. 15–26. doi:10.1007/978-3-642-37807-2_2.

12. Bailey M, Oberheide J, Andersen J, Mao Z, Jahanian F, Nazario J. Automated classification and analysis of internet malware. In: Kruegel C, Lippmann L, Andrew C, editors. Recent advances in intrusion detection. New York: Lecture Notes in Computer Science; 2007. p. 178–97. doi:10.1007/978-3-540-74320-0_10.

13. Jain AK. Data clustering: 50 years beyond K-means. Pattern Recogn Lett. 2010;31(8):651–66. doi:10.1016/j.patrec.2009.09.011.

14. Hartigan JA, Wong MA. Algorithm as 136: a K-means clustering algorithm. J Roy Stat Soc: Ser C (Appl Stat). 1979;28(1):100–8. doi:10.2307/2346830.

15. Bayer U, Comparetti P, Hlauschek C, Kruegel C, Kirda E. Scalable, behavior-based malware clustering. In: Proceedings of the 16th annual network and distributed system security symposium (NDSS). San Diego: Internet Society; 2009.

16. Yen TF, Reiter M. Traffic aggregation for malware detection. In: Zamboni D, editor. Detection of intrusions and malware, and vulnerability assessment. New York: Springer, Lecture Notes in Computer Science; 2008. p. 207–27. doi:10.1007/978-3-540-70542-0_11.

17. Chiang MMT, Mirkin B. Intelligent choice of the number of clusters in K-means clustering: an experimental study with different cluster spreads. J Classif. 2010;27(1):3–40. doi:10.1007/s00357-010-9049-5.

18. Kaufman L, Rousseeuw PJ, et al. Finding groups in data: an introduction to cluster analysis. Wiley series in probability and statistics, vol. 39. New Jersey: Wiley Online Library; 1990. doi:10.1002/9780470316801.

19. Pelleg D, Moore A. X-means: extending K-means with efficient estimation of the number of clusters. In: Proceedings of the seventeenth international conference on machine learning. San Francisco: Stanford; 2000. p. 727–34.

20. de Amorim RC, Mirkin B. Minkowski metric, feature weighting and anomalous cluster initializing in K-means clustering. Pattern Recogn. 2012;45(3):1061–175. doi:10.1016/j.patcog.2011.08.012.

21. de Amorim RC. Constrained clustering with minkowski weighted K-means. In: 13th international symposium on computational intelligence and informatics. Budapest: IEEE Press; 2012. p. 13–7. doi:10.1109/CINTI.2012.6496753.

22. Stanforth RW, Kolossov E, Mirkin B. A measure of domain of applicability for qsar modelling based on intelligent K-means clustering. QSAR Comb Sci. 2007;26(7):837–44. doi:10.1002/qsar.200630086.

23. France SL, Douglas CJ, Xiong H. Distance metrics for high dimensional nearest neighborhood recovery: compression and normalization. Inf Sci. 2012;184(1):92–110. doi:10.1016/j.ins.2011.07.048.

24. Aggarwal CC, Hinneburg A, Keim DA. On the surprising behavior of distance metrics in high dimensional space. In: Bussche JVD, Vianu V, editors. Database theory, vol. 1973. New York: Springer, Lecture Notes in Computer Science; 2001. p. 420–34. doi:10.1007/3-540-44503-X_27.

25. Beyer K, Goldstein J, Ramakrishnan R, Shaft U. When is nearest neighbor meaningful? vol. 1540. New York: Springer, Lecture Notes in Computer Science; 1999. p. 217–35. doi:10.1007/3-540-49257-7_15.

26. France S, Carroll D. Is the distance compression effect overstated? some theory and experimentation. In: Perner P, editor. Machine learning and data mining in pattern recognition, vol. 5632. New York: Springer, Lecture Notes in Computer Science; 2009. p. 280–94. doi:10.1007/978-3-642-03070-3_21.

27. Strehl A, Ghosh J, Mooney R. Impact of similarity measures on web-page clustering. In: Proceedings of the 17th national conference on artificial intelligence: workshop of artificial intelligence for web search. Austin 2000; p. 58–64.

28. Qian G, Sural S, Gu Y, Pramanik S. Similarity between euclidean and cosine angle distance for nearest neighbor queries. In: Proceedings of the 2004 ACM symposium on applied computing. Nicosia: ACM; 2004. p. 1232–7. doi:10.1145/967900.968151.
29. Zhao Y, Karypis G. Empirical and theoretical comparisons of selected criterion functions for document clustering. Mach Learn. 2004;55(3):311–31. doi:10.1023/B:MACH.0000027785. 44527.d6.

Chapter 19
Dynamic Monitoring of Composed Services

**Muhammad Asim, Bo Zhou, David Llewellyn-Jones, Qi Shi
and Madjid Merabti**

Abstract Service-Oriented Architectures (SOAs) are becoming a dominant paradigm for the integration of heterogeneous systems. However, SOA-based applications are highly dynamic and liable to change significantly at runtime. This justifies the need for monitoring composed services throughout the lifetime of the service execution. In this chapter we present a novel approach to monitor services at runtime and to ensure that services behave as they have promised. Services are defined as BPMN (Business Process Modelling Notation) processes which can then be monitored during execution.

1 Introduction

Modern software architectures are increasingly dynamic in nature. Among them, Service-Oriented Architectures are one of the most prominent paradigms. SOAs allow software components from different providers to be exported as services for

The research leading to these results has received funding from the European Union Seventh Framework Programme (FP7/2007-2013) under grant no 257930 (Aniketos)

M. Asim (✉) · B. Zhou · D. Llewellyn-Jones · Q. Shi · M. Merabti
School of Computing and Mathematical Sciences, Liverpool John Moores University,
Byrom Street, Liverpool L3 3AF, UK
e-mail: M.Asim@ljmu.ac.uk

B. Zhou
e-mail: B.Zhou@ljmu.ac.uk

D. Llewellyn-Jones
e-mail: D.Llewellyn-Jones@ljmu.ac.uk

Q. Shi
e-mail: Q.Shi@ljmu.ac.uk

M. Merabti
e-mail: M.Merabti@ljmu.ac.uk

C. Blackwell and H. Zhu (eds.), *Cyberpatterns*, DOI: 10.1007/978-3-319-04447-7_19,   235
© Springer International Publishing Switzerland 2014

external use. Service descriptions (both functional and non-functional properties) are published by service providers and are used by the potential users to discover services. A service composer is a service provider that is responsible for constructing service compositions and offering them to consumers. Service discovery is based on matching user requirements and security needs with the published service descriptions. Typically, service composers will have different needs and different requirements. They have varying business goals and different expectations from a service, for example in terms of functionality, quality of service and security needs. Given this, it's important to ensure that a service should deliver what it promises and should match the user's expectations. If it fails, the system should take appropriate subsequent reactions, e.g. notifications to the service invoker or service composer. However, SOA-based applications are highly dynamic and liable to change heavily at runtime. These applications are made out of services that are deployed and run independently, and may change unpredictably after deployment. Thus, changes may occur to services after deployment and at runtime, which may lead to a situation where services fail to deliver what has been promised. Traditional validation and verification techniques cannot foresee all of these changes as they are mainly pre-deployment activities. Therefore, there is a need to shift towards runtime monitoring of services [1].

Aniketos is an EU research project [2] that addresses trustworthy and secure service compositions with run-time monitoring and adaptation of services. The adaptation is needed due to changing operational, business or threat environments or due to changes in service quality and behaviour. Among the challenges is to monitor the services at runtime to ensure that services behave as promised. This chapter focuses on our proposed novel monitoring framework that is based on the runtime monitoring of a service to ensure that the service behaves in compliance with a pre-defined security policy. We mainly concentrate on monitoring service behaviour throughout the service execution lifetime to ensure that services behave as promised. The monitoring mechanism is based on the Activiti platform [3] and services are defined as BPMN [4] processes.

BPMN is widely used as a modelling notation for business processes. Before BPMN 2.0, analysts or developers used to receive a BPMN 1.x model for requirements or documentations but then they had to convert those models into an execution language such as Business Process Execution Language for Web Services (BPEL4WS, also known as BPEL) [5] for implantation. This might result into ambiguities and unexpected results. But, now we have BPMN 2.0 as a standard for both modelling business processes and implementing a process execution model. Both business oriented people and developers can speak with the same vocabulary and to share business models without the need of any conversion. Activiti on the other hand is an open-source light-weight workflow engine and Business Process Management (BPM) platform written in Java and helps business people, developers and system admins to execute various business process based on BPMN 2.0 specification.

Current monitoring methods applied to service execution environments focus on generating alerts for a specific set of pre-built event-types. However, the dynamic nature of SOAs also extends to the end-user security requirements. An ideal system might allow different users to be given the opportunity to apply their own security policies enforced through a combination of design-time and run-time checks. This might be the case even where multiple users are accessing the same services simultaneously. Current monitoring techniques [6–9] have not been set up with this flexibility in mind and in the work presented here we aim to address this by combining the flexibility of Complex Event Processing (CEP) [10] with the accuracy of a monitoring system that links directly in to the service execution environment. The result is a policy-driven framework that allows different user-specified policies to be monitored simultaneously at run-time.

The rest of the chapter is organized as follows. The next section presents an analysis of existing techniques. Section 3 describes the event model we propose for the monitoring framework. A monitoring approach is proposed in Sect. 4. Section 5 concludes the chapter and indicates the direction of our future work.

2 Related Work

As part of the work undertaken for the Aniketos project, we carried out a study on existing techniques relevant to the runtime monitoring of Service-Oriented systems. The result reveals that research in this area is still in its infancy and mainly conducted using xml based service composition languages, i.e. [6, 8, 9]. They do not consider the graphical representation of the business processes. This could introduce a semantic gap between the way of describing business process and the way implementing them with service composition.

The work presented by Baresi et al. [6, 7] is based on how to monitor dynamic service compositions with respect to contracts expressed via assertions on services. Dynamic service compositions are presented as BPEL processes which can be monitored at runtime to check whether individual services comply with their contracts. Assertions are specified with a special-purpose specification language called WSCoL (Web Service Constraint Language), for specifying constraints (monitoring rules) on service execution. The monitoring rules are then deployed with the process through a weaving procedure. The weaving introduces a proxy service, called monitoring manager; which is responsible for evaluating monitoring rules. If some constraints are not met, the monitoring manager will inform the BPEL process about the enforcement. In [8], authors proposed a solution to the problem of monitoring web services instances implemented in BPEL. The solution used a monitoring Broker to access web service runtime state information and calculates the QoS (Quality of service) property values. The Monitoring Broker is devised with the support of Aspect-oriented programming (AOP) that separates the business logic of web service from its monitoring functionality. In [9], an event-based monitoring approach for service composition infrastructure has been proposed. The framework intercept each message as an event of a particular type and leverages complex event processing technology to define and detect situations of interest.

While there are therefore a number of related techniques, we believe our framework introduces additional flexibility by using CEP techniques and is novel in its ability to monitor both atomic and composite services. It does not require assertions to define what needs to be monitored using a proprietary language. Our framework performs compliance monitoring by using a non-intrusive AOP mechanism and has direct access to the service execution environment. The service execution environment (Activiti engine) is extended to generate events for the services that are required to be monitored.

3 Event Model

The monitoring framework we propose is built around the concept of events. It is an event-driven approach that allows the monitoring system to analyze events and react to certain situations as they occur. Since the proposed monitoring approach is based on events generated by services, we use Complex Event Processing (CEP) techniques in order to identify situations leading to contract violation. Any viable monitoring system must have the capability to analyze and identify the correct events in a timely manner. In addition to providing more flexibility and scalability than batch approaches, CEP also allows analysis to be performed sufficiently fast for run-time monitoring.

Figure 1 displays a simplified version of our proposed event model. This organizes the different event types allowing us to reason about and provide a generic way to deal with them.

The Activiti engine provides an extension on top of the BPMN 2.0 specification allowing Execution Listeners to be defined. These listeners can be configured at the Process level, Activity level or Transition level in order to generate events.

Our event model is based on two types of process variables; Base Variables and Domain Specific Variables. Both types of variable are available during the execution of a business process and could be used for monitoring. The listeners have access to these process variables and can create events populated using their associated values, sending them to the CEP engine for analysis. The Base Variables inherit common attributes from the process itself e.g. the process ID, process name, activity ID, activity name, process start time etc. For example, to monitor the execution time of a particular service composition (described as a BPMN process), both process start and end events could be used along with the common variables: event start time and event end time. However, the Domain Specific Variables are user defined and may build upon the Base Variables. For example, to analyze the load on a particular service, we could accumulate all start process events for that service over the last hour. An alert message should be generated if the number of requests is more than a threshold value in the last hour. This threshold value is a user define attribute falling within the Domain Specific Variables.

In the following discussion, we try to determine the structure of events that should be received by the CEP engine for analysis. In our proposed framework, an overall process could represent a composite service and an Activity could represent a service component. Figure 2 shows events for a BPMN process executed in a specific order.

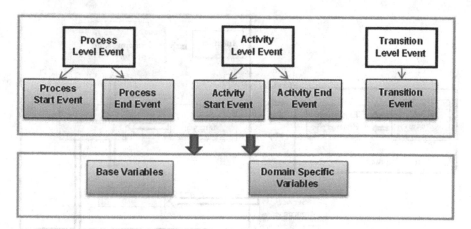

Fig. 1 Event model

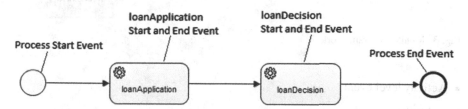

Fig. 2 Events flow

In this example, a loan business process is comprised of *loan application service task* and *loan decision service tasks*. Therefore, it is not possible to define a single structure for monitoring the overall process. For example, to monitor an Activity, we cannot wait for the whole process to complete. The monitoring of an Activity may need only the process ID, Activity start and end events.

In our proposal, an event structure describes the data and structure associated with an event. It helps in organizing the data that is required for monitoring. Below we define the event structure for our proposed monitoring framework.

- Process level event

  – Attributes
     processName
     eventLevel (processLevelEvent)
     eventName (Start or End)
     eventTime (Timestamp)
     Variable 0...n—domain specific variables

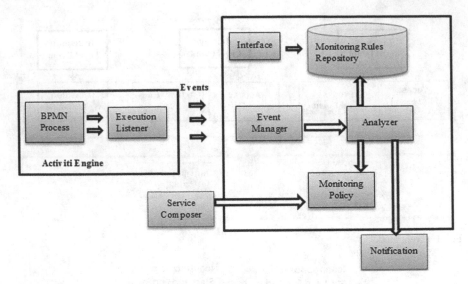

Fig. 3 Monitoring framework

- Activity level event
  - Attributes
    processName
    activityName (name of the Service or User Task)
    eventLevel (activityLevelEvent)
    eventType (Service Task or User Task)
    eventName (Start or End)
    eventTime (Timestamp)
    Variable $0\ldots n$—domain specific variables
    eventDate (e.g. 2013/04/05)
    eventTime (e.g. 1365158859238).

4 The Monitoring Framework

The general architecture of the monitoring framework that we use to monitor the
BPMN processes introduced in this paper is shown in Fig. 3. The Activiti engine
with the help of execution listeners throws events for the deployed BPMN process.
The framework consists of an analyzer that accepts a set of security requirements
(monitoring policy) for a particular process to be monitored. The monitoring policy
is defined by the service composer. The analyzer then recovers the monitoring patterns that are related to the requirements from the monitoring pattern repository and
checks whether the received events are consistent with the patterns and if it is not

Table 1 An overview of event types that can be configured in BPMN using listeners

BPMN construct	Event type	Description
Process	Start and end	A start and end event of a process instance can be captured with a process execution listener
Activity	Start and end	A start and end execution listener of an activity can be implemented
Transition	Take	A transition execution listener can catch a take transition event
User task	Create, assignment and complete	A user task throws events when the task assignment has been performed and when the user task has been completed

then it reports a violation through the notification module. The monitoring policy is defined using the language ConSpec [11]. However, the step for translating the CoSpec monitoring policy into monitoring patterns has not been implemented yet. The monitoring patterns are defined manually through the Drools Guvnor interface [12]. The components of the monitoring framework are shown in Fig. 3. The details of the monitoring unit are as follows.

Event Manager: This module gathers the events coming from the Activiti engine and passes them to the Analyzer. In Table 1 an overview is provided of the event types that can be configured in a BPMN 2.0 xml definition using the Activiti execution and Task listener extensions.

Monitoring policy: A set of requirements that specify what to monitor for a particular BPMN process. We suggest the language ConSpec to specify the monitoring policy. A policy written in ConSpec is easily understandable by humans and the simplicity of the language allows a comparatively simple semantics. This will enable the service composer to easily specify the monitoring requirements for their processes and monitor them using this framework. The Service Composition Framework (SCF) [13] (shown in Fig. 4) is a module available in the Aniketos project allowing service designers to build executable composition plans and specify their monitoring policy using the ConSpec editor shown in Fig. 5.

Consider the following example where a service composer creates a travel booking composition that consist of several tasks, such as ordering, booking hotel, booking flight, payment and invoice, and each task is performed by a component service. The service composer of the travel booking composition might want that the payment service component should only be invoked when it has a trustworthiness value $\geq 90\,\%$. This requirement could easily be specified using the language Conspec as shown below.

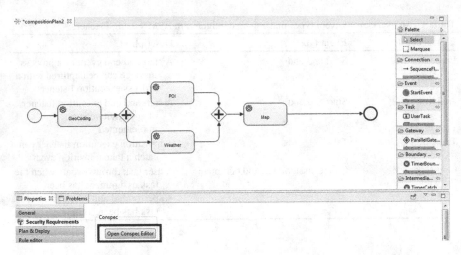

Fig. 4 Service composition framework

```
SCOPE method

SECURITY STATE
    Int trust_threshold=90%;
    /* assume trustworthiness is in [0%,..., 100%]*/

BEFORE invoke (service_A, args)
PERFORM
    (eval_Trustworthiness(service_A) >= trust_threshold)->
skip
```

In the ConSpec language, the state declaration section defines auxiliary variables that characterize the internal state of the automaton defined by the policy. Variables can be of Boolean, integer or string type. A modifier is one of the keywords BEFORE, AFTER, EXCEPTIONAL that identifies at which moment the action must be intercepted. As a requirement we have that there exists at least one statement in each update block (at least the command skip). In this way we consider both cases: in the case the value of a local variable is not changed (i.e. there is no state change) then the statement skip is used; on the contrary, if the statement is different from skip, the variable's value is updated.

Monitoring Pattern repository: Holds definitions for monitoring patterns, which are predefined. A monitoring pattern needs two pieces of information to be able to complete the requested verification: a monitoring ID and the data which will be used for verification. An example for a monitoring pattern might specify to continuously monitor the trustworthiness of the services and generate notification as soon as the trustworthiness value falls below a threshold value. These patterns are defined with the help of Drools expert [14]. Drools fusion [10] could also be used for monitoring events that requires a Complex Event Processing (CEP) environment. Consider the

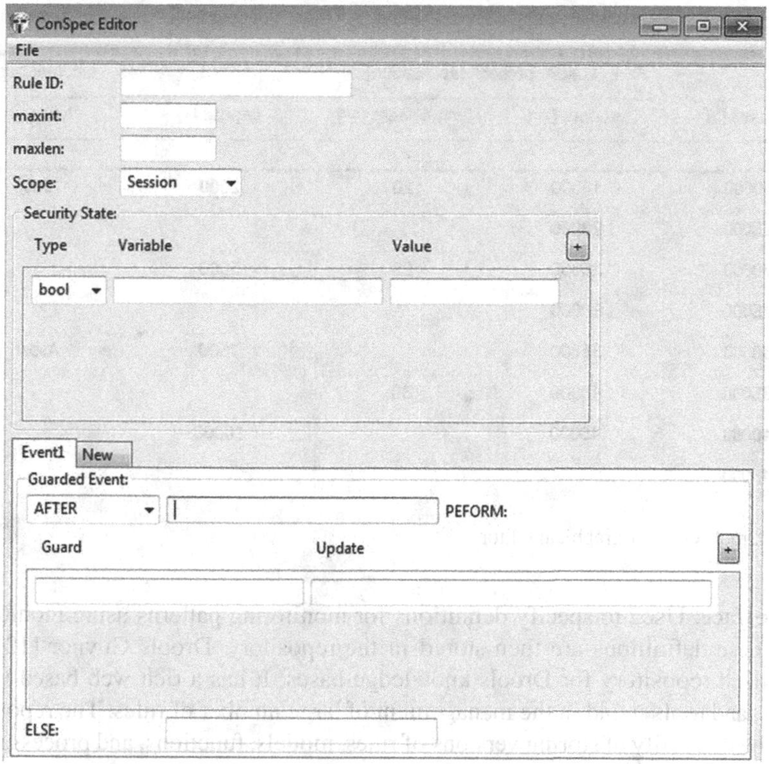

Fig. 5 ConSpec editor

example of travel booking process where a service composer put a requirement in the monitoring policy that the payment service component should only be invoked when it has a trustworthiness value ≥ 90 %. However, the trustworthiness of the payment service can be deteriorated during the execution. Therefore, it is necessary to continuously monitor the payment service and check its trustworthiness before it is used for processing any payment. The following drools rule evaluates the trustworthiness and can be used for the payment service.

```
rule "check trustworthiness"
@ruleID("4")
when
# condition such as - when trustworthiness > threshold
(90%)
then
#actions such as - access granted
```

Analyzer: Upon receiving events from the Event Manager, it analyses them by accessing patterns from the repository. It uses the monitoring policy to select the appropriate monitoring patterns for a particular process.

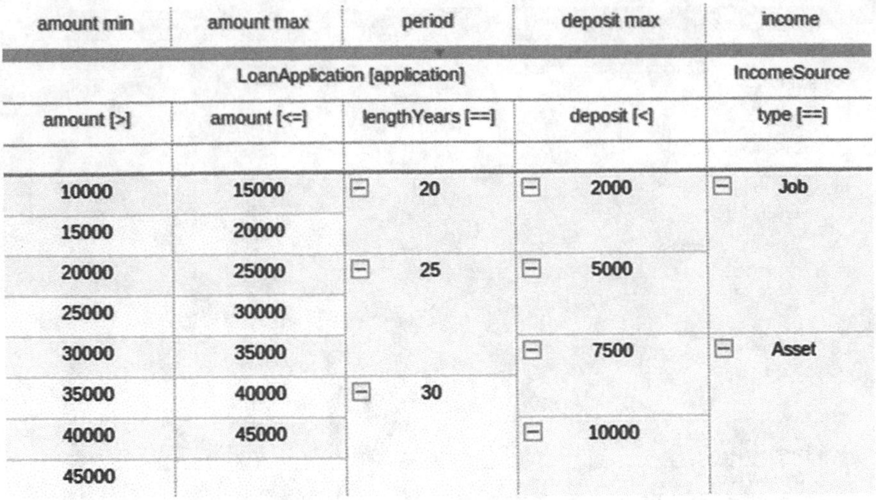

amount min	amount max	period		deposit max		income	
	LoanApplication [application]					IncomeSource	
amount [>]	amount [<=]	lengthYears [==]		deposit [<]		type [==]	
10000	15000	⊟	20	⊟	2000	⊟	Job
15000	20000						
20000	25000	⊟	25	⊟	5000		
25000	30000						
30000	35000			⊟	7500	⊟	Asset
35000	40000	⊟	30				
40000	45000			⊟	10000		
45000							

Fig. 6 Drools Guvnor graphical editor

Interface: Used to specify definitions for monitoring patterns using monitoring IDs. These definitions are then stored in the repository. Drools Guvnor [12] is a centralized repository for Drools knowledge bases. It has a rich web based GUIs, editors, and tools to aid in the management of large number of rules. The repository gives the flexibility of storing versions of rules, models, functions, and processes etc. (Fig. 6).

Notification Module: It is mainly used by the Analyzer to report any violations. The Notification Module [13] is implemented as a cloud service in the project Aniketos and is based on publish-subscribe paradigm that notifies the entities subscribed about contract violation.

5 Conclusion and Future Work

In this paper we presented our monitoring framework that applies both event filtering and event correlation in order to ensure that the service behaves in compliance with a pre-defined security policy. The monitoring framework is based on the Activiti platform to deploy BPMN services and generate events throughout the service execution lifetime. The platform supports a rich collection of events and attributes that apply at the level of services within a service composition. The events are monitored to ensure that a service behave in compliance with a pre-defined monitoring policy. A user friendly interface is provided for specifying monitoring policies as ConSpec rules. ConSpec is a simple and easily understandable language for specifying service contracts. The novelty of our work is based on the way monitoring information can be combined from multiple dynamic services in order to automate the monitoring of business processes and proactively report compliance violations.

Our future work will focus on the process of transforming ConSpec policies into monitoring patterns. Currently, monitoring patterns are defined manually through the Drools Guvnor interface. We would also like to evaluate our proposed framework for some real life scenarios.

References

1. Ghezzi C, Guinea S. Run-time monitoring in service oriented architectures. In: Baresi L, Nitto D, editors. Test and analysis of web services, Berlin: Springer; 2007, p. 237–64.
2. Aniketos (Secure and Trustworthy Composite Services), Available: http://www.aniketos.eu. Accessed 5 May 2012.
3. Activiti, Activiti BPM Platform, Available: http://www.activiti.org/. Accessed 5 May 2012.
4. Business Process Model And Notation (BPMN) Specification, Version 2.0, January 2011, Available: http://www.omg.org/spec/BPMN/2.0/. Accessed 5 May 2012.
5. OASIS, Web services business process execution language version 2.0, April 2007, Available: http://docs.oasis-open.org/wsbpel/2.0/wsbpel-v2.0.pdf. Accessed 5 May 2012.
6. Baresi L, Guinea S, Nano O, Spanoudakis G. Comprehensive monitoring of BPEL processes. IEEE Internet Comput. 2010;14(3):50–7.
7. Baresi L, Ghezzi C, Guinea S. Smart monitors for composed services. In: Proceedings of the 2nd international conference on service oriented computing. (ICSOC 2004), New York, USA; 2004. p. 193–202.
8. Haiteng Z, Zhiqing S, Hong Z. Runtime monitoring web services implemented in BPEL. In: International conference on uncertainty reasoning and knowledge engineering (URKE), Bạli, Indonesia, vol. 1; 2011. p. 228–31.
9. Moser O, Rosenberg F, Dustdar S. Event driven monitoring for service composition infrastructures. In: Proceedings of the 11th international conference on web information system engineering (WISE'10), 12–14 Dec 2010, Hong Kong, China; 2010.
10. Drools, Drools Fusion: Complex Event Processor, Available: http://www.jboss.org/drools/drools-fusion.html. Accessed 6 May 2012.
11. Aktug I, Naliuka K, ConSpec: a formal language for policy specification. In: Run time enforcement for mobile and distributed systems (REM 2007). Electonic notes in, theoretical computer science, vol. 197–1; 2007. p. 45–58.
12. Drools, Drools Guvnor, Available: http://www.jboss.org/drools/drools-guvnor. Accessed 6 May 2012.
13. Aniketos Consortium, Deliverable D5.2: Initial Aniketos Platform Integration, 2012, http://www.aniketos.eu/content/deliverables. Accessed 6 May 2012.
14. Drools, Drools Expert, Available: http://www.jboss.org/drools/drools-expert.html. Accessed 6 May 2012.

Chapter 20
Where has this Hard Disk Been?: Extracting Geospatial Intelligence from Digital Storage Systems

Harjinder Singh Lallie and Nathan Griffiths

Abstract Digital storage systems (DSS) contain an abundance of geospatial data which can be extracted and analysed to provide useful and complex intelligence insights. This data takes a number of forms such as data within text files, configuration databases and in operating system generated files—each of which require particular forms of processing. This paper investigates the breadth of geospatial data available on DSS, the issues and problems involved in extracting and analysing them and the intelligence insights that the visualisation of the data can provide. We describe a framework to extract a wide range of geospatial data from a DSS and resolve this data into geographic coordinates.

1 Introduction

Digital storage systems (DSS) contain an abundance of geospatial data (sometimes referred to as *geolocation data*). Geospatial data is any data that can identify a geographic location. This data is stored in a number of locations and formats in a digital storage system, such as EXIF-data (Exchangeable Image format) within images, the photographic images themselves if they can be resolved to particular locations and as zip-codes/postcodes within contact databases. Geospatial data can serve a number of benefits if processed and analysed correctly and can be useful to enterprises, marketing agencies, law enforcement agencies and the defence services.

Research has previously taken place into the value of geospatial data in other domains, for instance the value of geospatial digital intelligence in the business/marketing domain has been highlighted by Stanhope [1] who charts the

H. S. Lallie (✉)
Warwick Manufacturing Group (WMG), University of Warwick, Coventry CV4 7AL, UK
e-mail: h.s.lallie@warwick.ac.uk

N. Griffiths
Department of Computer Science, University of Warwick, Coventry CV4 7AL, UK
e-mail: Nathan.Griffiths@warwick.ac.uk

C. Blackwell and H. Zhu (eds.), *Cyberpatterns*, DOI: 10.1007/978-3-319-04447-7_20,   247
© Springer International Publishing Switzerland 2014

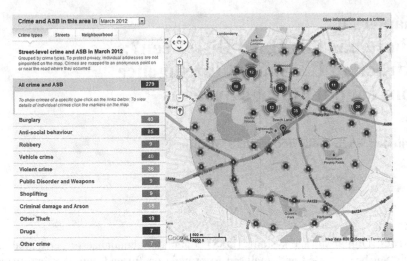

Fig. 1 Crime rate map for March 2012, B17 8AE

progression of web analytics from simple *web server log analytics*, through more formal *web analytics*, *digital analytics* through to *digital intelligence*. In this context companies are able to 'track' traffic and in particular the source of that traffic to create intelligence which assists in influencing business/marketing decisions and aiding 'know your customer' (KYC) solutions.

Geospatial data has proven valuable in medical research to identify cancer care and support needs and the way it links with socioeconomic, demographic and environmental factors and in particular the support needs within particular geographic areas [2–4]. Geospatial data generated by GPS (global positioning satellite) systems is used in a variety of applications including movement monitoring in sports [5, 6], monitoring movement of children [7], parcel/courier tracking [8], clock synchronisation [9], tracking sex offenders and bailed/paroled prisoners [10], in differentiated/mobility pricing to calculate insurance or road tax premiums [11–13] and perhaps most popularly in Satellite Navigation (SatNav) based systems [14].

In the area of law enforcement, geospatial data serves a useful purpose for Government for the analysis and publication of crime statistics [15], it is used by regional police forces to highlight crime rates in given postcode areas [16] (see Fig. 1) and is also used by American states for systems designed to publish addresses of sex offenders [17].

One area in which more research can be conducted is in analysing, extracting and processing a wider range of geospatial data from a DSS and in particular extracting knowledge of underlying social networks and digital intelligence of criminal homophily. This paper describes such a framework and explores the process involved in resolving this data into geographic coordinates which can be used in subsequent applications. We use the example of criminal homophily to demonstrate the value of such a system.

2 Geocoding

Geospatial data exists in one of two places on a DSS–as document data or application/configuration data.

Document data is textual references to places within user documents created in applications such as Word, Excel, Adobe Acrobat; in contact databases such as Microsoft outlook or data entered into online forms (stored as file fragments and cache). Within this category we also include photographic images which can be resolved to identify locations. The format of such data can be inconsistent, ambiguous and in many cases incorrect.

Application/Configuration data is data that has been input as part of the configuration process for an operating system, application or hardware to work, or which may be generated automatically by the operating system, an application or hardware such as a GPS receiver. Examples are: IP address information in particular applications and hardware, DNS data in web servers, email addresses, mail server details, cookies, cache generated by internet browsers and geo-tag data automatically stored in EXIF data in photographic images. An example of very precise geospatial data in this context is that generated by GPS systems in satellite navigation applications wherein precise coordinates are generated to demonstrate the receiver position and calculate the route. Application/Configuration data is structured to meet the standards of the application and is more easily resolved than document data.

Approaches towards geospatial data extraction from digital storage systems vary according to the location of the data on the storage system. Geospatial data may be located in specific, formally and precisely defined areas of files, such as records in databases or entries in operating system specific files (such as the registry in Microsoft Windows). An example is EXIF data, which can include geographic coordinates stored as metadata in images. This data represents precise geographical coordinates of the location where a photograph is taken. An example of this is shown in Fig. 2. Similarly, email client applications store mail server details, web browsing applications may store local DNS details and operating system specific configuration files and databases may store IP addresses and other geospatial data.

Before geospatial data can be used it has to be translated into coordinates, through a process known as *geocoding* that involves one or both of two stages: resolution and correlation. The process of geocoding is demonstrated in Fig. 3.

3 Resolving Geospatial Data

There are at least three instances where geospatial data needs to be resolved before it can be correlated. This is where the geospatial data is circumstantial/textual, is ambiguous or is a photographic image. In certain cases it may be necessary to resolve the data because of a combination of factors, for instance in the case of a photographic image which looks very similar to multiple locations or a misspelt location name

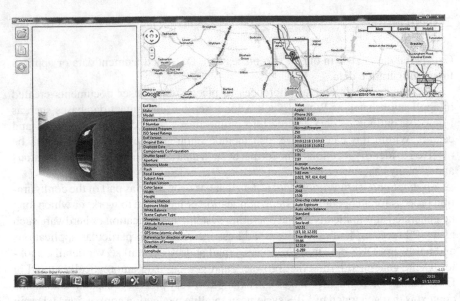

Fig. 2 Analysing GeoTags using TagView [18]

Fig. 3 Geocoding

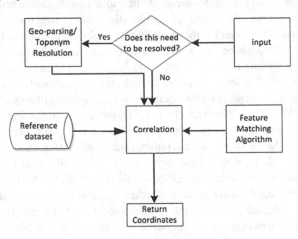

which first has to be 'corrected' before it can be resolved to one of a number of geographic existences of that place name.

- *Textual data.* Textual data has to be searched for the existence of geospatial data which then needs to be matched with a reference dataset of place names in order to establish that it is indeed a place name. This process of geo-parsing is well covered in the literature, and as far back as 1966 systems such as *GeoRef* were based on textual analysis and deployed to create geospatial systems for scientific use [19]. The growth of the internet further popularised research in this area. In 1994, Woodruff and Plaunt proposed *GIPSY*, a system which took parsed textual input to extract geographic terms and applied spatial reasoning and a degree of statistical analysis to arrive at a geo-position [20].

- *Toponym Resolution.* Occasionally a place name may be ambiguous because, for instance, it refers to more than one location that has the same name. As an example, Sheffield points to 28 geographic locations with most of them being in the USA [21]. In this case we must perform toponym resolution wherein through some contextual analysis we are able to better determine which instance of Sheffield the geospatial data refers to.

- *Photographic images.* Photographs may contain iconic landmarks which are in their own right geospatial data which can also be resolved automatically. This can be done through a process known as *scene matching* which was described by Hays and Efros and implemented in a system referred to as IM2GPS [22].

4 Correlation

The geocoding system receives input data such as an address, postcode or trilateration metrics (as in the case of GPS systems), applies a *feature/pattern matching* algorithm to this and correlates the input data with geographic coordinates present in a *geospatial reference dataset* (a gazetteer such as the US TIGER/Line Shapefiles [23]). The reference dataset contains data which allows for the coordinates to be plotted on a particular point of the map, i.e. it correlates the input with a point on the map.

In particular circumstances, multiple reference datasets may be used to increase the accuracy of the correlation process. However this also has contains the risk of introducing further ambiguities as the correlation process may present conflicting coordinates, in such a case, a *best* match can be calculated to return the most 'likely' or accurate set of coordinates [24].

Some of the features described herein are automated in online mapping systems such as Batchgeo, Google Maps, MapPostcode and Freemaptools [25–28] and the Geocoding system tends to be part of a larger system known as a *Geographic Information System (GIS)/Geographic Information Retrieval (GIR) System.*

The result of this process is either:

- A pair of specific longitude/latitude coordinates presented (for instance) to 8 decimal places which is accurate to within 1.11 mm of a physical geographic location, or
- Or a group of longitude/latitude coordinates which point to a range (such as a postcode) that may cover an area of a few hundred square meters.

We can see from this that the resulting coordinates may refer to a single point or a geographic range, and we refer to this as *geo-granularity*. The issue of geo-granularity is important and should not be confused with accuracy. A street name which produces a set of coordinates which point to the entire geographical range of that street, a business name which the application plots precisely to the business address or a set of longitude/latitude coordinates which are plotted precisely to that geographic coordinate are all accurate. However the plotted geographical *range* is different in each case. That said, there certainly are issues of accuracy and errors can be introduced during the process of geocoding. Methods of improving the accuracy of plotting have been proposed by Bakshi [29] and Goldberg and Cockburn [24].

Of the types of geospatial discussed herein, IP addresses present the greatest difficulty. Whilst IP addresses can provide a good indication of geospatial locality, they are also prone to a number of problems, for instance, IP addresses can be spoofed, they may point to the ISP instead of a user, they may be dynamically allocated and have other features which make it difficult to map more precisely. Further research needs to focus on how IP addresses can be used to provide more accurate geospatial locality. One method may be to use other contextual data to add value to the IP address.

5 The Value of Geospatial Analysis

The resulting data has applications in a number of fields, and we use the example of criminal homophily to demonstrate this. Geospatial data can be extracted from DSS to create what Bell refers to as a *forensic information pool* [30], which becomes an important source of intelligence in criminal investigation casework. The benefits that such a forensic information pool might present have not hitherto been explored. Some of the benefits may include:

- An analysis of geospatial data in the context of image hash datasets such as Child-base [31] to highlight geographic criminal trends and provide more efficient victim identification.
- If we treat geospatial data on a DSS as nodes, the geospatial data can be analysed to highlight social structures which show the density and intensity of communication between nodes, thus highlighting communication behaviour. This can in turn help to identify criminal homophily and further insights into geographic patterns in offending behaviour.
- Such systems have benefits outside of law enforcement as well. More detailed analysis of geospatial data can give better indications of consumer behaviour and habits.

Table 1 Range precision of geospatial data

Data type	Processing features
Geospatial data in images	Directly accessed from the appropriate field, high level of accuracy and requires no further processing
IP addresses	Must be interpolated back to the source in order to be used. May require further analysis before it can be used due to a potentially higher degree of ambiguity
Addresses in textual documents	Requires geo-parsing possibly followed by toponym resolution
Addresses in contacts databases	Directly accessible from appropriate fields in databases, may require geo-parsing possibly followed by toponym resolution
Telephone number prefixes in contact lists	Directly accessible from appropriate field. Needs to be interpolated to provide a geographic range. High level of geo-granularity
Routes calculated and/or followed by users of SatNav system	Often stored as coordinates so very precise, rarely requires further processing

6 Conclusions

Based on the discussions presented herein we can summarise the main elements of this paper in Table 1 which describes the range of geospatial data and the issues relating to processing the data therein. We can see that particular data types require a greater degree of processing

The resulting framework is illustrated in Fig. 3. An input (address, telephone number, IP address etc.) is analysed and considered for resolution. It may need to be resolved if it is ambiguous. The input (or resolved version thereof) is correlated against a reference dataset using a *feature matching algorithm*, which results in a set of coordinates. As an example, if the input data is a UK postcode, this may not need to be resolved and can proceed to the correlation phase. The reference dataset in this case may be a UK postcode gazetteer which would return a set of coordinates. However, a textual reference to a place name would first need to be identified as a place name followed by further resolution to a set of coordinates.

The main contribution of this paper has been the synthesis of a number of geospatial data translation methodologies into a single framework and the consideration of the complexities and issues in correlating the various geospatial data into a meaningful set of coordinates.

The next step of this research is to implement this framework into a system which can ultimately be designed as an application.

References

1. Stanhope DFJ, Dickson M. Welcome to the Era of digital intelligence. http://www.xplusone. com/uploads/case_studies/Welcome_To_The_Era_Of_Dig.pdf (2012).
2. Rushton G, Armstrong MP, Gittler J, Greene BR, Pavlik CE, West MM, Zimmerman DL. Geocoding in cancer research: a review. Am J Prev Med. 2006;30:S16–24.
3. Krieger N, Chen JT, Waterman PD, Soobader MJ, Subramanian S, Carson R. Geocoding and monitoring of us socioeconomic inequalities in mortality and cancer incidence: does the choice of area-based measure and geographic level matter? Am J Epidemiol. 2002;156:471–82.
4. Oliver MN, Smith E, Siadaty M, Hauck FR, Pickle LW. Spatial analysis of prostate cancer incidence and race in virginia, 1990–1999. Am J Prev Med. 2006;30:S67–76.
5. Coutts AJ, Duffield R. Validity and reliability of gps devices for measuring movement demands of team sports. J Sci Med Sport. 2010;13:133–5.
6. Ermes M, Parkka J, Mantyjarvi J, Korhonen I. Detection of daily activities and sports with wearable sensors in controlled and uncontrolled conditions. IEEE Trans Inf Technol Biomed. 2008;12:20–6.
7. AmberAlert. Locate via APP and computer: https://www.amberalertgps.com/ (2011). Accessed 7 Jul 2011.
8. Jung H, Lee K, Chun W. Integration of gis, gps, and optimization technologies for the effective control of parcel delivery service. Comput Industr Eng. 2006;51:154–62.
9. Sterzbach B. Gps-based clock synchronization in a mobile, distributed real-time system. Real-Time Syst. 1997;12:63–75.
10. Iqbal MU, Lim S. Legal and ethical implications of gps vulnerabilities. J Int Commercial Law Tech. 2008;3:178–87.
11. Link H, Polak J. How acceptable are transport pricing measures? empirical studies in nine European countries. In: AET european transport conference. Homerton College, Cambridge; 2001. p. 21.
12. Niskanen E, Nash C. Road pricing in europe–a review of research and practice. Road pricing, the economy and the environment. Berlin: Springer; 2008. p. 5–27.
13. Palma AD, Lindsey r. Traffic congestion pricing methodologies and technologies. Transp. Res. Part C: Emerg Technol. 2011;19:1377–99.
14. Strawn C. Expanding the potential for gps evidence acquisition. Small Scale Digit Device Forensics J. 2009;3:12.
15. Home Office: Recorded crime datasets. http://www.homeoffice.gov.uk/science-research/ research-statistics/crime/crime-statistics-internet/ (2012). Accessed 12 May 2012.
16. Police.uk. http://www.police.uk (2012). Accessed 12 May 2012.
17. Alaska Department of Public Safety: Sex offender/child kidnapper registration central registry. http://dps.alaska.gov/Sorweb/Search.aspx (2012). Acessed 12 May 2012.
18. Evigator Digital Forensics: TagExaminer. http://www.evigator.com/tag-examiner/ (2011). Accessed 28 Sep 2011.
19. American Geosciences Institute: About the GeoRef database. http://www.agiweb.org/georef/ about/index.html (2012). Accessed 16 May 2012.
20. Woodruff AG, Plaunt C. Gipsy: automated geographic indexing of text documents. J Am Soc Inf Sci. 1994;45:645–55.
21. Leidner JL. Toponym resolution in text:"which sheffield is it?". The workshop on Geographic Information Retrieval, SIGIR. Sheffield: ACM; 2004. p. 602.
22. Hays J, Efros AA. IM2GPS: estimating geographic information from a single image. In: IEEE conference on computer vision and pattern recognition (CVPR 2008), Anchorage, Alaska: Acm; 2008. p. 1–8.
23. United States Census Bureau: 2010 census TIGER/Line shapefiles. http://www.census.gov/ geo/www/tiger/tgrshp2010/tgrshp2010.html (2010). Accessed 11 May 2012.
24. Goldberg DW, Cockburn MG. Improving geocode accuracy with candidate selection criteria. Trans GIS. 2010;14:149–76.

25. Google: Google Maps. http://maps.google.com/ (2012). Accessed 11 May 2012.
26. FreeMaptools: Free Map Tools. http://www.freemaptools.com/ (2012). Accessed 11 May 2012.
27. Mappostcode: Mappostcode. http://mappostcode.com/ (2012). Accessed 11 May 2012.
28. BatchGeo LLC: BatchGeo. http://www.batchgeo.com/ (2012). Accessed 11 May 2012.
29. Bakshi R, Knoblock CA, Thakkar S. Exploiting online sources to accurately geocode addresses. In: 12th annual ACM international workshop on Geographic Information Systems, New York :Acm; 2004, pp. 194–203.
30. Bell C. Concepts and possibilities in forensic intelligence. Forensic Sci Int. 2006;162:38–43.
31. Walker D: Hi-tech tool against paedophiles unveiled. http://news.bbc.co.uk/1/hi/uk_politics/3091663.stm (2003). Accessed 10 May 2012.

Part VII
The Future

Chapter 21
Future Directions for Research on Cyberpatterns

Clive Blackwell and Hong Zhu

Abstract As patterns in cyberspace, cyberpatterns shed light on research on the development of cyber systems from a new angle. They can help us move from an improvised craft to an engineering discipline because they help to transfer knowledge about proven solutions in an understandable and reusable format. They allow innovative applications in cloud, cyber-physical and mobile systems, and novel methods of use with data patterns for observation and analysis of 'big data' problems. The ultimate aim of research on cyberpatterns is an overall framework for cyberpatterns integrating all the cyber domains to help develop a better-understood and effective cyberspace. However, there are many research questions in cyberpatterns that remain unanswered regarding both their conceptual foundation and practical use. This chapter concludes the book by exploring some of the most critical and important problems needing to be addressed.

Cyberpatterns are predictable regularities in cyberspace that may help us to understand, design, implement and operate successful and reliable cyber systems. In this chapter, we explore the possible future directions for research on cyberpatterns that we hope eventually leads to the development of a general framework. We group these research questions into two closely related sets of representation and engineering issues giving very brief summaries of the current state of the art.

C. Blackwell (✉) · H. Zhu
Department of Computing and Communication Technologies, Oxford Brookes University,
Wheatley Campus, Wheatley, Oxford OX33 1HX, UK
e-mail: cblackwell@brookes.ac.uk

H. Zhu
e-mail: hzhu@brookes.ac.uk

C. Blackwell and H. Zhu (eds.), *Cyberpatterns*, DOI: 10.1007/978-3-319-04447-7_21,   259
© Springer International Publishing Switzerland 2014

1 Representation Issues

Patterns are reusable knowledge about recurring phenomena in certain subject domains, including repeatable successful solutions to certain engineering problems. How to represent such knowledge is of critical importance for all aspects of a pattern-oriented methodology. The following are among the most important research questions associated with pattern representation.

1.1 Definition of the Semantics of Patterns

Ideally, the representation of patterns needs to package knowledge in a useful way to help both experienced and novice users alike. Moreover, it should also enable machine understanding and efficient processing. However, currently many patterns are inadequately documented with nature language, which are inevitably vague and incomplete. Thus, they typically lead to poorly implemented solutions and are hardly ever processed by computer. We need to design new pattern representation frameworks and languages to realise the full potential of cyberpatterns. A challenge in the design of pattern representation languages is that the real world phenomena and its digitalised presentation in the form of the data that a cyberpattern represents are often interpreted in the context of the environment and situation. Their semantics are not always clear, but heavily depend on human interpretation. Defining the semantics of patterns accurately enough for machine processing is a grave challenge.

1.2 Uniformity of Pattern Representation for All Sub-domains

In a complicated subject domain like cyberspace, there are a great number of patterns. In order to use them effectively, we must classify and categorise related patterns and understand their interactions within various cyberspace sub-domains as well as across sub-domain boundaries. Cyberpattern representation languages need to be expressive, extendable and flexible enough to apply to a range of potential problem contexts, but also needs standardisation, clarity and precision for knowledge acquisition and to aid automation. Another grave challenge in research on cyberpatterns is to meet these seemly conflicting requirements on pattern representation.

A good pattern representation language will allow effective and efficient investigation of the relationships and interactions between patterns so that they can be systematically classified, catalogued and organised for efficient retrieval and application through development of automated tools. An important research question is that, whilst patterns in different subject sub-domains demonstrate specific features of pattern interactions and relationships, is there a general framework or theory of pattern interaction applicable to all sub-domains and across the boundaries of sub-domains? Such a general framework or theory would help the development of tools for implementing patterns, detecting patterns in existing systems, and automated reasoning with patterns.

1.3 Integration of Different Pattern Representations

In the process of research in order to meet the above challenges, it seems most likely that different languages and frameworks will be proposed and advanced before a generally applicable framework or theory emerges. Different pattern knowledge bases will be, and in fact, some have already been, constructed by different vendors. If this does occur, the community will face another grave challenge, that is, how to investigate the relationships and interactions between patterns not only within one pattern representation language but also between different languages, not only within one pattern classification and cataloguing system but also across different systems.

2 Engineering Issues

Patterns help us move from an improvised craft to engineering discipline because they help to transfer knowledge about proven solutions in a comprehensible and reusable format. In order to advance such an engineering discipline, the following research problems must be addressed.

2.1 Validation, Verification and Testing Patterns

As a kind of knowledge representation, the correctness of patterns plays a critical role in their applicability. Validated cyberpatterns help to form a foundation for the study of cyberspace by encapsulating knowledge about the cyber world, analogous to scientific theories in the natural world. However, how to validate, verify and test the correctness of patterns is a grave challenge to research on cyberpatterns, on which little attention has been paid in the research community so far. We need to provide a solid theoretical foundation and to develop practical techniques to address these issues.

2.2 Pattern-Oriented Knowledge Bases

When patterns are formalised to give an adequate and unambiguous semantics, they can be stored and processed by computer systems for use as a knowledge base.

A question then arises how to organise such a knowledge base. In particular, what kind of relationships between patterns should be included in the knowledge base? For example, the most important relationships between design patterns are sub-pattern, uses, composition and alternative choice [1]. It is noteworthy that inheritance thoroughly pervades the classification of attack patterns [2] in the CAPEC schema [3], and therefore a theory of inheritance would be useful for both attack patterns and possibly other pattern types.

Should redundancy between patterns be removed from the knowledge base? And, in what sense is a pattern redundant? Design pattern composition has been formally modelled by extending the *Pattern:Role* graphical notation with composition represented as overlaps between pattern instances [4]. The composition and instantiation of design patterns was studied in finer detail using a set of six operators for precise expression [5]. Decomposition of patterns into their fundamental components is also important. Smith [6] demonstrated that some design patterns can be composed from more elementary patterns. Should a composite pattern (i.e. a pattern that is a composition of other patterns) be regarded as redundant? Should we only store atomic patterns? How do we detect whether a pattern is a composite of others? These questions deserve a thorough investigation since they are fundamental to the development of a practical pattern-oriented knowledge base.

2.3 Mechanisms for Pattern Interactions

Moreover, given the fact that there are a large number of patterns in each complicated sub-domain of cyberspace, each subject sub-domain may develop its own pattern knowledge base(s). We need to extend the existing work on pattern languages to consider the relationships and interactions between patterns in different pattern spaces. We can compose cyberpatterns across different pattern spaces using both existing composition operators and novel ones, such as the 'defeats' relation between security and attack patterns, where the security pattern resolves the security forces caused by attack patterns in the particular problem context. This is closely related to the pattern representation problem that requires compatible representation to enable associations between patterns across different cyber sub-domains to be meaningful and useful. There is some research to indicate that the existing formal modelling of design patterns may possibly be extended to cyberpatterns [2, 7].

2.4 Mechanisms for Efficient Application of Patterns

Patterns can be represented in descriptive or prescriptive ways. The descriptive view characterises the predictable structure and behaviour of patterns in deployed systems. Many novel types of cyberpattern such as attack patterns, machine patterns, network traffic patterns and user behaviour patterns are usefully considered descriptively.

In contrast, the prescriptive view provides recommendations of best practice to help develop general methods of providing solutions to recurring problems. Many patterns that have been developed, such as architectural and security patterns, are typically used prescriptively in building systems.

A special form of prescriptive representation of design patterns is as transformational rules. For example, Lano [8] proposed that a design pattern is represented as a set of transformation rules to refactor a system that contains design flaws. Refactoring alters the internal structure of an existing system to improve its quality without changing its externally observable behaviour [9]. Within the cyberpatterns domain, most of Hafiz's catalogue of security patterns could be seen as security-oriented transformations [10].

Each of the descriptive and prescriptive ways has its own advantages and disadvantages in the acquisition and application of pattern knowledge. The former helps to discover a pattern as repeated phenomena and makes it easier to detect occurrences of a pattern from observed data. Tools have been developed to support the uses of design patterns at the reverse engineering stage of software development to detect patterns in code and in design diagrams. The latter helps to generate instances of a pattern in a constructive way. Many tools have been developed to support uses of design patterns at the design stage and coding stage for instantiating patterns. A research question worthy of investigating is whether we can develop a general mechanism independent of application domain that enables us to instantiate patterns and detect patterns based on a pattern representation language.

Moreover, it will be redundant to store each pattern with two different representations: one descriptive and one prescriptive. This will not only consume more storage space and processing time, but also cause inconsistency between the two. More research is needed to reconcile these two approaches, for example, by developing a mechanism to enable transformation of one representation into another.

2.5 Mechanisms for the Automatic Acquisition of Patterns

With the advent of cloud computing, mobile computing and cyber-physical systems, a great quantity of data is now available as recorded observations of real world phenomena and human behaviour, as well as the interplay between them. There is also a great amount of work in the design and implementations of cyber systems. Such design knowledge is available in the form of program code, design diagrams, and operation manuals, etc. How to discover pattern knowledge in such big data or "big code" is the most challenging but also most important research question. The characteristics of cyberpatterns and their interrelationships suggest that we must go beyond the existing machine learning and data mining techniques. A new mechanism for automatic discovery of patterns from complicated combinations of structured and non-structured data is needed.

3 Conclusions

To conclude this book, let us quote Nobel Laureate Ernest Rutherford, who once asserted that *all science is either physics or stamp collecting*. By physics, Rutherford meant clean, succinct principles that apply to diverse phenomena, whereas by stamp collecting he meant the cataloguing and organising of large sets and varieties of observations. Being reusable knowledge about recurring phenomena, we believe patterns form a bridge that possibly spans the gap from stamp collecting to physics, because pattern-oriented research methods do not only recognise, catalogue and organise observations, but also discover regularities as well as interrelationships and interactions between such regularities. This knowledge is the mother of clean, succinct principles.

Rutherford also once said, *"Scientists are not dependent on the ideas of a single man, but on the combined wisdom of thousands of men, all thinking of the same problem, and each doing his little bit to add to the great structure of knowledge which is gradually being erected"*. The pattern-oriented research methodology offers such a platform for thousands of computer scientists to contribute to a structure of knowledge. We hope this book is only the start of the erection of a great structure of knowledge of cyberspace.

References

1. Zhu H. Cyberpatterns: a pattern oriented research methodology for studying cyberspace. In: Unifying design patterns with security and attack patterns. Springer; 2014.
2. Bayley I. Challenges for a formal framework for patterns. In: Cyberpatterns: unifying design patterns with security and attack patterns. Springer; 2014.
3. Mitre Corporation. Common attack pattern enumeration and classification (CAPEC). Mitre corporation. 2014. http://capec.mitre.org. Accessed 11 Jan 2014.
4. Taibi T. Formalising design patterns composition. IEE Proc Softw. 2006;153(3):126–53.
5. Zhu H, Bayley I. An algebra of design patterns. ACM Trans Softw Eng Methodol. 2013;22(3):1404–8.
6. Smith J. Elemental design patterns. UK: Addison-Wesley; 2012.
7. Zhu H. Design space-based pattern representation. In: Cyberpatterns: unifying design patterns with security and attack patterns. Springer; 2014.
8. Lano K. Design patterns: applications and open issues. In: Cyberpatterns: unifying design patterns with security and attack patterns. Springer; 2014.
9. Fowler M. Refactoring: improving the design of existing code. UK: Addison-Wesley; 1999.
10. Hafiz M. Security on demand. PhD dissertation. University of Illinois. 2011. http://munawarhafiz.com/research/phdthesis/Munawar-Dissertation.pdf

Printed in the United States
By Bookmasters